A CHECKLIST
OF AMERICAN
COVERLET
WEAVERS

Coverlet installation in the Abby Aldrich Rockefeller Folk Art Center featuring border sections of woven coverlets from the collections of: (1) Abby Aldrich Rockefeller Folk Art Center; (2) Abby Aldrich Rockefeller Folk Art Center, gift of Mr. and Mrs. Foster McCarl, Jr.; (3) Mr. and Mrs. George Dittmar, Jr.; (4) Mr. and Mrs. William Peto; and (5) Mr. and Mrs. Foster McCarl, Jr.

# A *Checklist of* American Coverlet Weavers

*compiled for the*
Abby Aldrich Rockefeller
Folk Art Center
by JOHN W. HEISEY

*Edited and Expanded*
*by* GAIL C. ANDREWS
and DONALD R. WALTERS

*Published by*
THE COLONIAL WILLIAMSBURG FOUNDATION
Williamsburg, Virginia

*Distributed by* The University Press of Virginia
Charlottesville, Virginia

© 1978 by
THE COLONIAL WILLIAMSBURG FOUNDATION

All rights reserved, including the right to reproduce
this book or portions of it in any form.
SECOND PRINTING, 1980
*Printed in the United States of America*

Library of Congress Cataloging in Publication Data

Heisey, John W.
    A checklist of American coverlet weavers.
    Bibliography: p. 139
    Includes index.
        1. Weavers—United States. 2. Coverlets—United States. I. Andrews, Gail C. II. Walters, Donald R. III. Abby Aldrich Rockefeller Folk Art Center, Williamsburg, Va. IV. Title.
TT848.H4    746.9'7    77-15968
ISBN 0-87935-048-2

**COVER**

*Coverlet border pattern featuring hunters, roosters, birds, and squirrels in trees; Beiderwand weave in red and blue wool and white cotton. Corner inscription: "S. B. Musselman Weaver Milford Bucks Co. No. 426," and "This Coverlet Belongs to Me Sary Meier 1843." Woven by Samuel Musselman, Bucks Co., Pa., in 1843. Collection of Mr. and Mrs. Foster McCarl, Jr.*

# Contents

| | |
|---|---|
| Foreword | v |
| Short-Title List | ix |
| Introduction | 1 |
| Checklist Explanation | 29 |
| Checklist | 31 |
| Supplement to the Checklist | 124 |
| Trademarks | 125 |
| Where To See Coverlets | 131 |
| Glossary | 135 |
| Bibliography | 139 |
| Index | 143 |

# Foreword

NINETEENTH-CENTURY technological improvements introduced efficient new methods that greatly changed many domestic crafts, including weaving. By 1830 the availability of a loom attachment, known as a Jacquard mechanism, made it possible for America's professional weavers to produce decorative textiles more rapidly and economically. This revolutionary device also encouraged imaginative operators to experiment with figured patterns.

Although the artistry varies according to each maker's feeling for design, color, and scale, coverlets woven by professional weavers between 1825 and 1875 provide an intriguing visual record of the interplay of folk motifs, such as animals, birds, flowers, sunbursts, humans, and buildings, with Victorian foliate medallions or complex, tilelike geometric configurations. Designs in the latest fashion were usually featured in the center of the coverlet, while more traditional elements were confined to border patterns and corner blocks. The end products were variously advertised as "damask coverlets," "patent coverlets," "carpet coverlets," or simply "fancy weaving."

These coverlets and the professionals who wove them are the subjects of this book. In recent years, several useful publications, ranging from pictorial surveys to closely researched regional studies, have focused on woven coverlets, their makers, and the evolution of weaving techniques. While still not definitive, this is the most ambitious systematic study attempted to date.

Donald R. Walters, curator of Williamsburg's Folk Art Center, conceived this project in the summer of 1973 while installing an exhibition of woven coverlets borrowed from the comprehensive and ever-expanding textile collection of Muriel and Foster McCarl, Jr., of Beaver Falls, Pennsylvania. The McCarls have long been recognized as discriminating pioneer collectors of American coverlets. Mr. and Mrs. McCarl enthusiastically endorsed Walters's concept of a handsomely illustrated, substantive handbook by funding the initial survey; they have been unreservedly generous in their continuing moral and financial support as the project developed.

*Coverlet border detail showing a fox and a dog at the base of a flowering tree in which there is a partridge; double weave in blue and white cotton. Woven by David D. Haring, Bergen Co., N. J., 1833. Collection of Mr. and Mrs. Foster McCarl, Jr.*

The Abby Aldrich Rockefeller Folk Art Center's research on professional coverlet weavers grew out of a study launched by the Historical Society of York County, Pennsylvania, under the direction of John W. Heisey and Janet G. Crosson. Thanks to the McCarls, Williamsburg's Folk Art Center subsequently commissioned Mr. Heisey to spend two years expanding the Pennsylvania listing. During this period, he compiled biographical information for most of the 942 weavers cited in the checklist entries. John and Mary Heisey also examined many of the 2,500 coverlets indexed during the study to establish weavers' working dates and locations and to record the motifs or trademarks an individual artisan employed. The checklist assembled from these findings is designed to help those interested in identifying the maker, provenance, or pattern of coverlets in their possession.

The scope of the project exceeded expectations, and in 1975–1976 Gail C. Andrews continued the coverlet study while serving as museum intern on a grant from the National Endowment for the Humanities. Her persistence in tracking down obscure leads and authenticating facts has generated a voluminous correspondence that continues to supply new data on weavers and coverlets.

An introductory essay, developed by Ms. Andrews and Mr. Walters from a draft prepared by Mr. Heisey, synthesizes and interprets the information itemized in the checklist and offers a fresh look at the lives and work of professional weavers who produced coverlets during the years of transition from traditional homecrafts to mass production.

The photographs that accompany the checklist section emphasize the inventive artistic qualities to be found in many of the individual motifs incorporated in well-designed woven coverlets. Most of the illustrations are the work of Frank J. Davis, a talented Colonial Williamsburg staff photographer. His pictures add richness and depth to the text by focusing on some of the unusual details often obscured by the impact of the overall design. A special acknowledgement of support is due Robert S. Davies who, as an extension of his late wife's interest in woven coverlets and the Folk Art Center itself, established the Margaret B. Davies Memorial Fund, which has made possible many of the color reproductions in this book.

The production of this handbook would not have been possible without the expertise and cooperation of the entire Folk Art Center staff, including Barbara Luck, registrar, Ann Brown, research associate, Douglas Canady and Osborne Taylor, preparators, and Cathy Gibbons and Joy Slepin, typists. The project is particularly indebted to Miss Mildred B. Lanier, Colonial Williamsburg's curator of textiles, for her objective analysis and constant counsel.

It is impossible to list all of the individuals and institutions that shared information and offered suggestions while this study was being prepared. However, the following people were so generous that they deserve special thanks here, since without their assistance this book could never have encompassed so much: Ms. Rita Adrosko, the Smithsonian Institution; Mr. Fred Brusher, Ann Arbor, Michigan; Dr. Eugene P. Bertin, Muncy Historical Society and Museum of History, Muncy, Pennsylvania; Mrs. Dorothy K. Burnham, Royal Ontario Museum, Ontario, Canada; Mrs. L. B. Caldwell, Ithaca, New York; the Children's Museum, Indianapolis, Indiana; Mrs. Janet G. Crosson, Lancaster, Pennsylvania; Mr. and Mrs. Randy Eisensmith, Charlottesville, Virginia; Ms. Suzanne Hall, Valentine Museum, Richmond, Virginia; Mrs. Mary F. Heisey, York, Pennsylvania; Ms. Ada M. Hodge, Vigo County Historical Association, Terre Haute, Indiana; Ms. Patricia McFerren, Hanover Public Library, Hanover, Pennsylvania; Mrs. George Martin, Lancaster, Ohio; Mrs. Christa C. Mayer-Thurman, Art Institute of Chicago; Mrs. Nancy Muller, the Shelburne Museum, Shelburne, Vermont; Mr. Cyril I. Nelson, E. P. Dutton & Co., New York City; staff of the Ohio Historical Society, Columbus, Ohio; Mrs. Virginia Partridge, New York State Historical Association, Cooperstown, New York; Mr. Dan Reibel, Old Economy Village, Ambridge, Pennsylvania; Mr. H. F. Riffle, Jr., Dayton, Ohio; Mr. Harry Rinker and staff of the Historical Society of York County, York, Pennsylvania; Mr. and Mrs. David Sapadin, Columbia, Maryland; Mrs. Margaret W. M. Shaeffer, Jefferson County Historical Society, Watertown, New York; Ms. Carol Steiro, Museum of New Mexico, Santa Fe, New Mexico; Ms. Marceline Szpakowski, Ontario Science Centre, Ontario, Canada; Mr. Otto Charles Thieme, Elvehjem Art Center, University of Wisconsin, Madison, Wisconsin; Mrs. C. C. Warren and Mrs. Ruth E. Wollet, The Colonial Coverlet Guild of America, Chicago; Mr. Harold Yoder, the Historical Society of Berks County, Reading, Pennsylvania.

The generous cooperation of many owners who agreed to lend their coverlets to the museum for study or photography is also deeply appreciated: Mrs. Robert Brooks; Clermont County Historical Society; Dr. and Mrs. Willard J. Davies; Mr. and Mrs. George Dittmar; The Glen Ellyn Historical Society; Iroquois County Historical Society; Mr. and Mrs. Robert C. Kelley; Ms. Cynthia Lanford; Mr. and Mrs. Foster McCarl, Jr.; Mr. F. James McCarl; Northern Indiana Historical Society; Mr. and Mrs. William E. Peto; Mrs. George M. Prescott; Mr. and Mrs. H. F. Riffle, Jr.; Mr. G. W. Samaha; Mr. S. F. Silver; Mrs. Gretchen Truslow; Mrs. Theo Van De Polder; Western Reserve Historical Society; Mrs. Elizabeth L. Williams; Mrs. Henry B. Wilson; Mrs. Joe W. Wilson; Margaret Woodbury Strong Museum.

BEATRIX T. RUMFORD
*Director, Abby Aldrich Rockefeller Folk Art Center*

# Short-Title List

**Art Institute of Chicago**

Mildred Davison and Christa C. Mayer-Thurman, *Coverlets: A Handbook on the Collection of Woven Coverlets in The Art Institute of Chicago.* Chicago: Art Institute of Chicago, 1973.

**Boyd's Business Directory,**
  **Adams–York**

William H. Boyd, *Business Directory of the Counties of Adams, Bucks, Chester, Cumberland, Dauphin, Delaware, Franklin, Lancaster, Montgomery, and York.* Philadelphia: William H. Boyd, 1860.

**Boyd's Business Directory,**
  **Berks–Schuylkill**

William H. Boyd, *Business Directory of the Counties of Berks, Lebanon, Lehigh, Northampton, and Schuylkill.* Philadelphia: William H. Boyd, 1860.

**Burnham and Burnham**

Harold B. and Dorothy K. Burnham, *"Keep Me Warm One Night": Early Handweaving in Eastern Canada.* Toronto: University of Toronto Press, 1972.

**C.C.G.A.**

The Colonial Coverlet Guild of America compiled a weaver checklist as part of its book, edited by Mrs. Luther M. Swygert, *Heirlooms From Old Looms.* Chicago: Colonial Coverlet Guild of America, 1955.

**French**

S. French et al., comps., *New York State Mercantile Union Business Directory Carefully Collected & Arranged for 1850–1851.* New York: S. French, L. C. & H. L. Pratt, 1850.

**Hall**
    Eliza Calvert Hall [pseud.], *A Book of Hand-woven Coverlets*. Boston: Little, Brown and Co., 1912.

**Hawes**
    George W. Hawes, comp., *George W. Hawes' Ohio State Gazetteer and Business Directory for 1859 and 1860*. Cincinnati: George W. Hawes, 1859.

**Kovel and Kovel**
    Ralph and Terry Kovel, *Know Your Antiques: How to Recognize and Evaluate any Antique—Large or Small—Like an Expert*. New York: Crown Publishers, 1973.

**Madden**
    Betty I. Madden, *Arts, Crafts, and Architecture in Early Illinois*. Urbana: University of Illinois Press, 1974.

**Montgomery**
    Pauline Montgomery, *Indiana Coverlet Weavers and Their Coverlets*. Indianapolis: Hoosier Heritage Press, 1974.

**O.H.S.**
    Ohio Historical Society, Columbus.

**W. W. Reilly & Co.**
    W. W. Reilly & Co., *Ohio State Business Directory for 1853–1854*. Cincinnati: Morgan & Overend, 1853.

**Reinert**
    Guy F. Reinert, *Coverlets of the Pennsylvania Germans*. Pennsylvania German Folklore Society Yearbook, 1948. Allentown: Pennsylvania German Folklore Society, 1949.

**Roberts**
    Charles Rhoads Roberts et al., comps., *History of Lehigh County, Pennsylvania, and a Genealogical and Biographical Record of Its Families*. Allentown: Lehigh Valley Publishing Co., 1914.

**Safford and Bishop**
    Carlton L. Safford and Robert Bishop, *America's Quilts and Coverlets*. New York: E. P. Dutton & Co., 1972.

**Weiss and Ziegler**
    Harry B. Weiss and Grace M. Ziegler, *The Early Woolen Industry of New Jersey*. Trenton: New Jersey Agricultural Society, 1958.

**White**
    Margaret E. White, "Weavers of New Jersey," New Jersey Historical Society, *Proceedings*, LXXXII (October 1964), pp. 283–288.

# Introduction

A STUDY of the history of textiles shows that as man began to develop utilitarian fabrics, he soon discovered how to use colors, patterns, and textures to express himself aesthetically. Bedcoverings were both utilitarian and decorative: often part of a crowded living space, beds required a covering that would be attractive and protective by day, yet warm at night.

Because they served the same function, people today often confuse two types of brightly patterned bedcoverings commonly used in nineteenth-century American homes, the quilt and the coverlet. A quilt is made up of distinct layers—a top, often pieced or appliqued with scraps to form a decoration or design, usually an interlining, and a backing. The layers are fastened together, that is, quilted, with small, regular stitches normally worked in orderly patterns. Unlike a quilt, which is wrought with a needle, a coverlid or coverlet, as defined in this study, is a bedcovering woven on a loom.

For centuries, individuals wove in the home and in small workshops, using simple looms to make fabric for clothing, bedcovers, and household linens. Weaving and fiber preparation were done as time permitted or necessity dictated, and were considered a part of the routine of everyday life. Woven on handlooms, the earliest American coverlets were constructed of the sturdiest and warmest fibers available. The warp threads, those threads that are stretched or "warped" vertically on a loom, are usually cotton that is undyed. Occasionally linen was used. Due to advances in the processing of cotton and the proliferation of cotton mills, even before

1825 cotton yarn was readily available to weavers and was relatively cheap.[1] Consequently, for the part of the coverlet woven from cotton thread, the tedious, time-consuming carding and spinning processes traditionally carried on in the home were becoming obsolete.

The threads that run horizontally across the loom, crossing the warp at right angles, are called the weft. Colored wool is used for the weft threads that form the pattern, while the alternating ground weft is of the same cotton used for the warp.

Dyeing is an important step in preparing the colored pattern weft threads. Until about the mid-nineteenth century, the three dyes used most frequently in American woven coverlets were indigo for blue and madder or cochineal for red. J. and R. Bronson, *Domestic Manufacturer's Assistant and Family Directory, in the Arts of Weaving and Dyeing*,[2] was one source of instruction for those wishing to familiarize themselves with the dyer's arts.

Indigo (*Indigofera tinctoria*) was described as "the most extraordinary and useful of all dyeing drugs; from its affording a blue color, that withstands in a very great degree the action of acids and alkalies. For these reasons indigo blue is chosen, and very properly, for dyeing various descriptions of goods that require to be often washed. Indigo is cultivated and manufactured in South America, the East Indies, Isle of France, Louisiana, Carolinas, etc. The best is brought from Bengal; and comes in pieces about two inches square." Madder, a red color derived from the plant root, "gives to woollen cloth, prepared with allum and tartar, the most durable of all reds, though not so bright as the cochineal scarlet; yet the red of madder has this important advantage, by enduring to be washed with soap, without producing any material change of color: whereas the cochineal scarlet by the same means used, becomes tarnished."[3]

The more costly cochineal, sometimes used in place of madder, is made by drying and crushing bodies of a small insect native to South America, *Dactylopius coccus*. According to the Bronsons, "That which is good, and has been well prepared, is plump and of a greyish color inclining to purple:

---

[1] Mildred Davison and Christa C. Mayer-Thurman, *Coverlets: A Handbook on the Collection of Woven Coverlets in The Art Institute of Chicago* (Chicago, 1973), p. 13; Verla Birrell, *The Textile Arts, A Handbook of Fabric Structure and Design Processes: Ancient and Modern Weaving, Braiding, Printing, and Other Textile Techniques* (New York, 1959), p. 39.

[2] Utica, N. Y., 1817.

[3] Ibid., pp. 188, 186.

that which has been damaged by sea water, appears of a dull crimson hue and is useless."[4] Fustic, quercitron (black oak bark), yellow dock, and hickory bark were used to obtain a yellow dye; all but fustic are native to the United States.[5] Until the early nineteenth century, green was a compound or two-dye process—blue over yellow or vice versa. Logwood occasionally was used for black; using wool from a black sheep eliminated the need for such a dye.

William Henry Perkins's 1856 discovery of a lavender dye made from aniline, a coal-tar product, soon terminated the commercial use of natural dyes and launched a synthetic dye industry that produced the wider palette of colors frequently seen in coverlets woven in the 1860s and 1870s.[6]

While the methods and techniques of fiber preparation do not always distinguish the work of an amateur or domestic home weaver from that of a professional, weave constructions and the looms and equipment that were required to produce them usually do. Many of the oldest surviving American coverlets were woven at home or in a small shop on a four-harness loom in the "overshot" weave.[7] The term overshot describes the long skips or passes of a supplementary weft thread that overshoots the ground, forming a geometric pattern with a raised, almost three-dimensional, effect.

"Summer and Winter"[8] refers to a closely textured weave constructed from a cotton warp woven with a pattern weft of wool (or half-wool, half-cotton) as in overshot weaving. Instead of forming long floats, the pattern is more closely interwoven with the warp threads and is reversible; however, its structure rather than its reversibility distinguishes this single cloth weave. "Summer and Winter" weaves usually were produced on looms having five or more harnesses; consequently, they generally were the work of a professional weaver trained to operate and make practical use of relatively complex equipment.

During the first half of the nineteenth century, many geometrically patterned American coverlets were produced in the technically complex dou-

---

[4] Ibid., p. 189.

[5] Rita J. Adrosko, *Natural Dyes in the United States,* United States National Museum Bulletin 281 (Washington, D. C., 1968), p. 13.

[6] For a discussion of dyes, see ibid and Brooklyn Botanic Garden, *Dye Plants and Dyeing—A Handbook* (Baltimore, 1964).

[7] See Davison and Mayer-Thurman, *Coverlets,* and Harold B. and Dorothy K. Burnham, "*Keep Me Warm One Night*": *Early Handweaving in Eastern Canada* (Toronto, 1972), for a more complete discussion and illustration of various coverlet weave constructions.

[8] Although this term is often thought to be modern, "Summer and Winter" coverlets were advertised by weaver Benjamin Hausman in the *People's Advocate* (York, Pa.), April 30, 1852.

ble cloth or double weave on multi-harness looms. This type of coverlet has two warps and two sets of weft threads. "In double-cloth weaving two cloths are woven simultaneously, one above the other, being interwoven at specified intervals to form an all-over patterned cloth in which the colors, of limited number, are reversible from front to back."[9] Although double weaving was technically within the ability of the home weaver, it was usually done by professionals. The fancy pictorial designs that are discussed in this study were certainly produced by skilled artisans.

Characterized by the ribbed vertical alignment of the pattern, another common color and pattern reversible coverlet weave used in America by professional weavers is a single weave also called "Beiderwand," from the German term for this type of construction. It consists of a warp-faced plain weave combined with a weft-faced plain weave. The vertically running ribs are produced by warp thread groupings of two, three, or four, plus a supplementary warp that is often light blue, tan, or natural.[10]

Many coverlets were woven in two or three strips, depending on the width of the loom and the breadth of the bed. The widths were designed so that the pattern matched and continued uninterrupted at the vertical seams. The strips were carefully positioned selvage to selvage and were whipstitched together by hand to form the full width of the coverlet. By the 1840s some coverlets were being woven full width on wide looms.[11]

The drawloom[12] was used to create intricately figured or pictorial textiles, including elegant and costly patterned woven silks and linen damasks, until the nineteenth century. Infinite variations could be created with the drawloom, but operating it was complicated and involved two individuals, a weaver and a drawboy. Working from a diagram, the drawboy raised the warp threads required to form the design. For many years attempts were made to mechanize the drawloom and to simplify the weaving process. These efforts culminated in the development of the Jacquard apparatus.

The Jacquard-type attachment is a mechanical apparatus which, when mounted on a multi-harness handloom, enabled weavers to create pictorial

---

[9] Mildred B. Lanier, *English and Oriental Carpets at Williamsburg* (Williamsburg, Va., 1975), p. 31.

[10] Davison and Mayer-Thurman, *Coverlets*, p. 66.

[11] To weave a full-width coverlet required a loom twice as wide as the regular one, and either a fly-shuttle or two weavers sitting at the loom and throwing the shuttle between them. Virginia D. Parslow, "James Alexander, weaver," *Antiques*, LXIX (April 1956), p. 348.

[12] The drawloom is a complicated handloom. The Jacquard loom was based on the principles of the drawloom. See Burnham and Burnham, "*Keep Me Warm One Night,*" pp. 317–327, for a detailed discussion of the drawloom and the workings of the Jacquard mechanism.

View of an old hand loom that has been mounted with a Jacquard attachment. According to the donor, it is supposed to be the first "Jacquard loom mounted in the United States, in 1826." The loom measures 9 feet high, 10 feet long, and 10 feet wide. Shelburne Museum, Shelburne, Vt.

A Jacquard apparatus has been mounted on a hand loom. The loom and apparatus originally belonged to the Canadian weaver, John Campbell. The mechanism was manufactured in Jersey City, N. J., by James Lightbody for Campbell in the 1840s. Ontario Science Centre, Toronto.

Coverlet corner block showing the lion trademark; double weave in mauve wool and white cotton. Woven by Harry Tyler, Jefferson Co., N. Y., 1859. Collection of Mr. and Mrs. Foster McCarl, Jr.

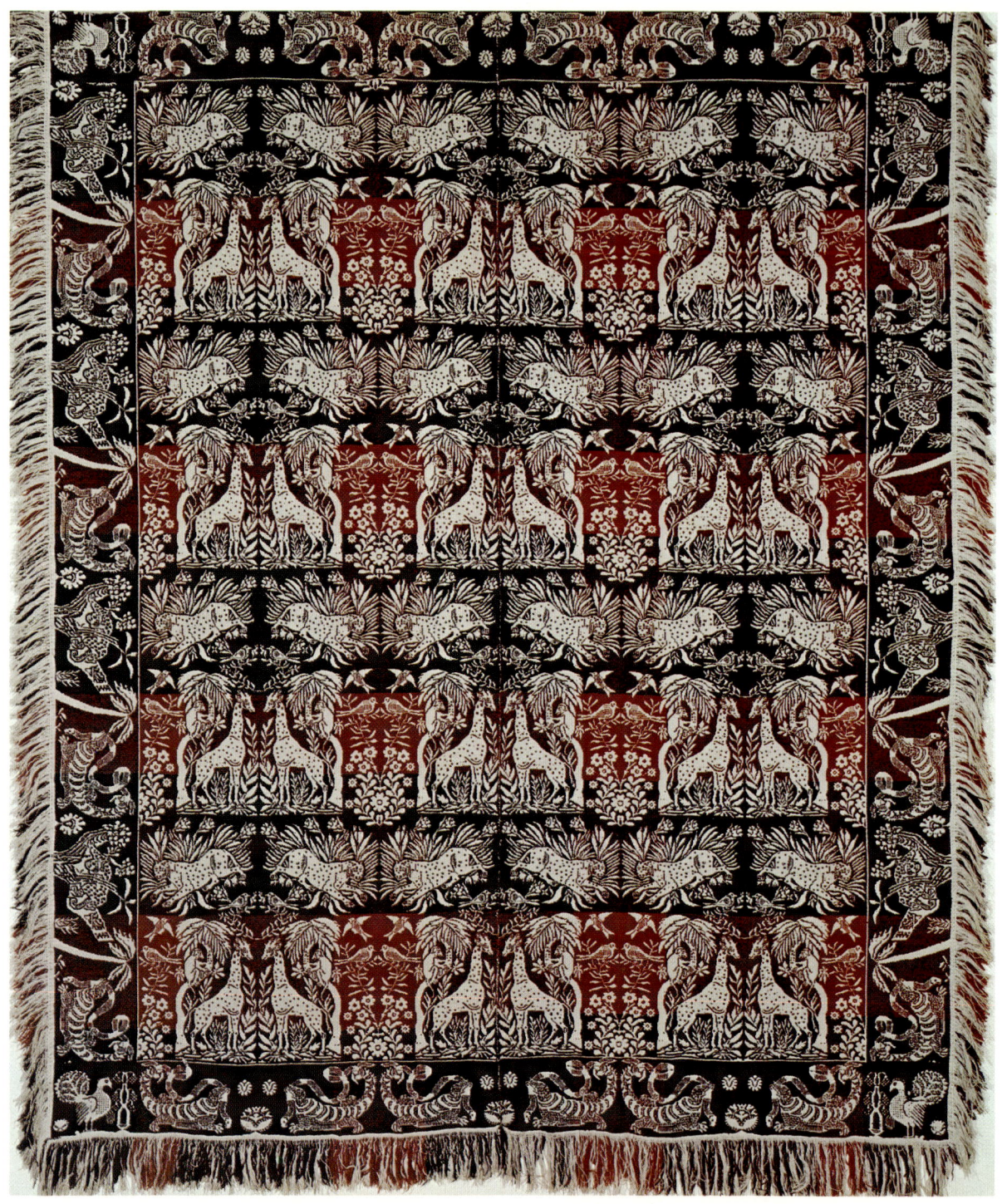

The interior design of this coverlet is composed of giraffes, monkeys, and birds, while the borders contain crocodiles, snakes, and leopards. Tropical foliage appears in both areas, and there is a turkey in each corner; double weave in red and blue wool and natural cotton. Weaver unidentified, possibly Ohio, ca. 1850. Courtesy of Mr. G. W. Samaha.

*A coverlet is being woven on the Campbell loom with the aid of the Jacquard mechanism. Ontario Science Centre, Toronto.*

designs more easily and rapidly and to move away from the traditional rectilinear patterns associated with the overshot, Summer and Winter, and geometric types of double weaves. The apparatus is named for Joseph-Marie Jacquard (1752–1834), the Frenchman who perfected it early in the nineteenth century.[13]

According to the William H. Horstmann Company, the Jacquard-type attachment was introduced in the United States by William Horstmann in

---

[13] Jacquard exhibited an automated loom that did not require a drawboy at the 1801 Paris Industrial Exposition. The French government declared the Jacquard loom public property in 1806, but several years passed before it could be employed practically. See "The Loom," *CIBA Review*, XVI (December 1938), pp. 562–563, and Birrell, *Textile Arts*, p. 22, for a discussion of the evolution of the loom and the individuals associated with it.

[7]

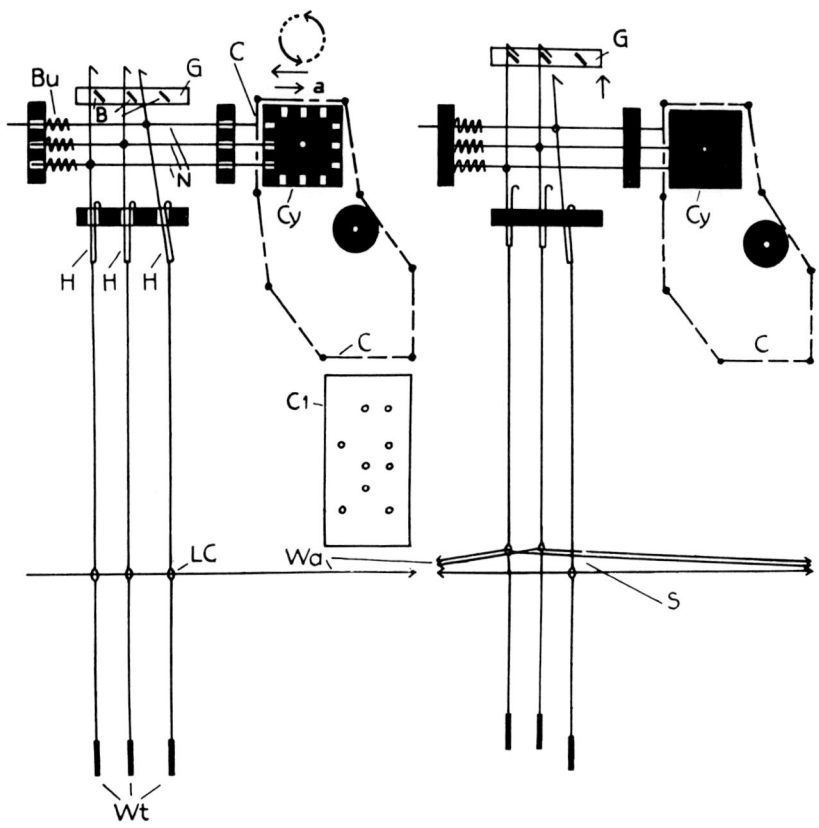

The frequently heard term "Jacquard loom" is misleading. It is not a loom but a comparatively small apparatus that may be mounted on any hand loom and is an automatic selective shedding machine for figured fabrics that is worked by a treadle. After the pattern of the drawloom, every warp thread (Wa) runs through the loop of a cord (LC), which is carried upward and is movable; each cord is held taut by a weight (Wt) attached to the lower end. Every cord is suspended from a wire, known as a lifter or hook (H), which is bent at the top to enable it to hook around the blades (B) of the griff (G). If no further provision were made, all the hooks would move every time the griff was raised. To prevent the raising of certain warp threads, the corresponding hooks must be thrust off the rising blades, which is done by means of the needles (N) that are connected to each hook. The spiral springs of the needles are contracted by means of a buffer (Bu). The automatic thrusting back of certain needles is achieved by means of the cylinder (Cy), a quadrangular block of wood upon which perforated cards (C) are placed, an example of which is shown in (C1). Only where the cards are perforated does the position of the needles remain unchanged. Only those hooks rise with the griff that have not been thrust into an oblique position. By this device a selective shed (S) corresponding to the details of the pattern is made, and the weft can be inserted and beaten down. To prepare the shed for the next stage in the pattern, the griff is lowered and the cylinder moved in the direction indicated by (a), at the same time executing a quarter revolution. The cards are connected in the form of a chain, and each rotary movement places a fresh card in position. The endless chain of cards allows the pattern to be repeated as often as desired. Information reprinted from "The Loom," CIBA Review, XVI (December 1938), pp. 562–563, by permission.

[8]

1824. Horstmann, a Philadelphia merchant who had trained as a weaver in Germany, saw the advantages of the attachment and was fascinated by its operation.[14] The apparatus soon gained wide acceptance in America, and coverlets woven on looms with the Jacquard-type attachment were produced in quantity from the 1830s onward.[15] American coverlets produced with the Jacquard-type attachment were usually woven either in double cloth or the Beiderwand or single weave constructions.

The Jacquard-type attachment required specialized weavers who could operate the equipment. The end result was that in many cases the weaving process was literally removed from the home and became the function of professionals, whose income depended on their skillful operation of efficient, mechanized looms.

While the traditional frame loom could be constructed by anyone with a modest understanding of weaving and carpentry, the Jacquard-type attachment required the purchase of ready-made parts and supplies from a specialized company. Furthermore, the equipment was costly.[16] Once a weaver acquired the machinery, he had to make it pay for itself, which seems to have involved fairly steady weaving and a ready market that was relatively free of competition. Seldom did more than two of the professional weavers recorded in this survey work in the same locale.

This apparent lack of competition may have been due partially to the issuance of patent rights. For example, Archibald Davidson specified that he had "purchased a patent right for the town of Ithaca, superior to any patent heretofore in the United States, for weaving Carpet and Carpet Coverlets."[17]

---

[14] Wm. H. Horstmann, *One Hundred Years, 1816–1916; the Chronicles of an Old Business House in the City of Philadelphia* (Philadelphia, 1916).

[15] A coverlet bearing a date of 1829 is the earliest piece woven with the aid of the Jacquard attachment recorded in this study. Earlier examples have been noted; however, they precede or coincide so closely with the introduction of the apparatus in America that they were probably woven on a drawloom.

[16] When Joseph Schnee of Snyder County, Pennsylvania, died in 1838, he left two "machine looms" valued at $55. Inventory, November 29, 1838, Union County Courthouse, Lewisburg, Pa. Daniel Bordner, of Berks County, Pennsylvania, died in 1842, leaving a coverlet loom and fixtures valued at $11.60, a loom valued at $2, and a coverlet loom "and its apparatus" valued at $143, plus "paist bord" valued at $2. This was probably the cardboard used for Jacquard-type pattern cards. Inventory, January 13, 1843, Berks County Courthouse, Reading, Pa. Thomas Weaver died in Lehigh County, Pennsylvania, in 1843, leaving a "pattent coverlit weaving loom" valued at $50, and a "common weaving loom" valued at $10. Inventory, May 8, 1843, Lehigh County Courthouse, Allentown, Pa.

[17] A variation of this practice was employed by two other weavers, George Detterich and Jonathon Conger, of Tompkins County, New York. On March 12, 1831, they were granted a patent

## STATES WHERE WEAVERS WORKED

| KNOWN BIRTHPLACES OF WEAVERS Country/State | Connecticut | Illinois | Indiana | Iowa | Kansas | Kentucky | Maine | Maryland | Michigan | Missouri | New Jersey | New York | Ohio | Pennsylvania | Rhode Island | West Virginia | Wisconsin | TOTALS |
|---|---|---|---|---|---|---|---|---|---|---|---|---|---|---|---|---|---|---|
| Alsace | | | 3 | | 2 | | | | | | | | 1 | 1 | | | | 7 |
| Connecticut | | | | | | | | | | | | | 2 | | | | | 2 |
| England | | | 5 | | | | | | | | | | 3 | 2 | | | | 10 |
| France | | | 1 | | | | | | | | | | 1 | | | | | 2 |
| Germany | | 2 | 14 | | 2 | | | 2 | | | | 1 | 23 | 27 | | | | 71 |
| Holland | | | | | | | | | | | | | | 1 | | | | 1 |
| Indiana | | | 2 | | | | | | | | | | | | | | | 2 |
| Ireland | | | 2 | | | | | | | | 1 | 1 | 6 | 1 | | | | 11 |
| Kentucky | | | 1 | | | | | | | | | | | | | | | 1 |
| Maryland | | | 2 | | | | | | | | | | | 1 | | | | 3 |
| Massachusetts | | | | | | | | | | | | | 1 | | | | | 1 |
| New Hampshire | | | | | | | | | | | | | 1 | | | | | 1 |
| New Jersey | | | 2 | | | | | | 1 | | 3 | | 1 | | | | | 7 |
| New York | | | 1 | | | | | | | | | 7 | 1 | | | | | 9 |
| Ohio | | | 1 | | | | | | | | | | 7 | | | | | 8 |
| Pennsylvania | | 1 | 10 | | | | | 1 | | | | | 30' | 129 | | | | 171 |
| Scotland | 2 | | 19 | | 1 | | | | | | | | 7 | 6 | | | | 35 |
| South Carolina | | | 2 | | | | | | | | | | | | | | | 2 |
| Virginia | | | 1 | | | | | | | | | | 6 | 2 | | | | 9 |
| Unknown | 1 | 22 | 21 | 3 | | 3 | 1 | 12 | 2 | 1 | 15 | 48 | 172 | 130 | 2 | 9 | 2 | 444 |
| TOTALS | 3 | 25 | 87 | 3 | 3 | 5 | 1 | 14 | 4 | 1 | 19 | 67 | 259 | 293 | 2 | 9 | 2 | |

[ 10 ]

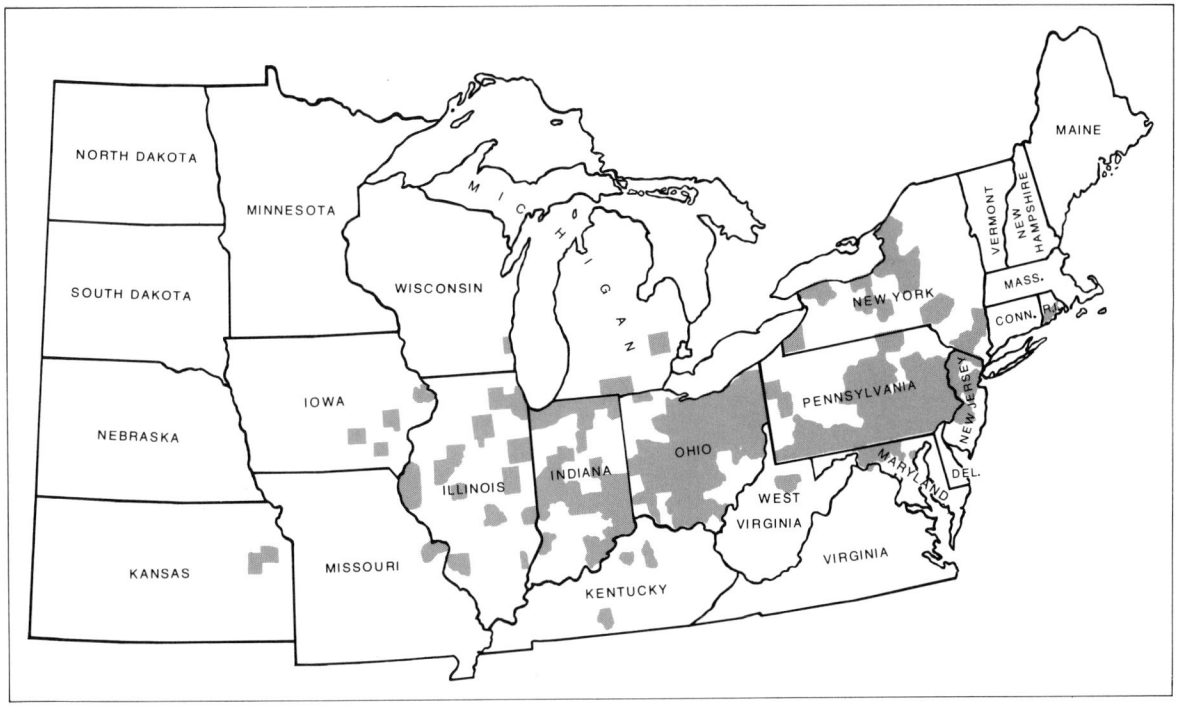

*Map showing geographic distribution and relative concentration of professional weavers recorded in this study.*

Once the new Jacquard mechanism began to be marketed in the United States in the late 1820s, numerous guild-trained European weavers ventured across the Atlantic seeking work. Research on the careers of some of these immigrants indicates that they generally settled in small towns and supported themselves by weaving for customers in nearby communities. Specific information is often hard to find, since there are few adequately detailed or relevant surviving records. The situation is further complicated by the fact that a weaver often had another occupation and may be listed in the records according to that activity, rather than as a weaver.

Like any cross section of nineteenth-century American craftsmen, professional coverlet weavers came from different regions and diverse back-

---

for a "new and useful improvement in the Machine for Weaving figured cloth." An addendum dated May 27, 1834, assigned exclusive rights to the device in Lansing, New York, to weavers Tichenor and Malloury. Mallory family tradition maintains that this was an improvement on a Jacquard-type device for lettering. Detterich and Conger apparently licensed other weavers to use their equipment, thereby creating a sort of nineteenth-century franchise for a specific area.

grounds. One advantage of compiling a checklist such as this is that it provides an opportunity for statistical analysis. Of the weavers cited here whose birthplaces are known, 102 were born in Europe,[18] 15 of whom are documented as having trained under guild systems in their respective countries before reaching the United States. Others doubtless received this kind of training, but adequate documentation has not yet been discovered.

Many German weavers settled in Pennsylvania, Maryland, and Ohio communities, finding permanent homes and good work, while British-born weavers often established themselves in New York state and Indiana. Most American-born coverlet weavers remained in the state where they were born, although some did relocate farther west to take advantage of unexploited markets. For example, we know that 171 professional weavers were natives of Pennsylvania. Of them, 129 worked in their home state, 30 moved to and worked in Ohio, 10 settled in Indiana, 1 in Michigan, and 1 in Illinois.

Few professional coverlet weavers were itinerant craftsmen.[19] The size and structure of the loom made moving about impractical, and weavers often farmed their own land or had some other business that tied them to a given locality. Studying a cross section of the available inventories and advertisements indicates that these artisans worked out of an established shop or another permanent location, where clients sought them out, bringing design preferences and sometimes spun and pre-dyed yarn for the item commissioned.[20] Even when records or the signature blocks found on coverlets indicate that a weaver worked in different places, it more often indicates that he relocated and not that he was an itinerant.

Although women continued to play a vital role in preparing materials, particularly the woolen portion, for the professional weaver after the intro-

---

[18] Of the European-born weavers recorded in this survey, 71 were born in Germany, 35 in Scotland, 11 in Ireland, 10 in England, 7 in Alsace-Lorraine, 2 in France, and 1 in Holland. (See chart, p. 10.)

[19] One possible exception may have been Abraham Frey, who worked in Mount Joy, Lancaster County, Pennsylvania, where he appears in tax lists as a peddler and, in 1857, as a "coverlid peddler." He was first described as a weaver in 1859.

[20] An advertisement by David Kennedy, which appeared in the *Western Herald and Steubenville Gazette* (Steubenville, Ohio), June 6, 1829, said, "Those who have any of the above work [carpet and coverlet weaving] to do, will please to call at his establishment." George Cosley placed an advertisement in the *Chambersburg Whig* (Chambersburg, Pa.), April 27, 1838, stating that "for the convenience of those at a distance, the subscriber will receive Wool and cloth at the following places . . . Written directions should be attached to each bundle."

duction of the Jacquard-type attachment,[21] it appears that few American women actually became professional weavers. The fact that some women provided weavers with prepared yarns has compounded the misconception that the individual who spun the yarn also wove the coverlet. So far, the only woman we can fully document as being a weaver is Sarah LaTourette of Indiana. Having assisted her father, John, with weaving until his death, she and her younger brother Henry subsequently managed their own flourishing business for some years.[22] Although other females have been included in the following checklist of professional coverlet weavers, no material evidence in the form of a fully documented coverlet woven with a Jacquard-type attachment has been found.

Professional weavers made a variety of items besides coverlets, and newspaper advertisements reveal that weavers produced carpets and small figured linens such as diaper and diaper damask, which is a type of fabric generally used for tablecloths and towels.[23] Coverlet and carpet patterns are frequently related, and after 1840 the design associations of large floral medallions or tilelike patterns becomes especially obvious. Illustrating clearly the stylistic and technical connections between coverlet and carpet production, the carpets created by Archibald Davidson, a New York state

---

[21] "Coverlet & Carpet Weaving By Harry Tyler, two miles South of Smithville, Jefferson County, N. Y.

Persons wishing the above work may be assured that all work entrusted to my care, shall be done as well, if not better, than by any other weaver in the state. But in order to do this the yarn must be prepared according to the following.

For coverlets:—Spin 60 knots to the pound in the oil. When doubled and twisted, 7 runs for one coverlet, or 13 runs for two coverlets in the same web. 3½ lbs. knitting cotton, No. 12, three threaded, for one coverlet, or 7 lbs. for two.

N.B. The wool may be spun crossband and not doubled, 30 knots to the pound.

For carpets:—Spin warp 40, and filling 30 knots to the pound in oil; when doubled and twisted, 13¼ knots each for a yard.

For weaving, do not twist your yarn very hard if you wish good work. Yarn should be scoured with old soap, and not allowed to lie in the suds any time, and rinse perfectly clean in clear water, to color scarlet.

For weaving one coverlet, $2.75; for more than one in the same web, $2.50 each. Ten shillings per coverlet for dyeing scarlet." Quoted in Jefferson County Historical Society, *Bulletin*, V (October 1964), pp. 12–13.

[22] Pauline Montgomery, *Indiana Coverlet Weavers and Their Coverlets* (Indianapolis, 1974), pp. 67–69.

[23] Weaver Josiah Meeks listed "Coverlet, Diaper, Janes [Jeans], Carpet and plain Weaving" in the April 12, 1838, issue of the *Western Reserve Chronicle* (Warren, Ohio); while another weaver, David Kennedy, agreed "also to manufacture per order, INGRAIN CARPETING of the newest patterns." *Western Herald and Steubenville Gazette*, June 6, 1829.

Coverlet interior pattern with a carpetlike design incorporating small drums; double weave in red and blue wool and white cotton. The interior pattern resembles the woven carpet designs also produced by professional weavers with the aid of the Jacquard apparatus. Weaver unidentified, possibly Ohio, 1849. Collection of Mr. and Mrs. Foster McCarl, Jr.

*The coverlet corner block reads, "Woven At The Ithaca Carpet Factory by Archd. Davidson 1838"; double weave in blue wool and white cotton. Woven by Archibald Davidson, Ithaca, N. Y., 1838. Collection of Mr. and Mrs. Foster McCarl, Jr.*

weaver, are inscribed "Woven At The Ithaca Carpet Factory by Archd. Davidson."

Prices charged for coverlets can be determined from inventories and advertisements. Andrew Kump stated that he was "prepared to weave Coverlets for $2 and will furnish the necessary Cotton Yarn, for each Coverlet for $1.62½."[24] An inventory shortly after the death of Thomas Weaver in 1843 included 47 coverlets valued at $140, while a similar inventory taken in 1880 on the death of Philip Schum listed 620 coverlets valued at $1,490.10. Coverlet prices varied, but over the years most appear to have sold for between two and three dollars.

Professional weavers' advertisements in local newspapers reveal much information about their work. The prices charged, the variety of materials woven, and any other services a weaver might provide, such as supplying the necessary cotton yarn or dyeing yarn to a client's taste, are described.

In addition, weavers often incorporated advertisements on the coverlets themselves by weaving inscriptions in corner panels or along borders. Andrew Kump of Pennsylvania and W. H. Gernand of Maryland signed cov-

---

[24] It is interesting to note that the purchaser was required to provide his or her own woolen yarn, while Kemp supplied cotton thread for warp and ground weft. See the advertisement from the *Spectator* (Hanover, Pa.), August 13, 1845, reproduced on p. 17. Since warping the loom was the most tedious part of the operation, it was cheaper to order more than one coverlet to be produced in the same warp. Harry Tyler issued a handbill dated September 25, 1856, that reads, "For weaving one coverlet, $2.75; for more than one in the same web, $2.50 each." See n. 21.

[15]

## American Manufactures.

## CARPET & COVERLET WEAVING.

THE Subscriber returns his thanks to his friends and the public in general, for the encouragement he has hitherto received, and is now in complete readiness to receive YARN for the above kind of work; also to manufacture, per order, INGRAIN CARPETING of the newest patterns from Boston, and of the very best of colors. He has now put on some elegant figures for COVERLETS, quite in a superior style. The work will be well executed, and on as good terms as possibly can be afforded. Those who have any of the above work to do, will please to call at his establishment, at the head of Adams Street, near Mr A. Wise's Machine Shop, were samples can be shown of the various figures.

### David Kennedy.

All orders from a distance will be thankfully received and punctually attended to. Those who furnish yarn will please provide Cotton Yarn No. 5, filling, and woollen yarn 14 cuts to the pound. D. K.

Steubenville, June 6, 1829—6m

Advertisement of David Kennedy, *Western Herald and Steubenville Gazette* (Steubenville, Ohio), June 6, 1829.

## ARCHIBALD DAVIDSON, FANCY WEAVER.

AT his Shop about 50 rods south of Otis Eddy's Cotton Factory, and a quarter of a mile east of the village of Ithaca, respectfully informs the publick that he has purchased a patent right for the town of Ithaca, superiour to any patent heretofore in the United States, for weaving Carpets and Carpet Coverlets of any pattern or figure that can be wove in the United States; and the work not inferiour to any in Europe or America.

He will weave the owners' name, date of the month and year, if required. If the yarn is good, and not cut, he flatters himself that he will show and give better work than has ever been by any patent loom heretofore invented. From his long experience and practice in the weaving line in Scotland and in the United States, and the great expense he has been at in procuring a patent so valuable, he hopes to merit the publick patronage.

Also, at his shop he weaves Broad Cloth, Sheeting, two and one half yards wide, in kersey or plain; Diaper of all kinds, and country work of every description done with punctuality and dispatch.

Yarn spun for coverlets ought to be spun 3 runs to the pound, douled and twisted, and cotton, No. 7, doubled and twisted. Carpet yarn spun two runs to the pound, douled and twisted, or one run to the pound, single. And he likewise, for their accommodation, will, if required, get their yarn coloured to suit the pattern. Ladies are requested to call and examine the work before they engage their weaving.

Nov. 9, 1831. 43tf

Advertisement of Archibald Davidson, *Ithaca Journal* (Ithaca, N. Y.), November 9, 1831.

[16]

### NEW STYLE OF
### DOUBLE-COVERLET WEAVING.

THE undersigned, living in Richmond, Wayne co. Ia. would inform the public, that he has went to considerable expense in procuring a

### JACQUARD MACHINE,

from New York, by which he can weave any kind of a FIGURE on COVERLETS and CARPETS that can be drawn upon paper. He will make the same kind of figures on Double-Coverlets that are made in Germantown, Dunlapsville, and Dayton, or any other place in the Western country, and at the same prices. Such figures as the Scotch fancy, with a beautiful Thistle in the border and a Flower in the centre; Also, Harrison's Fancy, with a border composed of a wreath of Tulips and Roses, and a handsome figure in the centre; the Eagle border and Bird of Paradise with a variety of other fine Figures.

Ladies wishing to exhibit their skill in their own American Manufacture, by making their own Parlour Carpets, can now have an opportunity; as I am prepared to weave the complete FIGURED, INGRAIN CARPETING, the same as the imported—provided they furnish good Yarn and good Colours.

Yarn will be received at the following places, and the goods returned free of extra charge:

E. Fisher's, Centreville; Mr. Bruce's, on the National Road, 4 miles west of Centreville; J. Baldwin's, Cambridge City; Cheesman's Mill, on West River; M. E. Reeves', Washington and Hagerstown; J. Monger's, Winchester; Dr. J. W Matchett's, Abington, Ia.; also, at G. W. Venneman's, New Paris; John Degroot's, Eaton; and Fouts' Factory, near West Alexandria, Ohio; William Grimes', New Boston, Indiana.

MATTHEW RATTRAY.

N. B. Persons having COVERLETS to weave, can have them done in a few weeks after the Yarn is received.

Richmond, Sept. 1841.—33-tf. M. R.

Advertisement of Matthew Rattray, *Palladium* (Richmond, Ind.), October 2, 1841.

### ANDREW KUMP,
### Damask Coverlet Weaver,

TENDERS to his friends and the public generally, his sincere acknowledgements for past favors, and respectfully informs them that he continues the

DAMASK COVERLET WEAVING,

at his old stand in Baltimore street, Hanover, in the shop adjoining the dwelling of Mr. John Beard, and a few doors from Dr. J. Culbertson's residence, where he is prepared to manufacture the latest and most improved patterns, of

### Damask Coverlets,

which in point of beauty and durability, are far superior to any heretofore made in this place.—He has lately added to his establishment, entirely new machinery of the latest eastern inventions, that supercede all others.

He is now prepared to weave Coverlets for $2, and will furnish the necessary *Cotton Yarn*, for each Coverlet for $1 62½. *Woolen Yarn*, if required, will be colored in a superior manner.

Twenty cuts of *Woolen Yarn* is required to each Coverlet.

A supply of COTTON YARN, of the best quality, always kept on hand.

He flatters himself that by strict attention to business, and a desire to please, he will be enabled to give general satisfaction to those who may favor him with their patronage, and merit a continuance of the same.

Hanover, Aug. 13, 1845.

N. B. Orders from a distance will be promptly attended to.

Advertisement of Andrew Kump, *Spectator* (Hanover, Pa.), August 13, 1845.

This coverlet border inscription reads, "Latest Stile Cov[erlet] Made By Henry K. Coble Colours Warranted"; Beiderwand weave in red, blue, green, and light blue wool and white cotton. Collection of Margaret H. Davies.

The coverlet border inscription reads, "Latest Improved P[atent] Warranted M[ade] By H. Stager Mount Joy"; Beiderwand weave in red, orange, and green wool and natural cotton. Woven by Henry Stager, Mount Joy, Pa., ca. 1850–1860. Collection of Mr. and Mrs. Foster McCarl, Jr.

erlets with their names and the designation "Damask Coverlet Manufacturer." Jay van Vleck of Ohio and Jacob Schnell of Pennsylvania used the more commonly encountered phrase "Manufactured by" as part of their signatures.

Since many of the weavers offered to dye the coverlet yarns for their customers, assurances of the dye's high quality might also be taken into consideration when composing an inscription for the signature block or border. Henry Stager used a variety of inscriptions in the corner blocks to guarantee his work, including "M. by H. F. Stager, Mount Joy, Lancaster Co., Pa., Fast Color No. 1." Another weaver, Henry Coble, signed his work with the legend, "Latest Stile Cov[erlet] Made By Henry K. Coble Colours Warranted."[25]

*This coverlet corner block, dated 1849, reads in part, "Fear God and Keep His Commandments," an inscription used consistently by Daniel Fisher, a professional weaver in South Bend, Ind. Beiderwand weave in red, black, and green wool and white cotton. Northern Indiana Historical Society.*

Some weavers also used inscriptions to express their sentiments. Jonathan Garber of Maryland was so proud of his work that he boasted "No man can better it" in woven words. Others were more pious. Daniel Fisher of Indiana used the legend, "Fear God and Keep His Commandments."

Considering the ethnic origins and backgrounds of the weavers, it is not surprising to find a mixture of German and English in some coverlet legends. In Upper Hanover Township, Montgomery County, Pennsylvania,

---

[25] Newspaper advertisements and inventories demonstrate that many weavers were familiar with the dyepot. George Cosley promised to "Dye INDIGO BLUE, warranted to stand, and all kinds of COLOURING done in the neatest manner." *Chambersburg Whig*, April 27, 1838. William Turner was listed in an 1850 census as a dyer and weaver in the fourth ward of Dayton, Montgomery County, Ohio. The will of George Nicklas declared that his "Looms and fixtures of my weaver shop including dye kettles" were to be sold to his nephew. January 24, 1860, Franklin County Courthouse, Pa.

W. Steier worked and wove "W. Steier, Ober Hanover in Montgomery." Peter Harting of Lancaster County, Pennsylvania, used the words "Der Depig W." ("The Coverlet Weaver") on at least one of his coverlets, while Michael Schwartz, also of Lancaster County, wove "Mate by M. Schwartz."

Perhaps because they believed that their work was well known to area residents, some weavers used only initials as identification. The Van Doren brothers, Garret William, Isaac William, and Peter Sutphen, had to abbreviate their long names and marked their coverlets "G.W.V.D., I.W.V.D., or P.S.V.D." David I. Grave of Indiana used the initials "D.I.G." on some coverlets, and his full name on others. Probably the most cryptic inscription was that used by Isaac Sheaffer. "Isaac Sheaffer, R.H.W.T.L.C." stood for "Isaac Sheaffer, Rabbit Hill, Warwick Township, Lancaster County, Pennsylvania."

Some weavers were poor spellers, and they inevitably made errors when they translated designs onto the pattern cards. In the case of popular designs, such mistakes could be corrected when the paperboard cards wore out and replacements were punched. The dimensional limits of a signature block might also affect the continuity of an inscription. For example, Martin Breneman of "Washingto Township, York, Count, Penn." had too many letters for the small space available, and thus the "n" and "y" were sacrificed. A few weavers consistently reversed letters or numbers—usually "n" and "3."

Several weavers identified themselves, not by using their names or initials, but with a trademark. For a number of years Harry Tyler, of Jefferson County, New York, used a regal lion to identify himself, later changing to a triumphant American eagle. Samuel Schreffler of Pennsylvania, Matthew Rattray of Indiana, and others used eagles. William Craig and his son William used a small courthouse with a cupola on top, while the Gilmour brothers identified themselves by weaving a sailboat into the corner block. Naturally it is sometimes difficult to distinguish a trademark from an element that is merely part of the pattern of the coverlet. A special section in this book illustrates many recognized trademarks and identifies the artisans who employed them. See page 125.

A few weavers not only signed their work but also numbered each coverlet. Absalom Klinger of Pennsylvania holds the known record. In 1843 he wove coverlet number 1,499; by 1855 he had completed number 2,003. It is not known whether he did all of the weaving himself or had assistance. Samuel B. Musselman, also of Pennsylvania, numbered his work, too—at least for a time. He wove coverlet number 852 in 1851 and he was still weaving but no longer numbering his coverlets by 1859. To date, no account books have been found with numbers that correspond to those on serialized coverlets.

In contrast to the folklore and traditions often associated with "family" or regional patterns woven on the less complex looms, weavers using the Jacquard-type attachment had no reason to be—and less ability to remain—secretive about their designs. Weavers could purchase ready-punched pattern or design cards,[26] but many made their own.[27] The advertisement of Abraham Van Vleet in the Connersville, Indiana, *Political Clarion*, April 20, 1830, promised coverlets "in the best and most fashionable manner," since he had "made arrangements with Eastern Shops for a regular supply of the newest patterns." Josiah Cass placed an advertisement in the *Freeman and Messenger*, Lodi, New York, November 22, 1841, stating that he was ready to weave coverlets of every description, having just received new designs from New York.

Due to the migration of weavers, the circulation of the coverlets themselves, and the availability of pre-punched pattern cards, it is difficult to determine definitive regional design differences. Although the distelfink, or thistlefinch, and tulip motifs are associated with Pennsylvania German weavers, these designs were known to others and appear on coverlets not woven in Pennsylvania and Maryland. In fact, by the 1840s identical designs appeared in Ohio, Indiana, and Canada.

A few generalizations about regional weaving techniques and weave structure may be made, however. For instance, coverlets made in New York, New Jersey, Indiana, and Illinois most often are double woven, while those from Pennsylvania and Maryland are generally single woven in the Beiderwand weave. The available data indicate that the majority of weavers who settled in the former group of states, especially New York and Indiana,

---

[26] Some of the companies manufacturing Jacquard loom attachments and equipment include John Scott and Cornelius McNeil in 1845; Walter C. Clark in 1850; Chambers and Riehl and W. P. Uhlinger and Co. in 1859—all Philadelphia companies—and James Lightbody, Paterson, New Jersey, before 1859.

[27] The advertisement of Matthew Rattray in the Richmond, Indiana, *Palladium*, October 2, 1841, states that he "can weave any kind of a FIGURE on COVERLETS and CARPETS that can be drawn upon paper." See advertisement on p. 17.

"Farmer's Fancy" coverlet; double weave in blue wool and white cotton. The interior is composed of repeats of a farmer at his plow, cabins, eagles, and the rising sun. The borders contain horses, trees, and meetinghouses. Woven by the LaTourette family, Fountain Co., Ind., ca. 1835. Collection of the Colonial Coverlet Guild of America.

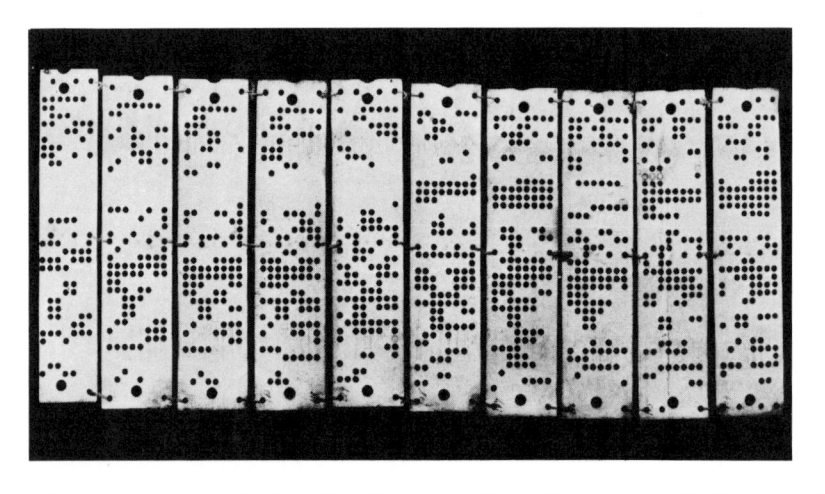

Jacquard-type pattern cards for the "Farmer's Fancy" coverlet. Collection of the Colonial Coverlet Guild of America.

came from the British Isles. Weavers in Pennsylvania and Maryland were usually German or of German heritage. Ohio weavers came from Great Britain and Germany in approximately equal numbers; consequently, the fact that Jacquard-type coverlets produced there are divided between single and double woven points to a fusion of the two traditions.[28]

The popular names of specific coverlet designs are often ambiguous, and the name of a particular pattern can seldom be cited with certainty because the terminology was and still is not universal, although some pattern books and weaver's drafts do spell out pattern names or give clues concerning pattern origin.[29] Occasionally the name of the design, such as "Peace and Plenty" or "Farmer's Fancy," was woven into a coverlet. It is clear that certain names were familiar to a local audience. Matthew Rattray advertised in an 1841 Richmond, Indiana, *Palladium* that he would weave figures such as "Scotch Fancy," "Harrison's Fancy," and the "Bird of Paradise" for his

---

[28] An intriguing and as yet unexplained regional difference is the fact that although few coverlets in New York are fringed, the majority of coverlets from other states include fringed borders, whether applied or self-fringed. This raises some interesting questions: did individuals pay extra for fringe in some areas? If so, did a client apply the fringe after the coverlet left the weaver? Or would weavers perform this service for an additional fee? As yet, there is no documentation to provide answers.

[29] Christian Frey's pattern book is privately owned; Abraham Serff's is in the Historical Society of York County, York, Pa.; and Heinrich Muhlenhoff's is in the Lycoming County Historical Society, Williamsport, Pa.

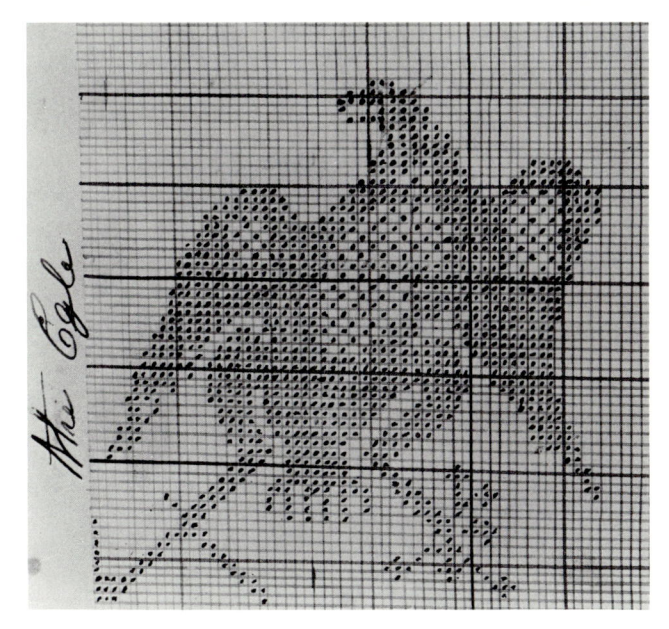

*Pen and ink draft of a coverlet design component titled "the E[a]gle"; drawn by weaver Henry Oberly, Womelsdorf, Pa. Historical Society of Berks County, Reading, Pa.*

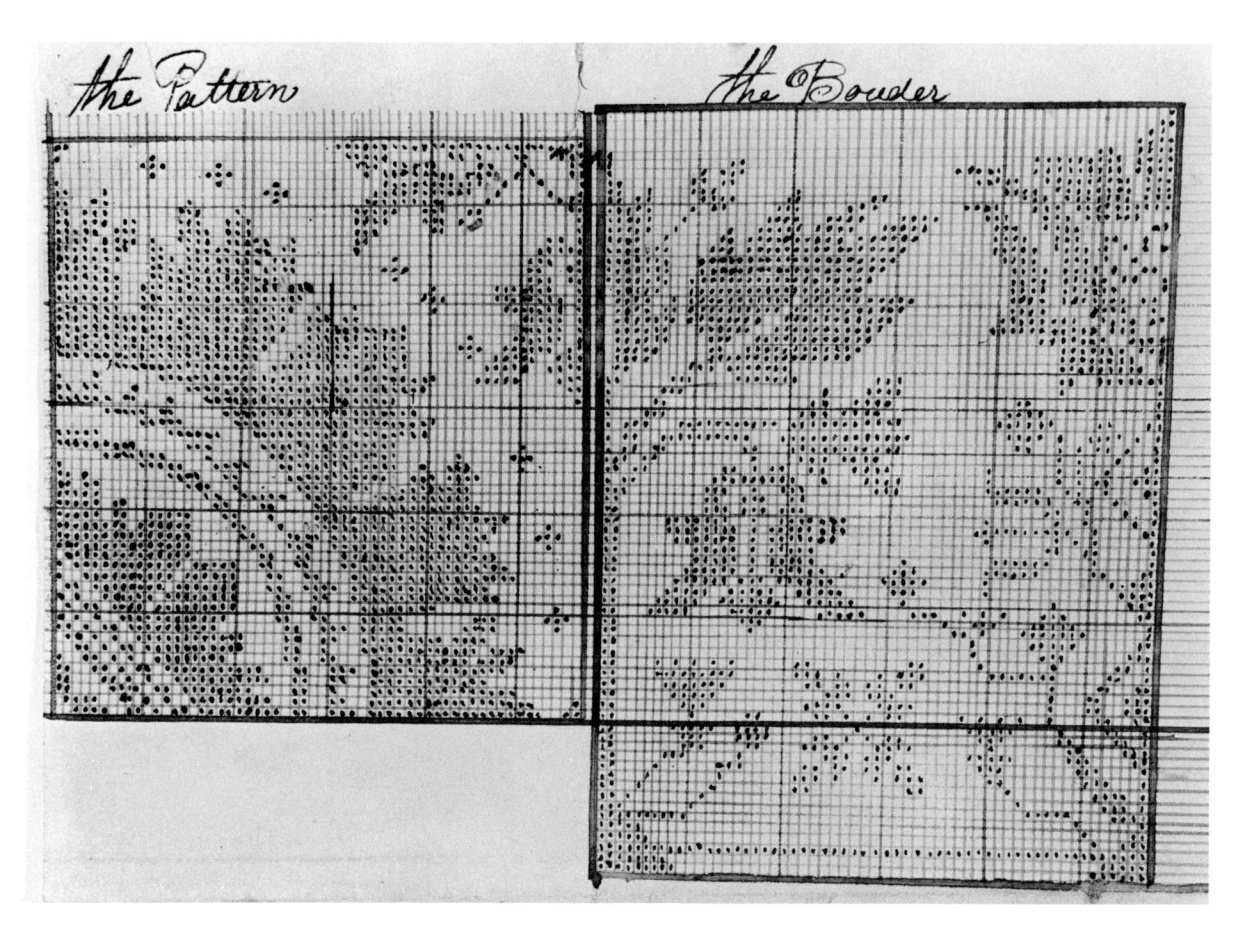

*Two pen and ink drafts for an interior "Pattern" design and a "Border" element for a woven coverlet; drawn by weaver Henry Oberly, Womelsdorf, Pa. Historical Society of Berks County, Reading, Pa.*

Wayne County, Indiana, customers.[30] Roses, eagles, lilies, a variety of birds, weeping willows, and stylized buildings were among the most common motifs.

Coverlet borders were often designed as separate units unrelated to interior patterns, and occasionally a coverlet takes its generic title from the border motif. Examples of such borders are "Eagle" and "Grapevine," two designs often used by Martin Breneman of Pennsylvania, who incorporated both names in the appropriate borders. Another popular border with several variations depicts the unlikely merger of a stylized New England town

---

[30] Montgomery, *Indiana Coverlet Weavers*, p. 85.

*Occasionally the weaver identified the border or interior pattern in the coverlet itself as seen in this example. The interior design of oak leaves and flowers repeats the name of the pattern, "Oak Leaf"; Beiderwand weave in red, blue, and green wool and white cotton. Woven by Joseph Turnbaugh, Luzerne Co., Pa., 1851. Collection of Mr. and Mrs. Foster McCarl, Jr.*

and an oriental village. Generally referred to today as "Boston Town," the pattern is also known as "Christian and Heathen."[31]

As the nineteenth century progressed, coverlet design was affected by the Victorian taste for lavish patterns. During the late 1840s and 1850s, huge floral medallions surrounded by foliate wreaths or geometric tilelike motifs appeared. Borders became more intricate and floral as well, and flowing vines and swirls were commonly employed. The Centennial of American Independence produced a rash of patriotic designs. Among the most common were those showing Memorial Hall, the 1876 exposition building in Philadelphia, and the United States Capitol. One design included a corner profile of George Washington, another featured a bust of General Ulysses S. Grant, while a third depicted silhouettes of Presidents Washington, Adams, Madison, Monroe, Jackson, Van Buren, and Harrison.

By the 1860s and 1870s, industrial growth and the accelerated needs of a rapidly expanding country terminated the careers of most individual weav-

---

[31] Boston's involvement with the China trade provides a reasonable explanation for the pictorial association of Boston harbor and oriental structures, although it must be kept in mind that "Boston Town" and "Christian and Heathen" cannot be documented as being nineteenth-century pattern names.

Patriotic double woven coverlet by J. Van Ness, Palmyra, N. Y., 1849, that features a center medallion with Liberty figures and flags surrounded by vines and floral motifs. "E Pluribus Unum" and eagles are repeated in the corners. Margaret Woodbury Strong Museum, Rochester, N. Y.

[ 26 ]

ers working hand-operated looms. Some moved farther west, while others migrated to Canada in search of new markets. But the era of the independent weaver was over, and handwoven coverlets were soon outmoded by the mechanized, large-scale production of textiles.

The data gathered in this project have increased our understanding of the life and work of the professional weaver, and we hope that our efforts will encourage further research and will prompt the discovery of other factual information about America's professional weavers and their coverlets. It has proven impossible to identify all of the skilled nineteenth-century craftsmen who wove Jacquard-type coverlets, and even weavers included in this checklist undoubtedly worked at other places and times. Readers with additional information are urged to send new or unrecorded data, with appropriate photographic evidence, to the Abby Aldrich Rockefeller Folk Art Center, Drawer C, Williamsburg, Virginia 23185, to add to our expanding index of professional weavers. Information on the whereabouts of Jacquard-equipped looms, Jacquard-type pattern cards or pattern books, account books, or advertisements of coverlet weavers is also welcome.

# Checklist Explanation

THE following is a checklist of professional weavers working in America primarily during the second and third quarters of the nineteenth century. Although skilled professional weavers played an important role in American coverlet production before 1825 and continued to produce coverlets in geometric weaves well into the nineteenth century, the primary focus of this study is on those weavers who used a loom with a Jacquard-type device. Professionals who utilized the Jacquard-type attachment and other patented variations of the invention were not necessarily more adept at their craft than earlier professional, semi-professional, or domestic weavers; they simply were skilled in a new phase of weaving technology that has been easier to document, mainly because the makers so often signed their products.

The names of the weavers are arranged alphabetically, last name first. When an individual's birth and death dates are known, they appear in parentheses. Where only an approximate date could be obtained, ca. is used. Other information about an artisan's life and work follows. Many entries incorporate findings from previous checklists and surveys; the abbreviated titles for sources cited frequently appear at the beginning of the checklist.

Each entry concludes with a number indicating how many coverlets by the weaver were recorded in this survey and the earliest and latest dates woven into them. For example, 4, 1838–1845 indicates that the individual discussed wove four recorded coverlets between 1838 and 1845. An asterisk signifies that no coverlets woven by that craftsman were recorded in this study.

When only one name appears in a signature block, and when only one coverlet has been recorded, it is sometimes impossible to distinguish the weaver of the coverlet from the client who commissioned it. It is too often assumed that a name or initials woven into corner blocks of some coverlets indicate that the piece was produced by that individual. A number of these puzzlers are included in the checklist in the hope that other coverlets or supporting documentation will appear to confirm some of the attributions.

During this survey, we attempted to note the weave structure, the interior and border patterns, and whether a specific coverlet was seamed in the middle or woven in one piece. Although the results have proved too fragmentary and inconclusive to warrant publishing here, the information is recorded on the individual coverlet cards that comprise the Abby Aldrich Rockefeller Folk Art Center's index to professional weavers working in the United States. Those readers desiring additional technical information may consult the museum. The data in this checklist have been obtained and verified through the interest and support of concerned individuals, and it is hoped that assistance from the public will continue.

# A

ADAM, ———. Adam is listed by the C.C.G.A., Safford and Bishop, and Kovel and Kovel as weaving in Greencastle, Pennsylvania (Franklin Co.), in 1821. *

ADOLF, Henry (ca. 1815–   ). Born in Alsace, France, Adolf worked in Montgomery County, Ohio, in 1838, moving to Wayne County, Indiana, by 1840 where, according to Montgomery, he was weaving with John Wissler near Milton. In 1844 he settled in Cambridge City and set up his own weaving shop. By 1849 he had purchased land near Noblesville, Indiana (Hamilton Co.), where he farmed and continued his weaving. When the land was sold in 1855, Adolf's residence was given as Mahaska County, Iowa. From inscriptions on his coverlets, it is evident that in 1866 he was weaving in Douglas County, Kansas, and in 1878 in Clinton, Kansas (Douglas Co.). (See also entry for John Klein.) 11, 1841–1878.

ADOLPH, Charles (ca. 1815–   ). Born in Alsace, France, Adolph immigrated to America in 1843 with his wife and brother George and settled in Williamsburg, Indiana (Wayne Co.). The 1850 U. S. census lists him as a weaver living in Green Township, Indiana (Wayne Co.), and gives his birthplace as Germany. Montgomery states that by the late 1850s he was in Henry County, Indiana; in 1870 he moved to Osage County, Kansas. He often wove a domed building or temple design in the corner blocks of his coverlets as a trademark. 8, 1845–1852.

ADOLPH, George (ca. 1822–   ). Born in Alsace, France, George Adolph immigrated to America with his brother Charles in 1843. He worked as a weaver in Wayne and Henry counties, Indiana. The 1850 U. S. census records George as a laborer, perhaps supporting Montgomery's contention that weaving was a part-time career for him. He is also listed by the C.C.G.A. and Safford and Bishop as weaving in Henry County, Indiana, in 1857. 2, 1848–1849.

AIKENS, James. Aikens was employed as a weaver by James Alexander (see entry) from July 1817 until March 1818. *

AKIN, Phebe. She is listed by Safford and Bishop as weaving in New York state in 1834. *

ALEXANDER, F. M. He is identified by the C.C.G.A. and Safford and Bishop as weaving in 1848; the location of his activity is unknown. This weaver may be T. M. Alexander (see entry). *

ALEXANDER, James (1770–1870). Born of Scottish parents in Belfast, Ireland, Alexander had seven years of training as a weaver before coming to America in 1798. Settling first in Connecticut, he soon moved to Little Britain, a village near Newburgh in Orange County, New York, where he farmed and also wove all sorts of fabrics including carpets, coverlets, and linens. At least initially, he used a drawloom to create intricate pictorial designs. Alexander employed several weavers over the years, and his account book, now preserved in the library of the New York State Historical Association in Cooperstown, lists a number of them and what they produced. Some of those who wove coverlets for him were James Robinson and John Wilson in 1806, Samuel Crothers in 1811, and John Gibbs in 1818 (see entries). Alexander died in Little Britain and is buried in St. George's cemetery in Newburgh. Many of his coverlets feature American eagles, Masonic emblems, or Independence Hall as part of the border designs. 9, 1821–1826. See Virginia D. Parslow, "James Alexander, weaver," *Antiques*, LXIX (April 1956), pp. 346–349.

ALEXANDER, Robert (1801–1880). Born in Kilmarnock, Ayrshire, Scotland, he worked in a shawl factory in Paisley, Scotland, before coming to the United States. He settled in Thompsonville, Connecticut (Hartford Co.), where he worked in the Bigelow-Sanford Carpet Factory. In 1849 he moved to Canfield, Ohio (Mahoning Co.), and opened a weaving shop; the 1850 U. S. census lists him as a weaver there. He is buried in the Canfield cemetery. Many of his coverlets have borders of houses alternating with huntsmen on horseback, dogs at their feet. 8, all undated.

ALEXANDER, Thomas M. (ca. 1813–   ). Born in Ohio, Thomas Alexander was weaving in Wayne County, Ohio, in 1848, according to the O.H.S. The 1850 U. S. census describes him as a coverlet weaver in Salt Creek Township, Ohio (Wayne Co.). 3, one dated 1848.

ALLABACH, Philip. The C.C.G.A., Safford and Bishop, and Kovel and Kovel describe Allabach as a weaver in Michigan; the dates of his activity are unknown. *

ALLEN, Abram. Allen is listed by the C.C.G.A. and Safford and Bishop as weaving in Ohio in 1840; in 1844 he was weaving in Hillsboro, Ohio (Highland Co.). The Art Institute of Chicago states that he was weaving near Wilmington, Ohio (Clinton Co.), and that he was the only man in the county using a flying shuttle. Allen paraphrased the Golden Rule in the inscriptions woven into the corners of his coverlets: "Be ye to others kind and true as you'd have others be to you and neither say or do to them what e'er you would not take again." 11, 1837–1844.

ALLEN, B. Hausman. He is listed by the C.C.G.A. and Kovel and Kovel as weaving in Groveland, New York (Livingston Co.), in 1839, which is probably a misreading and misinterpretation of an inscription woven on a coverlet by Benjamin Hausman (see entry). *

AMBROUSE, ———. The single coverlet by him recorded in this study indicates that Ambrouse was weaving in Greencastle, Pennsylvania (Franklin Co.), in 1836 with another weaver, Adam Bohn (see entry).

ANDREWS, Jacob. Reinert says that Andrews was weaving in East Hempfield Township, Pennsylvania (Lancaster Co.), in 1836. He also wove in Manor Township (Lancaster Co.), in 1836 and 1837. 3, 1836–1837.

ANDREWS, M. One coverlet with this name, the location of Millstone, New Jersey (Somerset Co.), and the date 1838 has been recorded; it is not known whether Andrews was the weaver or the client.

ANGSTAD, Benjamin (ca. 1806–1863). Born in Pennsylvania, he learned weaving from Joseph Schnee (see entry) at the Mount Pleasant Mills in Snyder County, Pennsylvania. Between 1836 and 1838 the two men wove together in Lewisburg, Pennsylvania (Union Co.), signing their work "Angstad & Schnee." After Schnee died in 1838, Angstad continued weaving alone in Lewisburg; according to the 1850 U.S. census, he was a weaver there. In his household at that time was a 28-year-old Pennsylvania-born weaver by the name of Nathaniel Angstadt (see entry), presumably a relative. A list of the awards given to exhibitors at the annual fair of the Union County Agricultural Society was published in the October 13, 1854, issue of the *Lewisburg Chronicle and West Branch Farmer*. Angstad received $2 for the best wool carpet, 50¢ for the second best rag carpet, and 50¢ for one pound of woolen yarn. Four coverlets woven by Angstad and Schnee that date from 1836 to 1838 have been recorded, and there are eleven by Angstad alone, dating from 1838 to 1849.

ANGSTAD, Jacob. His pattern book from Lewisburg, Pennsylvania, dated July 22, 1834, contains patterns for double weave and double face twill for 20-harness loom work, 28-harness work, and 32-harness work. Included are over 250 drafts for double and single woven coverlets as well as dye recipes. *

ANGSTADT, Nathaniel (ca. 1822– ). He is recorded in the 1850 U.S. census as a weaver living in the household of Benjamin Angstad (see entry). Among the exhibitors at the annual fair of the Union County Agricultural Society was "Nathan Angstadt," Lewisburg, who won $2 for the best wool carpet. *Lewisburg Chronicle and West Branch Farmer*, October 21, 1853. *

ANSHUTZ, Philip. Kovel and Kovel list Anshutz as weaving at Carrollton, Ohio, between 1820 and 1840. He is included in W. W. Reilly & Co. as a coverlet weaver in Carrollton, Center Township, Ohio (Carroll Co.). 7, all undated.

ANTIETAM FACTORY. See entry for Gabriel Baer.

ARAM, E. One coverlet with this name, Bethany, New York (Genesee Co.), and 1836 has been recorded; it is not known whether Aram was the weaver or the client.

*Coverlet border design of baskets of pears and flowers; double weave in red and blue wool. Woven by John Klein, Hamilton Co., Ind., 1868. Collection of Mr. and Mrs. Foster McCarl, Jr. See color plate facing page 70.*

[ 32 ]

Wreaths of flowers on a polka-dotted background dominate the interior of this coverlet, while the borders are composed of baskets of fruit and flowers; double weave in red and blue wool. Woven by John Klein, Hamilton Co., Ind., 1868. Collection of Mr. and Mrs. Foster McCarl, Jr.

Ardner, Jacob (ca. 1817– ). Born in Germany, he immigrated to America with his father, Jacob, and brother Michael, both of whom were weavers. The 1850 U. S. census includes all three as weavers living in Mt. Vernon, Ohio (Knox Co.), their name being spelled "Artner." Jacob and Michael are listed by the C.C.G.A., Safford and Bishop, and Kovel and Kovel as weaving in Mt. Vernon, Ohio, in 1858. 19 (Jacob and Michael), 1851–1859; 1 (Jacob alone), 1850.

Ardner, Michael (ca. 1821– ). Michael Ardner was born in Germany. (See entry for Jacob Ardner.) 19 (Jacob and Michael), 1851–1859.

Armbrust, Wilhelm (ca. 1807–1904). He was born in Germany. According to Burnham and Burnham, Armbrust was the first weaver to use Jacquard equipment in Canada (Lincoln County, Ontario) in 1834. He went to Canada from the United States, although nothing has been discovered about his training or work here. *

Armbruster, J. One coverlet with this name, a Miami County, Ohio, location, and the date 1839 has been recorded; it is not known whether Armbruster was the weaver or the client.

Armstrong, J. H. According to recorded coverlets, he was weaving in Erie County, Ohio, from 1844 to 1847. 3, 1844–1847.

Arnold, Daniel. According to the Art Institute of Chicago, Arnold was weaving in Chambersburg, Pennsylvania (Franklin Co.), from 1828 to 1844. 10, 1835–1846.

Arnold, Lorenz. One coverlet with this name and Wheeling, Illinois (Cook Co.), has been recorded; it is not known whether Arnold was the weaver or the client.

Artman, Abraham. He is listed by Safford and Bishop as weaving in Dansville, New York (Livingston Co.), in 1830. 1, undated.

Auburn Prison. The state prison in Auburn, New York (Cayuga Co.), is described in French as a maker of carpets and coverlids. 2, 1845–1850.

Ayrhart, Peter (ca. 1836– ). Born in Ohio, Ayrhart appears in the 1850 U. S. census as having no occupation, although he was living in the household of Thomas H. Sheldon, a tailor, in Columbus, Ohio (Franklin Co.). He later is listed in W. W. Reilly & Co. as a coverlet weaver in Canal Winchester, Madison Township, Ohio (Franklin Co.). *

B

Bachman, Anceneta. One coverlet woven by Bachman in Philadelphia in 1864 has been recorded. Philadelphia city directories for this period do not cite this individual.

Backer, Hiram. See entry for Solomon Kuder.

Backus, Thaddeus. Backus advertised that he was starting a weaving business and would weave single and double woven coverlets in the October 7, 1830, issue of the Marietta, Ohio (Washington Co.) *American Friend and Marietta Gazette.* *

Baden, C. The O.H.S. reports that Baden was weaving in Montgomery County, Ohio, from 1844 to 1846. 1, 1847.

Baer, Gabriel. The Franklin County, Pennsylvania, records indicate that Baer had a woolen factory there

*This coverlet border design is a flowering bush; double weave in blue wool and white cotton. Woven by Samuel Graham, Henry Co., Ind., 1849. Collection of Mr. and Mrs. Foster McCarl, Jr.*

[ 34 ]

in 1850; the 1856 tax records show him as a manufacturer in Washington Township, Franklin Co. The corner inscriptions of two of his coverlets, dated 1849 and 1856, state that they were woven by G. Baer at the "Antietam Factory" in Franklin County. 3, 1849–1856.

BAGLEY, S. One coverlet with this name, a Pekin, New York (Niagara Co.), location, and the date 1840 has been recorded; it is not known whether Bagley was the weaver or the client.

BAIRD, James (ca. 1788–    ). Born in Ireland, he is listed by the C.C.G.A. and Kovel and Kovel as weaving in Switzerland County, Indiana; Safford and Bishop locate him there in 1830. Montgomery states that he was in America by 1827 but is not known to have been a professional weaver. *

BAKER, Daniel, Jr. (1820–1905). He was a weaver in Carroll Township, Pennsylvania (York Co.), from 1841 to at least 1850, and is buried in the Salem (Barrens) cemetery, Washington Township, York Co. *

BAKER, David (1816–    ). He is listed by the O.H.S. as weaving in Columbus, Ohio (Franklin Co.), in 1843 and 1844, and he is described as a Virginia-born weaver living in the first ward of Columbus in the 1850 U. S. census. The Columbus city directory for 1850–1851 includes him as a weaver on Fourth Street between Spring and North streets. (See also entry for John Baker.) *

BAKER, Eliza Jane. Madden indicates that she was a weaver in New City (now part of Chicago), Illinois; the dates of her activity are unknown. *

BAKER, John. The O.H.S. lists Baker as weaving in Columbus, Ohio, in 1843 and 1844; the Columbus city directory for 1843–1844 shows that he was located on Fourth Street between Spring and North streets. (See also entry for David Baker.) *

BALANTYNE, Abraham (1835–1904). Born in Pennsylvania, he was a son of Samuel Balantyne (see entry), also a coverlet weaver. Montgomery states that the family moved to Lafayette, Indiana (Tippecanoe Co.), where Abraham worked awhile for his father. Some coverlets attributed to this family possibly were made by Abraham but are not so marked. 4 (Balantyne family), 1845–1847; most undated.

BALANTYNE, John (ca. 1812–    ). Born in Scotland, Balantyne is listed in the 1850 U. S. census of Eel Township, Indiana (Cass Co.), as a weaver. His relationship to Abraham and Samuel Balantyne is not known. *

BALANTYNE, Samuel (1808–1861). Born in Scotland, he was weaving in Indiana by 1850. Montgomery states that he came to America in 1832 with his wife and several children. They settled first in Canonsburg, Pennsylvania (Washington Co.), but by 1834 had moved to Cincinnati, Ohio (Hamilton Co.). By 1839 the family was in Reading, Ohio (Hamilton Co.), and had moved to Lafayette, Indiana (Tippecanoe Co.), by 1845. Samuel later moved to White County, Indiana, where he died.

*This coverlet interior design is composed of leaves with flower buds; Beiderwand weave in blue wool and white cotton. Weaver unidentified, possibly Pennsylvania or Ohio, ca. 1850. Collection of Mr. and Mrs. Foster McCarl, Jr.*

The 1850 census of manufacturers lists him as having a weaving establishment with three looms, where he employed two men and one woman. 4 (Balantyne family), 1845–1847; 1 signed S. Balantyne and dated 1847; 1 attributed to S. Balantyne.

BALDWIN, H. He appears in W. W. Reilly & Co. as a coverlet weaver in Medina, Ohio (Medina Co.). *

BALIOT, Abraham. One coverlet with this name and the date 1840 has been recorded; it is not known if Baliot was the weaver or the client.

BALL, H. H. Ball is listed by the C.C.G.A., Safford and Bishop, and Kovel and Kovel as weaving in Orange County, New York, in 1830. *

BALSAMAN, Isaac. The O.H.S. indicates that he was weaving in Springfield, Ohio (Clark Co.), around 1845. *

BARRETT, ———. He is listed by Reinert and Kovel and Kovel as weaving in Howard, Pennsylvania (Centre Co.), about 1850. The name Barrett does not appear in the 1850 U. S. census for that part of Centre County, nor have any coverlets bearing this name been found. *

BARTH, Andrew. Barth is cited by the O.H.S. as weaving in Columbus, Ohio (Franklin Co.), in 1843 and 1844, and appears as a weaver in the Columbus city directory for those years. *

BARTLER, Joseph. W. W. Reilly & Co. includes Bartler as a coverlet weaver in North Georgetown, Knox Township, Ohio (Columbiana Co.). *

BARTLET, Jerusha. She is listed by Safford and Bishop as weaving in 1855, but no location is given. *

BAUER, William. One coverlet with this name and Martinsburg, Virginia (Berkeley Co.), has been recorded. Presumably it was woven prior to 1863, since Martinsburg became part of West Virginia at that time.

BAUGHMAN, John. John Baughman is listed in W. W. Reilly & Co. as a coverlet weaver in Lexington, Ohio (Richland Co.). *

BAYARD, Jacob. W. W. Reilly & Co. describes Bayard as a coverlet weaver in North Lima, Ohio (Mahoning Co.). *

BEAN, ———. A Mrs. Bean is listed in W. W. Reilly & Co. as a coverlet weaver in Medina County, Ohio.*

BEARD, M. Reinert identifies him as weaving in 1842; Beard's location of activity is unknown. *

BEARD, William. Beard appears in W. W. Reilly & Co. as a coverlet weaver in Dunlevy, Ohio (Warren Co.). *

BEATTY, Gavin I. Beatty advertised that he was in business weaving coverlets and other materials. *Oracle of Dauphin and Harrisburgh Advertiser* (Harrisburg, Pa.), July 25, 1798. By February 1811 he was in debt and sold all his possessions and weaving equipment to George Beatty and David Scarlet. Among the items were a "warpin machine," reeds, gears, shuttles, temples, "reales," spools, and "the other tackling and weaving apparatus thereto belonging."

*A solid color vase with flowers and fruit alternates with a checkered vase of flowers and perching birds in this coverlet border design; Beiderwand weave in red wool and light blue cotton. Weaver unidentified, probably Pennsylvania or Ohio, ca. 1850. Abby Aldrich Rockefeller Folk Art Center, bequest of Margaret H. Davies.*

Dauphin County Courthouse. *

BECHTEL, John. According to Reinert, Bechtel was a weaver in Springfield Township, Pennsylvania (Bucks Co.). *

BECK, Augustus. He is listed by Madden as weaving in Quincy, Illinois (Adams Co.); the dates are unknown. *

BEERBOWER, William. The O.H.S. says that he was weaving in Steubenville, Ohio (Jefferson Co.), in 1837. *

BEIL, David (ca. 1811– ). Born in Pennsylvania, Beil wove in New Hamburg, Pennsylvania (Mercer Co.), from 1845 to 1868. The 1850 U. S. census lists him as a weaver in Delaware Township, Mercer Co. The C.C.G.A., Safford and Bishop, and Kovel and Kovel include a "B." Beil weaving in 1846; furthermore, a coverlet dated 1843 woven by "D. Bell" has been recorded. Both of these variations may be misreadings of inscribed coverlets by David Beil. 10, 1843–1868.

BELLMAN, Henry. See entry for Emanuel Meily, Jr.

BENDER, David (1824– ). He was weaving in Johnson County, Iowa; the dates are unknown but he may have been active as late as 1874. His coverlet pattern book dated 1846 and his daybook are now in the Museum of International Folk Art, Santa Fe, N. M. 1, 1874.

BENNETT, R. According to the O.H.S., he was weaving at Monroeville, Ohio (Huron Co.), in 1852 and 1853. 2, 1852–1853.

BENNETT, S. A. He was weaving in 1833; the location of his activity has not been determined, but possibly it was in New York state. 1, 1833.

BERRY, ———. Berry is listed by Madden as weaving in Bluff Springs (now Watseka), Illinois (Iroquois Co.); the dates are unknown. *

BERTHALEMY, Jacob. W. W. Reilly & Co. lists him as a coverlet weaver in New Berlin (now North Canton), Ohio (Stark Co.). *

BEWFORD, Elias (ca. 1819– ). Born in Pennsylvania, he had a carding and fulling mill in Union Township, Pennsylvania (Union Co.). The 1850 census of manufacturers locates him there and indicates that he made woolen coverlets. *

BICHEL, W. By 1843 Bichel was weaving in Newark, Ohio (Licking Co.), and by 1847 in Logan, Ohio (Hocking Co.). His name is also spelled "Bickel" or "Buechel" on his coverlets. "Pyna Rose" is one design he used, and the name of this pattern is woven into the corner panels of some of his coverlets. At least five of Bichel's coverlets are known. 2 ("Bichel"), 1843; 1 ("Bickel"), 1843; 2 ("Buechel"), 1847.

BICK, John (ca. 1822– ). Born in Germany, the O.H.S. lists Bick as weaving in Rome, Ohio (Seneca Co.), in 1850, and the 1850 U. S. census indicates that he was a weaver in London Township, Seneca Co. 2, 1850 and 1853.

BICKEL, W. See entry for W. Bichel.

BIESECKER, Jacob, Jr. (1806–1865). Born in Pennsylvania, this weaver is listed by Reinert, the C.C.G.A., and Safford and Bishop as weaving in Franklin Town-

Large and small pots of roses alternate in this coverlet border design; double weave in blue wool and white cotton. Weaver unidentified, Darien, Genesee Co., N. Y., 1850. Glen Ellyn Historical Society, Glen Ellyn, Ill.

[ 37 ]

ship, Pennsylvania (Adams Co.), from 1839 to at least 1852. His pattern book of coverlet patterns is owned by a descendant. Inscriptions on some of the coverlets themselves boast that he was using a "New Invention" in the weaving process. An inventory taken a short time after Biesecker's death includes three weaver's looms and fixtures valued at $15, a lot of old carpet valued at $1.25, and 187 yards of carpet valued at $4.50. Adams County Courthouse. 5, 1839–1852.

BIGHAM, David (1788–1847). Born in Lancaster County, Pennsylvania, he moved with his family to Cincinnati, Ohio (Hamilton Co.), in 1809. The following year they relocated on a large tract of land bordering Hamilton, Ohio (Butler Co.). After his father's death in 1815, Bigham inherited a section of the land, upon which he built his home and a woolen factory. James McBride, *Pioneer Biography: Sketches of the Lives of Some of the Early Settlers of Butler County, Ohio* (Cincinnati, 1869–1871). 1, 1844.

BIRCH, S. A. He is listed in W. W. Reilly & Co. as a coverlet weaver in Morristown, Ohio (Belmont Co.). *

BISHOP, P. Bishop was weaving in Fayetteville, Pennsylvania (Franklin Co.), in 1846. 1, 1846.

BISSET, William (1822–1888). Leaving Scotland, Bisset went to Canada and then came to the United States. According to information gathered by Montgomery, he worked for a time at the Auburn Prison (see entry), Auburn, New York (Cayuga Co.). He relocated in Franklin, Indiana (Johnson Co.), where he continued to weave. After the Civil War, he left Indiana, and his last home was Chillicothe, Missouri (Livingston Co.). *

BIVENOUR, M. He is listed by the C.C.G.A., Safford and Bishop, and Kovel and Kovel as weaving in 1842; the location is unknown. *

BLACK, G. He is listed by the O.H.S. as weaving in Springfield, Ohio (Clark Co.), in 1843. *

BLACK, William. The O.H.S. lists him as weaving in Ohio in 1868. *

BLOCHER, S. (or B.). From recorded coverlets, it has been discovered that Blocher was weaving in Bolivar, Ohio (Tuscarawas Co.), in 1848. The inscription on one of the coverlets reads "B. Blocher" rather than "S," although all were woven in Tuscarawas County. (See also entry for S. Flocher.) 3, all 1848.

BOALT, James (ca. 1820– ). The 1850 U. S. census lists Boalt as a coverlet weaver in Washington Township, Pennsylvania (Franklin Co.). *

BOARDMAN, E. One coverlet has been recorded with this name, the location Farmerville (county and state undetermined), and the date 1832; it is not known whether Boardman was the weaver or the client.

BODEN, C. See entry for C. Baden.

BOESHOR, Heinrich. He is listed by Reinert as weaving in 1819; the location of his activity is not known. *

BOETTGER, Carl (1823–1900). Born in Germany, he came to the United States and settled in Millerstown (now Macungie), Pennsylvania (Lehigh Co.). Boettger wove coverlets in his early years, but turned to weaving carpets later. He worked with another weaver, Charles B. Fliehr (see entry); they signed their work "Fliehr & Boettger." The 1860 U. S. census locates Boettger in Millerstown, spelling his name "Charles Bedger." He is buried in the Solomon church cemetery, Macungie. 3 (in partnership with Fliehr), undated.

BOHN, Adam (ca. 1808– ). Bohn was born in Penn-

*Coverlet border design with baskets of flowers alternating with flowering plants; double weave in blue wool and white cotton. Woven by Samuel Graham, Henry Co., Ind., 1849. Collection of Mr. and Mrs. Foster McCarl, Jr.*

[ 38 ]

sylvania. He was weaving in Greencastle, Pennsylvania (Franklin Co.), in 1836 with another weaver by the name of Ambrouse (see entry). One of their coverlets has been recorded. Bohn continued weaving in Greencastle through the 1840s. The 1850 U. S. census lists him as a weaver in Antrim Township, Franklin Co., living in the household of Adam Wingert, a farmer. 1 (Bohn and Ambrouse), 1836; 4 (Bohn alone), 1838–1846.

BOHN, Jacob W. One coverlet woven by Bohn in Greencastle, Pennsylvania (Franklin Co.), in 1846 has been recorded; his relationship with Adam Bohn (see above) is undetermined.

BOLTON, Thomas. Montgomery mentions that Bolton advertised he was starting a weaving business in Brookville. *Brookville Enquirer* (Brookville, Ind.), September 11, 1824. By 1850 he was farming in Blooming Grove, Indiana (Franklin Co.). *

BONE, Elihu. He is listed by Madden as weaving in Menard County, Illinois, dates unknown. *

BORDNER, Daniel (1807–1842). In April 1834 he bought partial rights to a new "weaving machine" from Emanuel Meily, Jr., John Mellinger, and Samuel Mellinger, who had taken out a patent on the machine earlier that year (see entries). He is listed by Reinert as weaving in Millersburg (now Bethel), Pennsylvania (Berks Co.), in 1835; Safford and Bishop also show him in the same location in 1839. An inventory taken shortly after his death includes a "cord" (carding?) machine, a warping machine, and a "'coverlid loom and its apparatus," as well as "1 lot of paist bord," probably for the pattern cards. (See n. 16, p. 9.) Inventory, January 13, 1843, Berks County Courthouse. (See also entry for Absalom Klinger.) 7, 1839–1843.

BOWER, L. He is listed in W. W. Reilly & Co. as a coverlet weaver in New Springfield, Ohio (Mahoning Co.). *

BOWMAN, Henry B. (d. 1863). A surviving coverlet indicates that Bowman was weaving in 1840, but the location is unknown. He is listed in the 1859–1860 city directory of Lancaster, Pennsylvania (Lancaster Co.), as weaving "coverlids" in Neffsville, Pennsylvania (Lancaster Co.). An inventory of his estate gives Bowman's home at the time of his death as Providence, Lancaster Co. Lancaster County Courthouse. The inventory includes 10 coverlets, 14 woolen blankets, 140 yards of rag carpeting, and 121 yards of linen cloth. 1, 1840.

BRAND, D. Although listed by the C.C.G.A. and Safford and Bishop as weaving in 1838, location unknown, it appears that D. Brand was not a weaver. The only mention of this name is on coverlets dated 1838 and 1841 made by John Brosey, Jr., of Manheim, Pennsylvania (Lancaster Co.). Presumably the coverlets were made *for* D. Brand.

BREESWINE, Peter N. (ca. 1816–1895). Peter Breeswine was born in Germany. The 1850 U. S. census shows him as a weaver in West Manchester Township, Pennsylvania (York Co.), with his name spelled "Breastbein." The 1850 census of manufacturers includes him as a coverlet weaver. Using two hand-powered looms and employing one man, the establishment produced coverlets valued at $600 annually and "some carpets." *Boyd's Business Directory, Adams–York*, lists Breeswine as a weaver near Market

*Fruit trees with a picket fence make up this coverlet border design; double weave in red wool and white cotton. Woven by Harry Tyler, Jefferson Co., N. Y., 1841. Collection of Mr. and Mrs. Foster McCarl, Jr.*

[ 39 ]

Street in York, and the 1856 York city directory describes him as "N. P. Bresswine," weaving at 365 West Main Street. He is included as a carpet weaver in the York city directories from 1882 to 1888. *

BREHM, Henry. He is listed by Reinert as weaving in Womelsdorf, Pennsylvania (Berks Co.), in 1834, and by Safford and Bishop and Kovel and Kovel in the same location in 1836. 8, 1835–1837.

BREIDENTHAL, P. From the nine coverlets recorded, it has been concluded that Breidenthal was weaving in Wayne County, Ohio, in 1839–1841.

BRENEMAN, Martin B. (1803–1889). Born in Lancaster County, Pennsylvania, he was the son of a weaver and the descendant of at least four previous generations of weavers; he was weaving in Washington Township (York Co.) from 1835 to 1861. (See p. 20.) An inventory of his estate lists eight coverlets worth $9.75 and "weaving machinery" valued at $1.50. York County Courthouse. Two border patterns that he often used are labeled "Eagle" and "Grapevine" on the coverlets themselves. 31, 1835–1862.

BRICK, Zena. Brick is listed by the C.C.G.A., Safford and Bishop, and Kovel and Kovel as weaving in 1833; the location of this weaver's activities is unknown. *

BRINK, R. J. One coverlet, dated 1832, gives this name and the location of New York; it is uncertain if Brink was the weaver or the client.

BRINKMAN, Henry (ca. 1806– ). Born in Germany, he is listed as a weaver in the 1850 U. S. census of Hopewell Township, Ohio (Seneca Co.). He is also listed in W. W. Reilly & Co. as a coverlet weaver in Bascom, Ohio (Seneca Co.). *

BRONSON, J. He appears in the C.C.G.A., Safford and Bishop, and Kovel and Kovel as weaving in New York state in 1817 with his brother R. Bronson; Safford and Bishop place them in Utica. The Bronsons published a treatise on the art of weaving, *The Domestic Manufacturer's Assistant, and Family Directory, in the Arts of Weaving and Dyeing* (Utica, 1817). *

BRONSON, R. See entry for J. Bronson. *

BROSEY, John, Jr. (ca. 1812– ). Born in Pennsylvania, he was the son of a weaver, John Brosey, Sr. From 1835 to 1860 he was weaving in Manheim, Pennsylvania (Lancaster Co.); the 1850 and 1860 U. S. census reports locate him in Manheim borough as a weaver. 14, 1835–1854.

BROSEY, John, Sr. (ca. 1790– ). He is listed in the 1850 U. S. census for Manheim, Pennsylvania (Lancaster Co.), as a Pennsylvania-born weaver. *

BROSEY, William (d. 1884). Possibly the son of John Brosey, Jr., he was weaving in Manheim, Pennsylvania (Lancaster Co.), from 1846 to 1860. *Boyd's Business Directory, Adams–York*, lists him as a weaver on North Charlotte Street, Manheim. 1, 1846.

BROWN, David (ca. 1819– ). Born in Pennsylvania, he is listed by Reinert as a weaver in Mount Joy, Pennsylvania (Lancaster Co.), in 1846. The 1850 U. S. census describes him as a coverlet weaver and locates him in Tulpehocken Township, Pennsylvania (Berks Co.). 1, 1841.

BROWN, Isaac (ca. 1799– ). Pennsylvania born, the O.H.S. says that he was weaving with his brother, W. W. Brown (see entry), in Ashland, Ohio (Ashland Co.), in 1840. The 1850 U. S. census also lists him as a coverlet weaver in Ashland. *

BROWN, John. The C.C.G.A., Safford and Bishop, and Kovel and Kovel indicate that he was weaving in New York state in 1843. 2, 1 dated 1843.

*Coverlet border pattern of potted flowering bushes; Beiderwand weave in red and green wool and natural cotton. Weaver unidentified, probably Pennsylvania, 1854. Collection of Mr. and Mrs. Foster McCarl, Jr.*

Brown, W. W. He is listed by the O.H.S. as weaving in Ashland, Ohio (Ashland Co.), in 1840 with his brother Isaac (see entry). *

Brubaker, (or Brubker), A. He is listed by the C.C.G.A., Safford and Bishop, and Kovel and Kovel as weaving in 1847; the location is unknown. *

Brubaker, Isaac (d. 1887). According to Reinert, he was weaving in New Holland, Pennsylvania (Lancaster Co.), in 1834. 8, 1832–1838.

Brumman, David. W. W. Reilly & Co. describes him as a coverlet weaver in Shreve, Ohio (Wayne Co.). *

Buchwalder, A. Reinert says that he was weaving in 1845; the location is unknown. *

Buechel, W. See entry for W. Bichel.

Bundy, Hiram. According to Montgomery, Bundy advertised that he had taken over the weaving business of Abraham Van Vleet (see entry). *Political Clarion* (Connersville, Ind.), April 27, 1831. *

Burkerd, E. He is listed by the C.C.G.A., Safford and Bishop, and Kovel and Kovel as weaving in La Porte County, Indiana, in 1845. Perhaps E. Burkerd and Peter Burkerd (see entry) are the same person. 2, 1845 (1 crib coverlet).

Burkerd, Peter (1818– ). Born in Pennsylvania, he was weaving in Fulton County, Ohio, in 1843. A coverlet made by him there has the inscription "Whoffe by P. Burkerd Fulton S. County Ohio 1843." Montgomery states that a Peter Burkherd was weaving in La Porte County, Indiana, from 1845 to 1850, but he does not appear in the Indiana census after 1850. 3, 1843–1849.

Burkhardt, P. H. According to the O.H.S., he was weaving in Canal Dover, Ohio (Tuscarawas Co.), in 1831. *

Burkholder, Isaac (ca. 1801– ). Born in Pennsylvania, he advertised his weaving business in the October 25, 1825, issue of the Brookville, Indiana, *Franklin Repository*. Montgomery states that his weaving career was brief and unsuccessful; by 1850 he was practicing law. *

Burns, James (ca. 1819– ). A native of Virginia, he is listed by the O.H.S. as weaving in St. Clairsville, Ohio (Belmont Co.), in 1831. He appears as a weaver in Chillicothe, Scioto Township, Ohio (Ross Co.), in the 1850 U. S. census. W. W. Reilly & Co. cites him as a coverlet weaver in Ross County. 1, undated.

Burns, Martin. He is listed by the C.C.G.A., Safford and Bishop, and Kovel and Kovel as weaving in West Virginia in 1851, when he is said to have made a coverlet commemorating the Hemfield Railroad, but it does not bear his name.

Burnside, John (ca. 1784– ). Born in Ireland, he is listed by the O.H.S. as weaving in Cincinnati, Ohio (Hamilton Co.), in 1844. The 1850 U. S. census locates him as a carpet weaver in the sixth ward of Cincinnati; also living in his household was John Craig, an Irish-born carpet weaver. *

Burrough, Mark. In 1836 Burrough advertised in a Camden, New Jersey (Camden Co.), newspaper that he had begun a weaving business "in Plum between Third and Fourth Streets," according to Weiss and Ziegler. He is described as a carpet weaver in the 1850 Camden directory. *

Bury, Daniel (ca. 1802– ). Bury was born in Penn-

*The coverlet border design includes baskets of flowers and fruit; double weave in red and blue wool. Woven by John Klein, Hamilton Co., Ind., 1868. Collection of Mr. and Mrs. Foster McCarl, Jr.*

sylvania and appears in the 1850 U. S. census as a coverlet weaver in Youngstown, Ohio (Mahoning Co.). W. W. Reilly & Co. identifies him as a coverlet weaver in Cornersburgh, Ohio (Mahoning Co.); dated and inscribed coverlets indicate that he wove in New Portage, Ohio (Summit Co.), before relocating in Cornersburgh in the late 1840s. 16, 1830–1851.

BUSCHONG, W. F. One coverlet with this name and the date 1835 has been recorded. It is not known if Buschong was the weaver or the client.

BUSH, W. He is listed by Reinert as weaving in 1840, probably in Bucks or Montgomery County, Pennsylvania. *

BUTTERFIELD, J. According to the C.C.G.A., Safford and Bishop, and Kovel and Kovel, Butterfield was weaving in New Hartford, New York (Oneida Co.), dates unknown. *

BUTTERFIELD, Samuel. Before 1835 he was weaving with James Cunningham (see entry) in New Hartford, New York (Oneida Co.). After 1835, and until at least 1850, he wove by himself in Oneida County. A reference in Daniel E. Wager, ed., *Our County and Its People: A Descriptive Work on Oneida County, New York* (Boston, 1896), p. 486, may refer to Butterfield: "A man named Butterfield established a factory for making ingrain carpets early in the century, his product being claimed as the first of the kind made in this state; he removed later to Oriskany." He employed patriotic motifs and many of his coverlets have a corner design showing Washington on horseback with the mottoes "United We Stand Divided We Fall" and "Under This We Prosper." These same elements and mottoes were used by James Cunningham. 8, 1834–1855.

BYSEL, Phillip. He is listed by the O.H.S. as weaving in Shanesville, Ohio (Tuscarawas Co.), in 1846. 1 (Holmes Co.), 1839; 2 (Tuscarawas Co.), 1846.

## C

CALISTER, James C. Safford and Bishop indicate that Calister was weaving in Jefferson County, New York, in 1853. *

CAMPBELL, Daniel. He is listed by the C.C.G.A., Kovel and Kovel, and Safford and Bishop as weaving at Bridgeport, Virginia (now in Harrison County, West Virginia), in 1839. In 1850 he is supposed to have woven a coverlet commemorating the opening of the Hemfield Railroad. 1, 1850.

CAMPBELL, James (ca. 1810– ). Campbell came to America from Ireland about 1845 and was working in Ohio by 1846. He is listed as a weaver in the 1850 U. S. census of New Philadelphia, Ohio (Tuscarawas Co.), and W. W. Reilly & Co. still shows him there in 1853–1854. *

CAMPBELL, John. Born in Paisley, Scotland, he came to the United States in 1832 and settled near Syracuse, New York (Onondaga Co.). He worked there as a weaver until 1859, when he moved to Canada, settling near London, Ontario. His hand loom, modified to do Jacquard weaving, may be seen in the Ontario Science Centre, Toronto. It is the only known Jacquard-modified hand loom still in existence in North America. Also on file there are his punched pattern cards and account book. 1, undated.

CASEBEER, Aaron (ca. 1825– ). A native of Pennsylvania, his father was Abraham Casebeer, a farmer and weaver in Somerset County, Pennsylvania. Aaron Casebeer probably was weaving in 1848 with the unidentified "Hoffman" in western Pennsylvania, possibly in Somerset County. The two men signed their work "Casebeer and Hoffman." The 1850 U. S. census lists Aaron Casebeer as a weaver in Somerset Township, Somerset Co. In his household at the time was Moses Zufall, a young Pennsylvania-born weaver. Also working in the household was David Menser, another young Pennsylvania-born weaver

*Coverlet border design of a grapevine; Beiderwand weave in blue green wool and natural cotton. Woven by John Klinhinz, Ohio, 1848. Collection of Mr. and Mrs. Foster McCarl, Jr.*

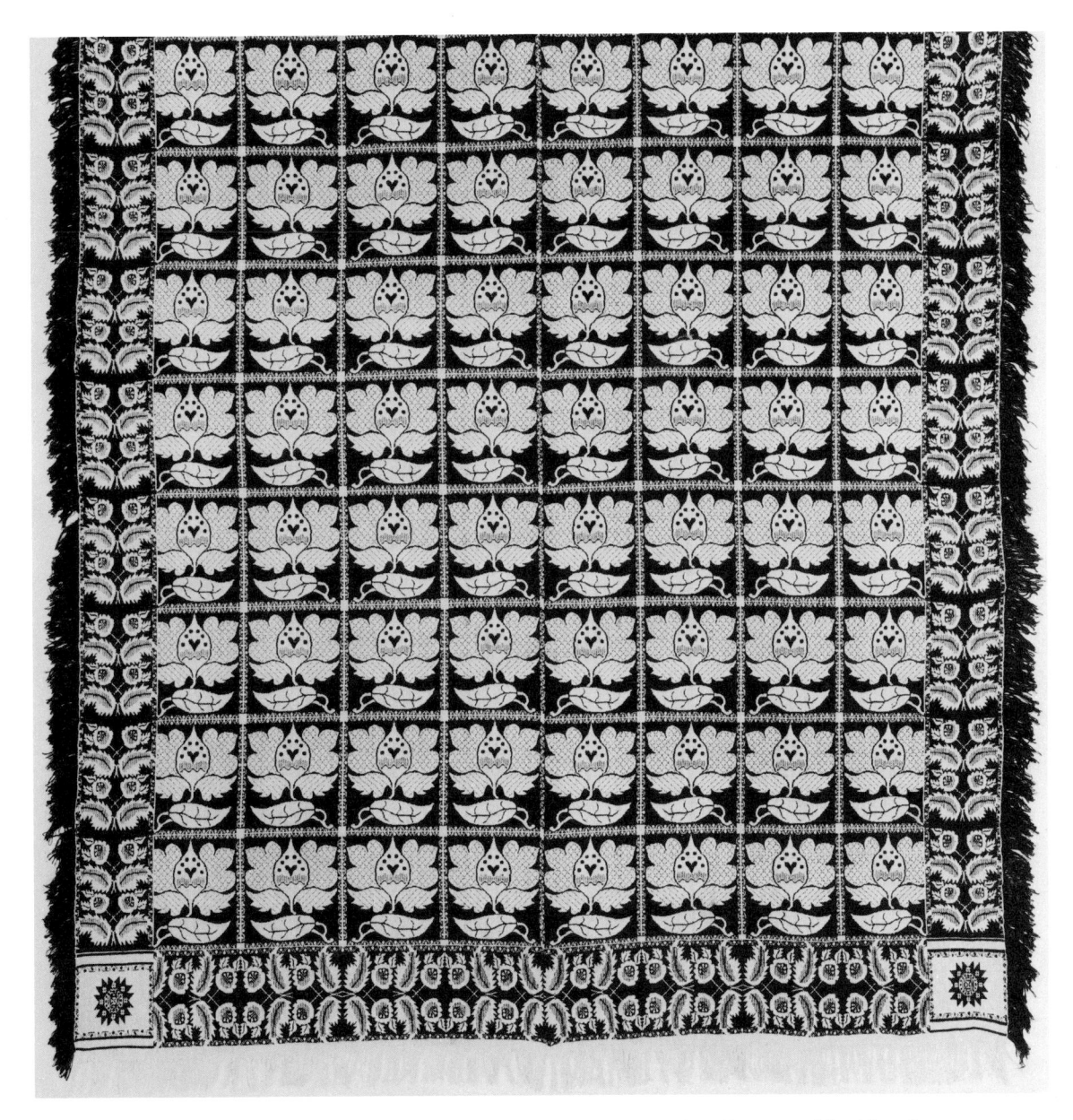

This coverlet combines a leaf and bud interior pattern with a flower and leaf border and star corner blocks; Beiderwand weave in blue wool and white cotton. Weaver unidentified, possibly Pennsylvania or Ohio, ca. 1850. Collection of Mr. and Mrs. Foster McCarl, Jr.

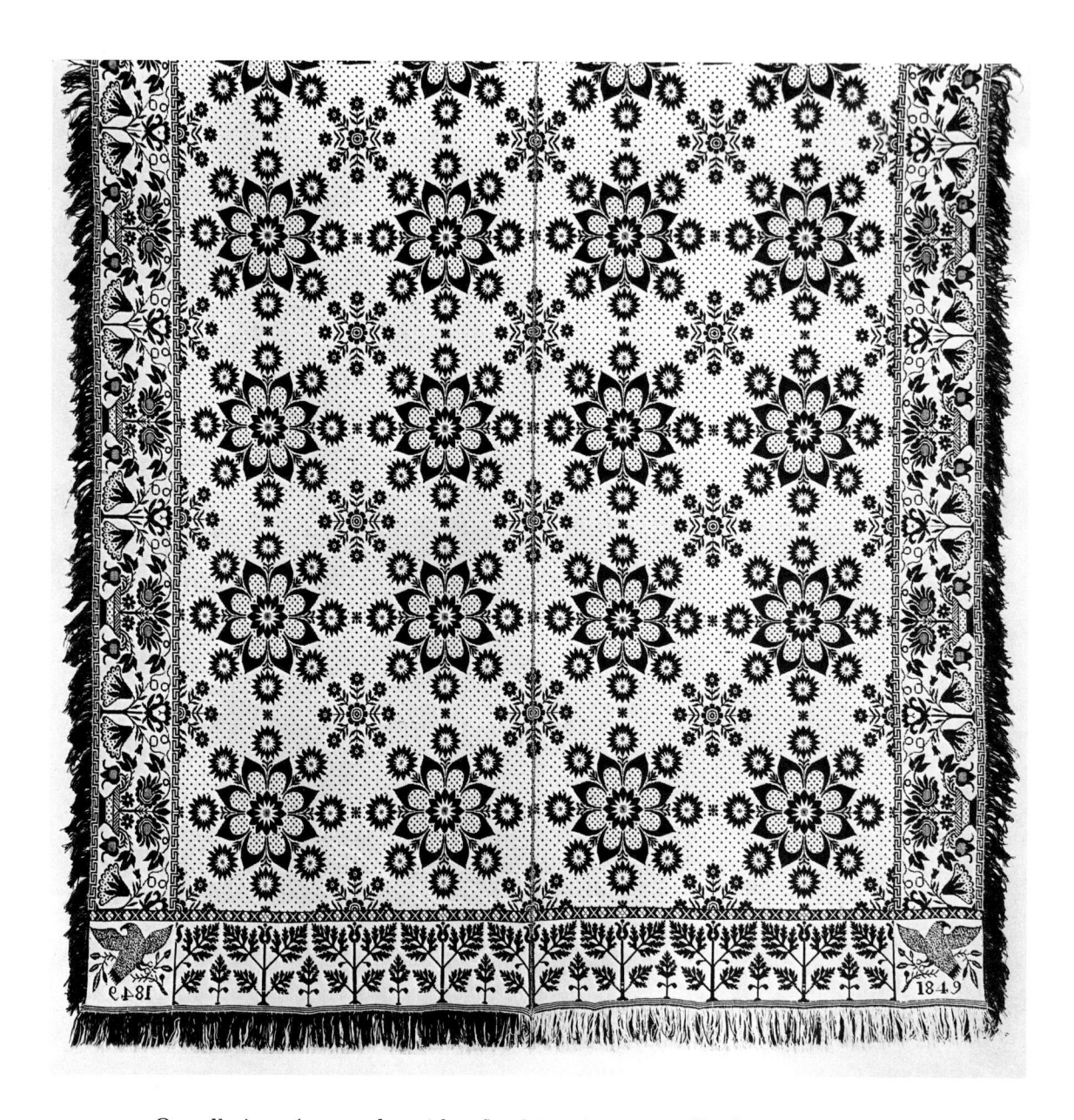

Overall view of a coverlet with a floral interior on a polka-dotted background and borders of flower baskets and leafy flowering shrubs; double weave in blue wool and white cotton. Woven by Samuel Graham, Henry Co., Ind., 1849. Collection of Mr. and Mrs. Foster McCarl, Jr.

(see entries). 4 (Casebeer and Hoffman), all 1848.

CASS, David (ca. 1825–   ). Born in New York state, he appears in the 1850 U. S. census for Lodi (now Gowanda), New York (Cattaraugus Co.), as a weaver. Apparently he was the son of Josiah Cass (see entry). *

CASS, Josiah (ca. 1798–   ). Cass is listed in the 1850 U. S. census for Lodi (now Gowanda), New York (Cattaraugus Co.), as a New Hampshire-born weaver. In an advertisement Cass announced that "having purchased looms for 'Fancy and Ingrain carpeting' would inform his old customers, and the public generally, that he is now prepared to weave Double and Single Carpets, and Coverlets of every description and figure . . . and has recently received direct from the city of New York, a large variety of figures, both for carpets and coverlets, of the latest styles, many of which cannot fail to suit the taste of the most fanciful, which will be wove to order. He has also made arrangements for Coloring Yarn for Fancy Carpets." *Freeman and Messenger* (Persia, N. Y.), November 22, 1841. Cass moved to Lodi, New York, in the early 1830s. With his son Nathan (see entry), he formed a partnership that continued after Josiah's death until 1880. 1, 1834; 1 (attributed), 1838.

CASS, Nathan (ca. 1820–1888). Born in New York state, he is listed in the 1850 and 1870 U. S. censuses for Lodi (now Gowanda), New York (Cattaraugus Co.), as a weaver, but in the 1880 census as a gardener. Nathan formed a partnership with his father, Josiah, that lasted until 1880. *

CASSEL, Joseph H. (ca. 1819–   ). He was born in Pennsylvania and was weaving there in Skippack Township (Montgomery Co.) in 1846, according to Reinert. In the 1850 U. S. census he is listed as weaving in East Lampeter Township, Pennsylvania (Lancaster Co.); he was in Strasburg, Pennsylvania (Lancaster Co.), in 1859. 2, 1846–1859.

CHAPMAN, Ernst. Hall identifies him as weaving in Clark's Falls, Connecticut (New London Co.); the dates of his activity are unknown. The only coverlet attributed to him is a geometric patterned coverlet, and he may not have had a Jacquard-equipped loom.

CHAPPELEAR, Mary. She is listed by Safford and Bishop as weaving in 1856; the location is unknown. *

CHATHAM'S RUN FACTORY. See entry for John Rich.

CHATTIN, Benjamin. One coverlet bearing this name and the date 1850 has been recorded; it is not known whether Chattin was the weaver or the client.

CHENNE, Joseph. This weaver is listed by Madden as weaving in Nauvoo, Illinois (Hancock Co.); the dates of his activity are unknown. *

CHORE, L. One coverlet with this name, the location Lisbon, Ohio (Columbiana Co.), and the date 1838 has been recorded. It is not known whether Chore was the weaver or the client.

CHRISTIE, I. The name is also spelled "Christy" on some of his coverlets. He was weaving in Bergen County, New Jersey, in 1834 and 1843. A small two-leafed white rose in a square in the corners of his coverlets may be his trademark as his name appears beneath or somewhere near it. The same mark was used by David D. Haring (see entry), and Christie's designs are similar to Haring's. 5, 1834 and 1843.

CHRISTMAN, G. According to Reinert, he was weaving in Hereford Township, Pennsylvania (Berks Co.), in 1842. 4, 1842–1844.

CHRISTMAN, W. F. He appears in *Boyd's Business Directory, Berks–Schuylkill*, as a coverlet weaver on Turner Street between Eighth and Ninth streets in Allentown, Pennsylvania (Lehigh Co.). *

CLAPHAM, J. One coverlet with this name and the inscription "West Buffaloe Factory Union Co. Penn 1849" has been recorded. Clapham is not included in the 1850 U. S. census of Union County.

CLARK, Jacob N. He was weaving in Richland County, Ohio, about 1835, and may also have worked in Newark, Ohio (Licking Co.). 2, undated.

CLEARFIELD TEXTILE MILL. According to the legend on the only coverlet recorded from this mill, it was operating in Knox County, Ohio, in 1849. However, the coverlet was not woven with a Jacquard-type attachment. 1, 1849.

CLEEVER, John. Reinert locates Cleever in Forks Township, Pennsylvania (Northampton Co.), in 1843. He is included in tax lists for 1850 as a weaver with a house and lot in Lehigh Ward, Easton, Northampton Co. His house and frame weaving shop were sold on August 24, 1855. Northampton County Courthouse. 4, 1843–1845.

CLELLAND, ———. See entries for J. McClellan and William McClellan.

COBLE, Henry K. He worked with another man by the name of Keener, and they signed their work, "Latest Stile Cov. Made by Coble and Keener Colours Warrented." (See entries for Henry Keener and Jacob Keener; see also pp. 18–19.) 1 (Coble), undated; 1 (Coble and Keener), undated.

COCKEFAIR MILLS. According to Montgomery, the mill was built in Harmony Township, Indiana (Union Co.), in 1816, and was remodeled in 1841 by Elisha Cockefair. At first the mill did only carding and fulling, but later it was converted to weaving. It used water-powered looms and employed seven men. From the coverlets recorded, it appears that the mill used a cross-hatched corner block as its trademark. Dismantled in 1911, the mill was taken to Greenfield Village in Dearborn, Michigan. 7, 1844–1856, although Montgomery states that one woven in 1870 has been located.

COLE, Anthony. He is listed by the O.H.S. as weaving in Cincinnati, Ohio (Hamilton Co.), in 1840. The

[45]

1844 Cincinnati city directory describes him as a carpet weaver. *

Cole, J. C. The C.C.G.A., Safford and Bishop, and Kovel and Kovel list him as weaving in Vernon Township, Ohio (Crawford Co.), in 1861. 4, 1851–1852.

Collings, S. Safford and Bishop list him as weaving in 1834; the location is unknown. *

Colman, Peter. According to the C.C.G.A., Safford and Bishop, and Kovel and Kovel, he was weaving in Ohio. Recorded coverlets indicate that he was in Chesterville, Ohio (Morrow Co.), in 1851, and in Thornville, Ohio (Perry Co.), in 1853–1854. 4, 1851–1854.

Conger, Daniel (ca. 1813–    ). Born in New York, he appears in the 1850 U. S. census as a weaver in Wolcott, New York (Wayne Co.). Living in his house at that time were two other New York-born weavers, William Spencer and Edwin Huntington (see entries). Presumably they were working for Conger. 5, 1856.

Conger, Jonathon. John H. Selkreg, *Landmarks of Tompkins County, New York* (Syracuse, N. Y., 1894), states that Conger was an early settler in Groton, New York (Tompkins Co.), and was a weaver and farmer. Letters patent dated March 12, 1831, reveal that a patent was granted to George Detterich and Jonathon Conger for a "new and useful improvement in the Machine for Weaving figured cloth, which improvement they state has not been known or used before in their application." Another patent of May 27, 1834, places Conger in Groton. (See n. 17, p. 9.) De Witt Historical Society, De Witt, N. Y. By 1839 he had relocated in Southport, New York (Chemung Co.), two miles south of Elmira. He advertised that he was continuing his business of "weaving and coloring ingrain and Venetian carpets, Double carpet and Float Work Coverlets." *Elmira Gazette*, November 1839. Safford and Bishop also state that Conger was weaving in New York in 1839. 2, 1830.

Conner, C. S. He is listed by Safford and Bishop as weaving in 1839; the location is unknown. *

Conoly, David. According to the O.H.S., he was weaving in Farmington, Ohio (Belmont Co.), in 1838. *

Cook, Harvey. Cook is listed by the C.C.G.A., Safford and Bishop, and Kovel and Kovel as weaving in 1851 in an area of Virginia that is now West Virginia, where he is supposed to have woven one of the Hemfield Railroad patterned coverlets.

Cook, John. One recorded coverlet by this weaver has an inscription that reads "Independence of the United States John Cook Weaver Ohio 1842." 3, 1840–1851.

Cook, Valentine (ca. 1820–1869). Born in Germany, his naturalization papers give his birthplace as the grand duchy of Hesse-Darmstadt, and his name as "Koch." The 1850 U. S. census lists him as a weaver living in the household of Andrew Kump (see entry), a coverlet weaver in Hanover, Pennsylvania (York Co.); Cook is included in tax lists for Hanover from 1852 to 1854. The 1860 U. S. census locates him in Germany Township, Pennsylvania (Adams Co.). During the Civil War he served in the 76th Regiment Pennsylvania Infantry from 1864 to 1865. In 1868 he advertised in the *Hanover Citizen* that he was prepared to carry on "the weaving Business in all its branches." The June 3, 1869, issue reports his death from drowning. Cook is buried in the Mount Olivet cemetery, Hanover. *

Cooper, Teunis. According to the New Jersey Historical Society, he was weaving in Englewood, New Jersey (Bergen Co.), in 1831. 1, 1831.

Corick, Andrew (ca. 1790–1863). He was a weaver in Middletown, Maryland (Frederick Co.); the dates of his activity are unknown. Corick is buried in the Reformed cemetery, Middletown. 4, undated.

Corick, Joshua (ca. 1820–    ). Born in Maryland, he was weaving at Middletown, Maryland (Frederick Co.); the dates are unknown. His relationship to

*Coverlet corner block showing the lion trademark; double weave in mauve wool and white cotton. Woven by Harry Tyler, Jefferson Co., N. Y., 1859. Collection of Mr. and Mrs. Foster McCarl, Jr. See color plate facing page 6.*

[ 46 ]

A lion is in the corner blocks of a coverlet that combines a daisy and star interior with a fruit tree and picket fence border; double weave in mauve wool and white cotton. Woven by Harry Tyler, Jefferson Co., N. Y., 1839. Collection of Mr. and Mrs. Foster McCarl, Jr. See color plate facing page 6.

[ 47 ]

Coverlet border pattern featuring hunters, roosters, birds, and squirrels in trees; Beiderwand weave in red and blue wool and white cotton. "S. B. Musselman Weaver Milford Bucks Co. No. 426" and "This Coverlet Belongs to Me Sary Meier 1843" are the corner inscriptions. Woven by Samuel Musselman, Bucks Co., Pa., 1843. Collection of Mr. and Mrs. Foster McCarl, Jr.

Andrew Corick (see entry) has not been determined. 5, undated.

COSLEY, Dennis (1816–1904). Born in Virginia, in 1831 he went to Fort Loudon, Pennsylvania (Franklin Co.), where he learned spinning, dyeing, and weaving. In 1837 he operated a mill in Bridgeport, Pennsylvania (Chester Co.), which later burned. After acquiring the necessary funds, he opened another mill in Fayetteville, Pennsylvania (Franklin Co.), in 1844. It also burned. In 1846 he and his brother George (see entry) moved to Xenia, Ohio (Greene Co.), where they built a log loom house behind Dennis Cosley's home and produced a number of coverlets. Art Institute of Chicago. The 1850 census of manufacturers for District 44, Greene County, Ohio, lists Cosley as owning a coverlet and carpet factory that employed three men. It produced 500 coverlets annually, valued at $3,000, and 1,500 yards of carpets worth $750. Cosley left Xenia in 1864 and ran a woolen mill in Miami County, Ohio, for three years. Later he had a store in Troy, Ohio (Miami Co.). Cosley retired in 1890. 29, 1846–1859.

COSLEY, George. George worked with his brother Dennis (see entry) in Fayetteville, Pennsylvania (Franklin Co.), and he advertised that he had rented the Franklin Woolen Factory one mile east of Fayetteville where he intended to do all sorts of weaving and dyeing. *Chambersburg Whig* (Chambersburg, Pa.), April 27, 1838. (See n. 20, p. 12, and n. 25, p. 19.) The brothers moved to Ohio, where the C.C.G.A., Safford and Bishop, and Kovel and Kovel include him as weaving in Xenia (Greene Co.), in 1851. No coverlets by George alone have been recorded; perhaps he helped make some of the coverlets that have his brother's name woven into the signature blocks.

COULTER, George. He is listed by the C.C.G.A., Safford and Bishop, and Kovel and Kovel as weaving in what is now West Virginia in 1851. He supposedly made one of the Hemfield Railroad patterned coverlets. Only one coverlet attributed to him is known.

COVEY, Harriet. According to the C.C.G.A., Safford and Bishop, and Kovel and Kovel, she was weaving in New York state in 1840. *

COWAM, Donald. He is cited by Safford and Bishop as weaving in Switzerland County, Indiana, in 1820; Montgomery does not list him. *

CRAIG, James (1819–1896). Born in Kilmarnock, Ayrshire, Scotland, he came to America in 1845 and settled in Washington County, Indiana. Montgomery states that he was probably a cousin of William Craig, Sr. (see entry). In 1852 he was working with Matthew Young (see entry) in Canton, Indiana (Washington Co.). They used a small building with a cupola on top that looks like a courthouse as a trademark, and did not date their coverlets. The same trademark was used by other Craig family weavers, but they dated their work. James later sold his interest in the business to Young and moved to Brazil, Indiana (Clay Co.), where he lived the rest of his life. 7, undated and attributed to Craig and Young.

CRAIG, James (1823–1889). Born in South Carolina, a son of William Craig, Sr. (see entry), James moved to Indiana with his family in 1839. Montgomery says that he moved to Andersonville, Indiana (Franklin Co.), soon after his marriage in 1846. He wove there until 1854 when he moved to Decatur County, Indiana, where he continued to weave until the 1860s. He signed his coverlets "J. Craig 2 miles N East of Greensburg, D. C. IA," and may be the J. Craig listed by the C.C.G.A., Kovel and Kovel, and Safford and Bishop who was weaving in Floyd Coun-

*Coverlet border design of horsemen and dogs; Beiderwand weave in blue wool and natural cotton. Woven by Robert Alexander, Canfield, Ohio, ca. 1850. Collection of Mr. and Mrs. Foster McCarl, Jr.*

[49]

ty, Indiana, in 1850 and 1851, signing his work "J. Craig, Andersonvill. Fl. C. IA." 12, 1846–1855.

CRAIG, John (ca. 1828–    ). Born in Ireland, he appears in the 1850 U. S. census for Cincinnati, Ohio (Hamilton Co.), as a carpet weaver living with John Burnside (see entry), who also was born in Ireland and was a carpet weaver.

CRAIG, Robert (ca. 1802–    ). Born in Ireland, he is listed by the Newark Museum, Newark, N. J., as weaving in Bethlehem Township, New Jersey (Hunterdon Co.), in 1850. *

CRAIG, William, Jr. (1824–    ). He was born in South Carolina, the son of William Craig, Sr. (see entry). In 1845 William, Jr., moved from the family farm in Decatur County, Indiana, to Greensburg, Indiana (Decatur Co.), where he established a weaving shop that his father subsequently took over in 1853, when Montgomery states that the son's weaving career ended, perhaps due to health problems. The Craigs used various trademarks, the best known of which is the courthouse. William, Jr., inscribed his coverlets "W. Craig Greensburg D. C. IA." accompanied by the date of manufacture. 8, 1850–1852.

CRAIG, William, Sr. (1800–1880). He was born in Kilmarnock, Ayrshire, Scotland, and came to America in 1820, landing in South Carolina. In 1821 his brothers and sisters joined him, bringing their weaving equipment with them. In 1830 Craig, married and with two sons, James and William, Jr. (see entries), moved to Franklin County, Indiana. The records of the Cincinnati firm of Foote and Bowlen indicate that Craig purchased substantial amounts of "coverlid yarn," or cotton warp, according to Montgomery. In 1840 he moved once more, this time to Decatur County, Indiana, three and one-half miles northeast of Greensburg, where he continued to weave and farm, assisted by his sons. In 1853 he took over the weaving shop in Greensburg that had been established by his son William, Jr. (see entry). Sometime in the 1860s he moved to Milford, Indiana (Decatur Co.), where he spent the remainder of his life; he appears in the 1870 U. S. census as a retired weaver. The best known trademark of the Craig family is the courthouse that appears in the corner block of many of their pieces. William, Sr., inscribed some of his coverlets "W. Craig W V" and included where they were made. The "W V" distinguishes his work from that of his son William, Jr. 49, 1842–1863.

CRANSTON, Thomas (ca. 1835–1899). Born in Scotland, he had seven years of training as a weaver before he came to the United States. He worked at his trade for three years in Lowell, Massachusetts (Middlesex Co.), before moving to Switzerland County, Indiana, according to Montgomery. He is listed by the C.C.G.A., Kovel and Kovel, and Safford and Bishop as weaving in Switzerland County in 1855. From 1863 to 1865 he served in the 3rd Indiana Cavalry Regiment. After the Civil War, he moved to Shelby Township, Indiana (Jefferson Co.), where he was a farmer and weaver. In 1881 he moved to Crawford County, Kansas, when it appears that he

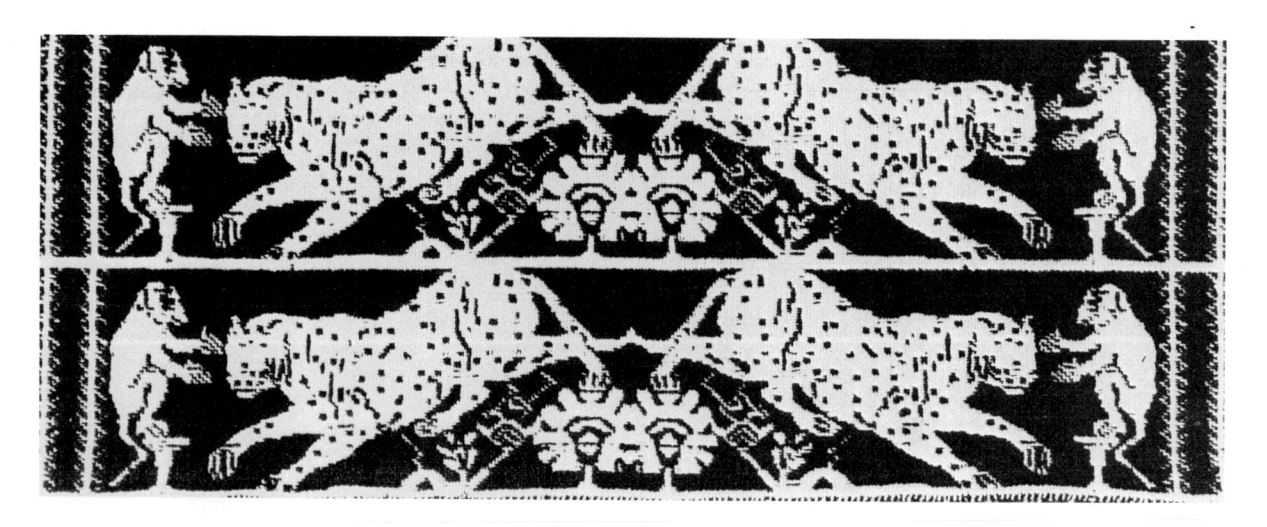

*Coverlet border design of leopards and monkeys; double weave in blue wool and white cotton. Weaver unidentified, possibly New York or Ohio, ca. 1830–1840. Collection of Mr. and Mrs. Foster McCarl, Jr.*

stopped weaving. As a trademark he often used an American eagle in the corner blocks. 7, undated.

CROSSLEY, Robert. The Art Institute of Chicago states that Daniel Stephenson (see entry) was apprenticed to a weaver named Crossley for two years about 1850 in Springfield, Ohio (Clark Co.). *

CROTHERS, Samuel. According to the account book of another weaver, James Alexander (see entry), Crothers was weaving coverlets, carpets, and blankets for Alexander in 1811 in Orange County, New York. *

CROZIER, John. He is listed by Kovel and Kovel and Safford and Bishop as weaving at Cadiz, Ohio (Harrison Co.), in 1830 and 1840. One coverlet inscription indicates he was still active there in 1845. 2; 1 undated and 1 dated 1845.

CUMBIE, ———. Kovel and Kovel say that Cumbie was weaving in Indiana before 1850. Montgomery states that the Cumbie family was reported to have been weaving in Alamo, Indiana (Montgomery Co.), in the 1840s, but this could not be confirmed. *

CUNNINGHAM, James (ca. 1797– ). Born in Scotland, Cunningham settled in New Hartford, New York (Oneida Co.), where he worked with Samuel Butterfield (see entry) on South Street (now Oxford Road) until Butterfield left in 1835. The 1835 U. S. census of New Hartford lists Cunningham, noting, "15 yds fulled cloth made in domestic way during year past. 30 yds flannel and other woolen cloth not fulled made during year past." He appears as a weaver in the 1850 U. S. census for New Hartford, while the 1865 census gives him as having no occupation. Cunningham's early double woven coverlets show Washington on horseback and the slogans "United We Stand, Divided We Fall," and "Under This We Prosper." Around 1840 he began to employ an adaptation of the New York state seal and "Excelsior" in the corners of his coverlets, although he continued to use Washington on horseback. 34, 1834–1848, some undated.

CURRY, Sam. He is listed by Hall as being an itinerant coverlet weaver in the Kentucky counties of Scott, Fayette, and Bourbon during the 1850s. The only known coverlet attributed to him is geometric, double woven, undated, and unsigned.

## D

DANHOUSE, F. He was weaving in 1862; the location of activity is unknown. 1, 1862.

DANNER, Philip. According to the O.H.S., he was weaving in Canton, Ohio (Stark Co.), between 1830 and 1840. *

DANNERT, Henry (ca. 1790– ). Kovel and Kovel and Reinert list him as weaving in Allentown, Pennsylvania (Lehigh Co.); the dates of his activity are unknown. The 1850 U. S. census for Allentown includes a Henry Danner (no "t"), whose occupation is not given. 1, undated.

DARE, Robert (ca. 1800–ca. 1839). According to the Art Institute of Chicago, he was born in 1800 and

*Coverlet corner block featuring a cow; double weave in blue wool and white cotton. Weaver unidentified, probably New York, 1824. Collection of Mr. and Mrs. Foster McCarl, Jr.*

[51]

worked in Union County, Indiana. Montgomery states that Dare lived in Fairfield, Indiana (Franklin Co.), and is reputed to have "plied his shuttle and wove 'fancy coverlits.'" Several coverlets with a latticelike corner block have been attributed to Dare (dated 1842 and 1847), although Montgomery believes the attribution to be incorrect; furthermore, Dare's estate was settled in 1839. No signed coverlets have been recorded.

DARON, Jacob (ca. 1805–    ). Born in Pennsylvania, he was weaving in Strinestown, Conewago Township, Pennsylvania (York Co.), in 1839; from 1840 to 1848 the location of manufacture is not indicated on his coverlets. 9, 1837–1848.

DARROW, J. M. He was weaving in Ithaca (probably New York) in 1832 or 1833. 1, 1832 or 1833.

DAVIDSON, Archibald. Born in Scotland, he learned the weaver's craft before coming to America. Davidson settled in Ithaca, New York (Tompkins Co.), where he was master weaver at the Ithaca Carpet Factory, a small establishment just outside town. In 1831 Davidson advertised in the *Ithaca Journal* that he would weave coverlets and carpets. (See p. 16.) Equipped with several looms and employing a number of workmen, the factory was in operation until the Civil War. After 1838 many coverlets bear the inscription "Woven at Ithaca Carpet Factory." Patriotic motifs are prevalent. 30, 1830–1848.

DAVIDSON, J. Two coverlets woven by this individual in Asbury (state unknown) in 1834 and 1835 have been recorded.

DAVIDSON, J. M. Safford and Bishop located him in Lodi, Ohio (Medina Co.) in 1837. From recorded coverlets, it is known that he was weaving in Lodi in 1836 and 1839 and in Ovid in 1840, but the state is not designated in the inscriptions. There are two towns with the names Lodi and Ovid in both New York and Ohio. 6, 1836–1840.

DEAVLER, Joseph (1809–1886). Born in Pennsylvania, Deavler's name is also found spelled as "Devler," "Dealer," "Deuler," and "Doebler" on his coverlets and in city records. He is listed by Reinert as weaving in Lititz, Pennsylvania (Lancaster Co.), in 1843, and the U. S. censuses of 1850 and 1860 include him as a weaver in Warwick Township, Pennsylvania (Lancaster Co.). His tombstone in the Salem Lutheran cemetery, Kissel Hill, Pennsylvania (Lancaster Co.), has his name as "Daveler." 4, 1838–1843.

DEEDS, William (ca. 1808–    ). Born in Pennsylvania, he had moved to Coshocton County, Ohio, by 1831. He purchased land in Miami County, Indiana, in 1848 and was listed in the 1850 U. S. census as a cabinetmaker there. Montgomery suggests that Deeds acquired his weaving equipment from J. Snider (see entry), of Harrison Township (Miami Co.). 5, 1850–1859.

DEHART, John, Jr. (ca. 1808–    ). Dehart was born in Pennsylvania. He is listed in the 1850 U. S. census as a weaver in the south ward, Harrisburg, Pennsylvania (Dauphin Co.), and is included in *Boyd's Business Directory, Adams–York*, as a carpet weaver "on the railroad near Paxton" [Street] in Harrisburg. One coverlet draft, marked with his name, is in the Berks County Historical Society, Reading, Pa. *

DEITSCH, Andrew. See entry for William Ney.

DENGLER, John (ca. 1812–    ). Born in Germany, Dengler was weaving in 1850, according to the C.C.G.A. Safford and Bishop also state that he was weaving in Newry, Blair County (probably Pennsylvania), in 1850. He appears in the tax records of Blair Township, Pennsylvania (Blair Co.), his name being spelled "Dangler." The 1850 U. S. census shows that a young German-born weaver, Joseph Hickenour, was living in his household. 1, 1850.

DENHOLM, John. Denholm is listed by the Art Institute of Chicago as weaving in Pennsylvania, although the places of manufacture are not inscribed on the coverlets recorded in this survey. 7, 1837–1861.

*Leaping stags alternate with large trees in this coverlet border design; double weave in blue wool and white cotton. Woven by Archibald Davidson, Ithaca, N. Y., 1838. Collection of Mr. and Mrs. Foster McCarl, Jr.*

DETTERICH, George. See entry for Jonathon Conger. 1 (Lansing, New York), 1832.

DEUEL, Elizabeth. She appears in Kovel and Kovel as weaving in Saratoga (now Saratoga Springs), New York (Saratoga Co.), around 1790. *

DEYARMON, Abraham. According to the C.C.G.A., Safford and Bishop, and Kovel and Kovel, he was weaving in Lexington, Kentucky (Fayette Co.), in 1825. *

DILLER, P. He is listed by Reinert as weaving in 1843; the location is unknown. 2, 1846.

DORNBACH, Samuel (ca. 1796–  ). Born in Pennsylvania, he was weaving at Sugarloaf, Pennsylvania (Luzerne Co.), between 1844 and 1848, spelling his name "Dornbach." In 1848 he apparently changed the spelling of his name to "Turnbaugh," since coverlets of that date reflect both spellings. He was working with Joseph Turnbaugh (see entry), probably his son, as early as 1849, because they made at least one coverlet inscribed "Made by J. & S. Turnbaugh, Sugarloaf, Luzerne Co." In the 1850 U. S. census, Samuel, described as a farmer, is located in Black Creek Township, Luzerne Co., assisted by Joseph Turnbaugh, a coverlet weaver. 12 ("Dornbach"), 1844–1848; 2 ("Turnbaugh"), 1848; 2 ("J. & S. Turnbaugh"), 1849–1851.

DORWARD, John (ca. 1812–ca. 1861). Born in Pennsylvania, Reinert lists him as weaving in Washington Township, Pennsylvania (Lehigh Co.). The 1850 U. S. census of Washington Township describes Dorward as a "slater" and his 16-year-old son Joshua as a weaver. Dorward's inventory includes one weaving loom and two spooling wheels. January 14, 1862, Lehigh County Courthouse. *

DORWARD, Joshua (ca. 1835–  ). See entry for John Dorward. *

DOUGLASS, Charles. From a recorded coverlet, it has been learned that Douglass was weaving in 1838 at Brownsville, Pennsylvania (Fayette Co.), with J. Packer (see entry), and in 1841 by himself, location unknown. 1 (Packer & Douglass), 1838; 2 (Douglass alone), 1841.

DUBLE, Jonathan. One coverlet woven prior to 1863 with this name and the location "Martinsburg, Berkeley County, Virginia" (now West Virginia) has been recorded. It is uncertain whether Duble was the weaver or the client.

DUDDLESON, C. He is listed by W. W. Reilly & Co. as as a coverlet weaver in Upper Sandusky, Ohio (Wyandot Co.). *

DUDLEY, Samantha C. Kovel and Kovel locate her as a weaver at Roxbury, Massachusetts (Suffolk Co.), in 1830. *

DUNLAP, William S. According to Montgomery, Dun-

*Coverlet border design of a fox and hound with a partridge in a flowering tree alternating with potted plants; double weave in blue wool and white cotton. Woven by David D. Haring, Bergen Co., N. J., 1833. Collection of Mr. and Mrs. Foster McCarl, Jr.*

lap advertised that he was opening a weaving shop in Richmond, Indiana (Wayne Co.), where he would make coverlets, carpets, and other woven items. *Richmond Palladium,* January 29, 1831. *

## E

EARNEST, Joseph. In an 1820 issue of the *New Jersey Mirror and Burlington County Advertiser* (Mount Holly, N. J.), Earnest announced that he was weaving double coverlets, figure work coverlets, bedspreads, diaper, double diaper, point work, line work, and other woven goods at the shop of Isaac A. Curtis in Garden Street, Mount Holly (Burlington Co.). *

ECKERT, Gottlieb (ca. 1809– ). Born in Germany, he emigrated to New York City in 1833. After his German partner, August Vogel (see entry), arrived in 1834, they both moved to Franklin County, Indiana; in 1836 Eckert, Vogel, and Jacob Walter (see entries) leased the G. W. Kimble Woolen Factory in Franklin County, but, according to Montgomery, the partnership was short-lived. *

ECKLER, Henry (ca. 1815– ). The 1850 U. S. census lists Eckler as a German-born weaver working in Columbiana County, Ohio. He is also listed in W. W. Reilly & Co. as a coverlet weaver in New Chambersburg, Ohio (Columbiana Co.). *

EICHMAN, Michael. From recorded coverlets it has been discovered that Eichman was weaving in Juniata County, Pennsylvania, between 1831 and 1860. 9, 1831–1860.

EICHNER, William (ca. 1807– ). A native of Germany, he appears in the 1850 U. S. census for Chester Township, Ohio (Wayne Co.), as a coverlet weaver. Living in his household at the time was a German-born coverlet weaver, Michael Leykauff. 6, 1839–1850. A number of coverlets marked "Berlin" (Holmes Co.), Ohio, with various dates from 1840 to 1848 may also have been woven by Eichner. See Stanley A. Kaufman, "William Eichner: Jacquard Coverlet Weaver, Holmes County, Ohio, 1840–1849," *Historic Shaefferstown Record,* X (April 1976), pp. 18–26.

ENDERS, Henry (1828–1902). Born in Germany, he came to America and settled in Sidney, Ohio (Shelby Co.), about 1850. He wove in his home on Brooklyn Avenue, and later sold real estate. Safford and Bishop locate him in Sidney as late as 1876. 5, 1855–1873.

ENDY, Benjamin (1811–1879). Born in Berks County, Pennsylvania, he spent his life there weaving linens, coverlets, and carpets. Morton L. Montgomery, comp., *Historical and Biographical Annuals of Berks County, Pennsylvania* (Chicago, 1909). Most of his coverlets give his location as "Friedensburg." Endy's pattern book for harness weaving, dated 1829, and some Jacquard patterns drawn on graph paper are

Coverlet border design featuring prancing horses and eagles with stars above; double weave in blue wool and white cotton. Woven by Archibald Davidson, Ithaca, N. Y., 1835. Private Collection.

*Coverlet border design of willow trees with horses and birds; double weave in blue wool and white cotton. Weaver unidentified, probably Pennsylvania or Ohio, 1839. Collection of Mr. and Mrs. William Peto. See frontispiece.*

*Coverlet border design of running foxes with eagles and stars; double weave in blue wool and white cotton. Attributed to David D. Haring, Bergen Co., N. J., 1831. Courtesy of Gretchen S. Truslow.*

*Leopards, a crocodile devouring a snake, and palm trees appear on this coverlet border design; double weave in blue and red wool and natural cotton. Weaver unidentified, possibly Ohio, ca. 1840. Courtesy of Mr. G. W. Samaha.*

[ 55 ]

in the Berks County Historical Society, Reading, Pa. He died in Oley Township (Berks Co.) and is buried in the Oley cemetery. 5, 1834–1843.

ENGEL, G. From recorded coverlets it has been determined that Engel was working in Newark, Ohio (Licking Co.), in 1830. His name is spelled "Engle" on some coverlets. 8, 1830–1855.

ETNER, Reuben. He is listed in W. W. Reilly & Co. as a coverlet weaver in Richland County, Ohio. *

ETTINGER, Emanuel (1801–1889). Born in Pennsylvania, he is listed by Reinert and Kovel and Kovel as weaving in Centre County, Pennsylvania, from 1820 to 1860, and is located by Safford and Bishop in Centre County from 1834 to 1841. In 1834 he purchased partial rights to a patent for a weaving machine for coverlets, carpets, diaper, and so forth. (See entries for Daniel Bordner, Emanuel Meily, Jr., John Mellinger, and Samuel Mellinger.) The 1850 U. S. census describes Ettinger as a weaver in Haines Township, Pennsylvania (Centre Co.); in his household were two younger men, Jacob Fisher, born in Pennsylvania, and John Folk, born in Germany, both weavers. Beginning in 1841, Ettinger signed most of his coverlets "E Ettinger & Co."; it is possible that Fisher and Folk had been working with him since then. The following reference is made to Ettinger in John Blair Linn, *History of Centre and Clinton Counties, Pennsylvania* (Philadelphia, 1883), p. 303: "Emanuel Ettinger, located at Aaronsburg in 1820, and for 40 years thereafter engaged in the occupation of coloring and weaving." He is buried in the Lutheran cemetery, Aaronsburg (Centre Co.). 33, 1834–1863.

ETTINGER, John. One coverlet has been recorded with this name, Springfield, Ohio (Clark Co.), and 1837; it has not been determined whether Ettinger was the weaver or the client.

ETTINGER, William (ca. 1825– ). Born in Pennsylvania, he is found in the 1850 U. S. census as a coverlet weaver in Shrewsbury borough, Shrewsbury Township, Pennsylvania (York Co.). Tax records for 1851 and 1852 show him as a weaver, but he does not appear thereafter. Because no deeds, estate settlements, or other county records mention him, Ettinger may have moved away. However, he may be the same William Ettinger (see entry) who was a coverlet weaver in Aaronsburg, Pennsylvania (Centre Co.). *

ETTINGER, William. He was weaving in Aaronsburg, Pennsylvania (Centre Co.), from 1863 to 1867 and possibly earlier. He may be the same William Ettinger who was recorded in York County, Pennsylvania, in 1851 and 1852 (see entry). William appears in the 1870 U. S. census as a carpet weaver in Haines Township, Centre Co. He may have been associated with Emanuel Ettinger (see entry) as part of "Ettinger & Co.," and he may be the William Henry Ettinger cited in Emanuel's will. 7, 1863–1867.

EYRE, John. He was weaving in Cincinnati, Ohio (Hamilton Co.), between 1840 and 1844, according to the O.H.S. Eyre may have been a carpet weaver. *

# F

FAIRBROTHERS, William (ca. 1800–1876). Born in England, he immigrated to America, living first in Ohio and then in Henry County, Indiana. He appears in the 1850 U. S. census as a farmer in Henry County, while the 1860 U. S. census describes him as a carpet weaver. The C.C.G.A., Safford and Bishop, and Kovel and Kovel include Fairbrothers as a coverlet weaver in Henry County; the dates are unknown. *

FASIG, A. Two coverlets woven by Fasig in Clark County, Illinois, have been recorded. His relationship to

Coverlet corner block featuring a peacock in a flowering tree, a pair of dogs below; double weave in blue wool and white cotton. The coverlet was made for Phebe J. Tripp. Weaver unidentified, probably New York or New Jersey, 1856. Collection of Theo Van De Polder, Lawton, Mich.

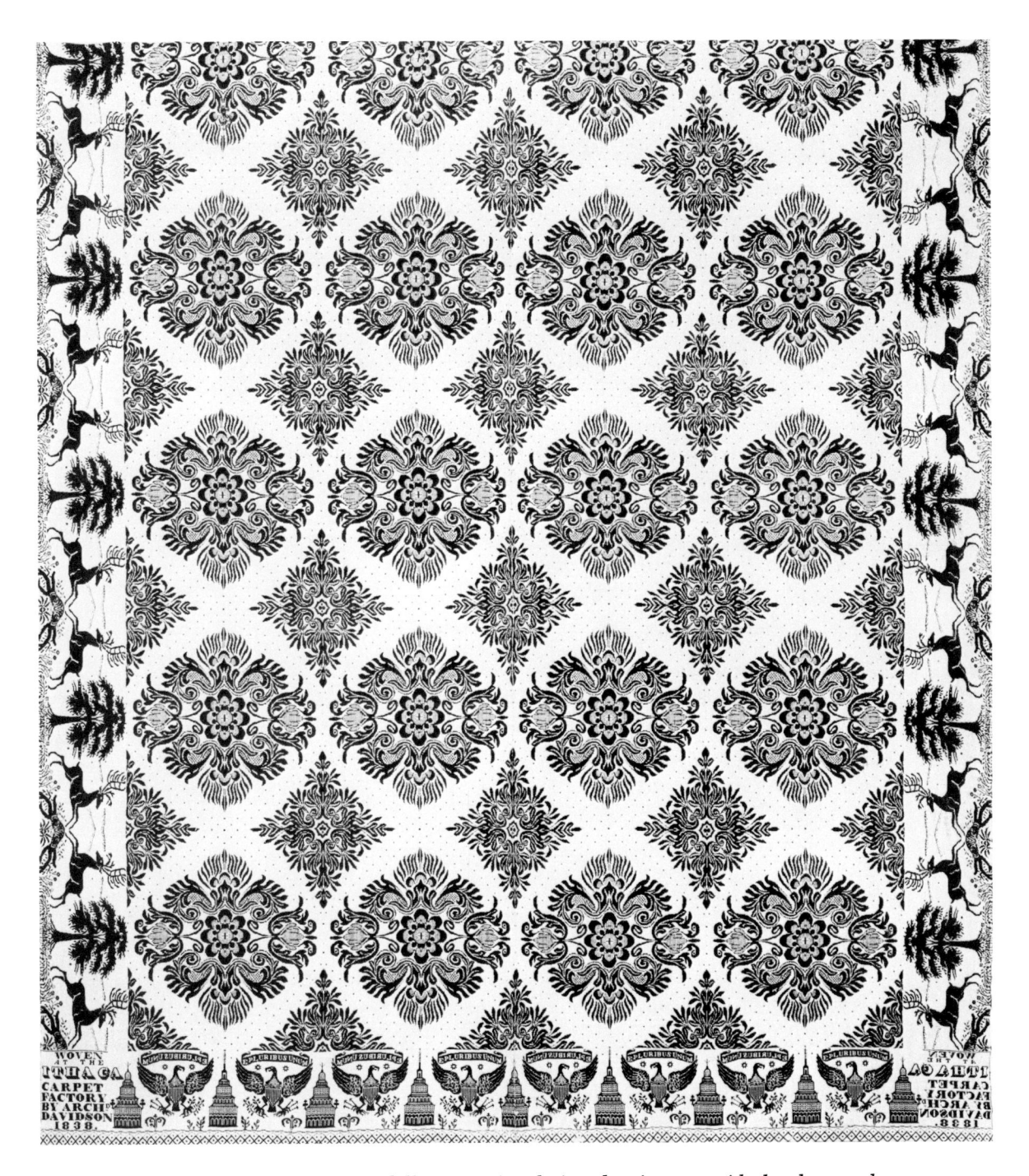

This coverlet has a floral medallion interior design, leaping stag side borders, and an eagle and capitol border at the base; double weave in blue wool and white cotton. Woven by Archibald Davidson, Ithaca, N. Y., 1838. Collection of Mr. and Mrs. Foster McCarl, Jr.

[ 57 ]

the two other Fasigs (see entries) has not been determined. 2, 1853 and 1854.

FASIG, Christian (ca. 1825–    ). He was weaving in Clark County, Illinois. His relation to A. Fasig and William Fasig (see entries) has not been determined. 2, 1853.

FASIG, William (ca. 1801–    ). Born in Lebanon County, Pennsylvania, Fasig moved to Wayne County, Ohio, in 1824 and was there until 1834, when he moved to Richland County, Ohio. In 1847 he moved to Missouri, finally settling in Martinsville, Illinois (Clark Co.), where he continued to weave. Some confusion has arisen over the Fasigs, their dates, and their relation to one another. There is a strong possibility that the three were brothers, all of whom were born in Pennsylvania and worked in Clark County, Illinois, as weavers. Eight coverlets have been recorded, three woven in Richland County from 1845 to 1846, and five woven in Clark County from 1850 to 1858.

FATSINGER, Adam. He is listed by Reinert as weaving in Lehigh County, Pennsylvania, in 1843. *

FAVORITE, Elias (ca. 1796–    ). Favorite was born in Maryland. He is listed as a coverlet weaver in the 1850 U. S. census for Dalton Township, Indiana (Wayne Co.); Montgomery believes that he may have worked in the Test Woolen Mills (see entry), which were nearby. *

FEHR, Abraham (ca. 1822–    ). Born in Pennsylvania, he was weaving in Emmaus, Pennsylvania (Lehigh Co.), with Thomas Fehr (see entry). The 1850 U. S. census lists him as a coverlet weaver in Salisbury Township, Lehigh Co. The 1860 U. S. census includes Fehr as a coverlet weaver in Emmaus, although he is described as a carpet weaver there in *Boyd's Business Directory, Berks–Schuylkill*. His name is sometimes spelled "Fahr" or "Fahre"; his recorded coverlets have the inscription "Manufactured by A. & T. Fehr in Emaus, Lehigh County." 5, all undated.

FEHR, Charles. According to recorded coverlets, he was weaving in Emmaus, Pennsylvania (Lehigh Co.), from 1836 to at least 1845. 13, 1836–1845.

FEHR, Thomas (ca. 1815–    ). According to recorded coverlets, this Pennsylvania-born weaver was in Lower Saucon Township, Pennsylvania (Northampton Co.), from 1838 to 1842. Tax lists for 1841 for Lower Saucon Township indicate that he was a weaver, and the 1850 U. S. census for Salisbury Township, in adjacent Lehigh County, describes him as a coverlet weaver, his name being spelled "Fare." (See also entry for Abraham Fehr.) 5 (A. & T. Fehr), all undated; 3 (T. Fehr alone), 1838–1842.

FEHR & KECK. They are listed by Reinert and Kovel and Kovel as weaving in Emmaus, Pennsylvania (Lehigh Co.), where Reinert locates them in 1844. From recorded coverlets, it has been determined that the two were weaving in Emmaus from at least 1843 to 1848. "Fehr" may have been Abraham, Charles, or Thomas (see entries); Keck has not been identified fully. 10, 1843–1848.

FENNELL, Michael (ca. 1826–    ). Montgomery states that a weaver named Fennell or Pennell may have been weaving in Indiana, but that no mention of him was found in any Indiana census records. A Michael Fennell appears in the 1850 U. S. census of Salem Township, Pennsylvania (Westmoreland Co.), as a "coverlid weaver." 2 (location of manufacture unknown), 1846 and 1851.

FERNBERG, Samuel. He is listed by Madden as a weaver in Mendota City, Illinois (La Salle Co.); the dates are unknown. *

FETTER, E. One coverlet has been recorded with this name and the date 1840. It has not been determined whether Fetter was the weaver or the client.

FINDLAY, Robert. According to the O.H.S., he was weaving in Cincinnati, Ohio (Hamilton Co.), in 1844. The 1844 Cincinnati city directory includes Findlay as a carpet weaver. *

FISCHER, Samuel. According to Reinert and to a recorded coverlet, he was weaving in Upper Bern Township, Pennsylvania (Berks Co.), in 1835, when he was using the inscription "Samuel Fischer, Oberbern Township ner By thebelmans church" ("Upper Bern Township nearby the Belman's Church"). 1, 1835.

FISHER, Daniel (ca. 1822–    ). Although Montgomery states that Pennsylvania-born Fisher moved to South Bend, Indiana (St. Joseph Co.), in 1846, an attributed coverlet inscribed "South Bend, 1845" seems to indicate that he was weaving there earlier. The 1850 U.S. census lists him as a weaver in St. Joseph County, Indiana, where Daniel and his brother Levi wove coverlets for ten years. The coverlets bear either the inscription "Daniel Fisher, South Bend, Indiana," and the date, or, more often, "Fear God and Keep His Commandments, South Bend," and the date. The Fishers left South Bend in 1857; there is no record of their activities thereafter, according to Montgomery. 17 (3 of which bear Daniel Fisher's name), 1845–1855.

FISHER, Jacob. See entry for Emanuel Ettinger.

FISHER, Levi (ca. 1829–    ). He was born in Pennsylvania. (See entry for Daniel Fisher.)

FLANIGAN, George (ca. 1798–1874). He is listed by Kovel and Kovel as weaving at Mill Hall, Pennsylvania (Clinton Co.), about 1850. He is described in the 1850 U. S. census of Mill Hall as a laborer, born of Irish parents "on the Atlantic Ocean." Tax lists for Bald Eagle Township (Clinton Co.) for 1860 and 1861 cite him, but do not identify his occupa-

"Lilies of France" interior design and standing lion borders; double weave in blue wool and white cotton. Woven by B. French, Waterville, N. Y., 1835. Abby Aldrich Rockefeller Folk Art Center, gift of Mr. and Mrs. Foster McCarl, Jr. See frontispiece.

The interior design of this coverlet is composed of giraffes, monkeys, and birds, while the borders contain crocodiles, snakes, and leopards. Tropical foliage appears in both areas, and there is a turkey in each corner; double weave in red and blue wool and natural cotton. Weaver unidentified, possibly Ohio, ca. 1850. Courtesy of Mr. G. W. Samaha. See color plate facing page 7.

tion. From 1860 to 1863 he appears as George, Sr., since there was also a George L. Flanigan in the same township. Flanigan is buried in the Cedar Hill cemetery, Lamar Township, near Salona (Clinton Co.). *

FLECK, Joseph (ca. 1825– ). Born in Germany, he is listed in the 1850 U. S. census as a weaver in English Township, Ohio (Hancock Co.). 1, undated.

FLECK, William. According to the O.H.S., he was weaving in Findlay, Ohio (Hancock Co.), in 1860. 1 (attributed), ca. 1860.

FLIEHR, Charles B. (ca. 1824–1885). Born in Midweitz, Saxony, Germany, he came to America about 1845, settling first in Millerstown (now Macungie), Pennsylvania (Lehigh Co.). He worked there as a coverlet weaver with Carl Boettger (see entry), signing their coverlets "Manuf: by Fliehr & Boettger, Millerstown, Lehigh Co., Pa." From Lehigh County he moved to Weissport, Pennsylvania (Carbon Co.), where he wove coverlets and carpets. According to Roberts, he gave up the occupation of weaver, however, and became an Evangelical minister around 1863. He died at Macungie and is buried at Emmaus. 3, undated.

FLOCHER, S. One coverlet, woven in Bolivar, Ohio (Tuscarawas Co.), in 1840, has been recorded with this name. S. Flocher is presumably the Blocher (see entry) who was weaving in Bolivar in 1848. 1, 1840.

FLOWERS, Peter (ca. 1805– ). A coverlet has been recorded with this name, Newark, Ohio (Licking Co.), and 1850. The 1850 U. S. census lists Peter Flowers as a carder and fuller. He was born in Pennsylvania and worked in Reading Township, Ohio (Perry Co.). 1, 1850.

FOGLE, Lewis. See entry for Samuel Slaybaugh.

FOLK, John. See entry for Emanuel Ettinger.

FOLTZ, Harry. He is listed by Reinert as weaving in Lititz, Pennsylvania (Lancaster Co.), dates unknown. *

FORDENBACH, E. One coverlet bearing this name and the date 1843 has been recorded; it has not been determined whether Fordenbach was the weaver or the client.

FORRER, Martin (ca. 1815–1890). He was born in Pennsylvania. Montgomery states that he lived near Massillon, Ohio (Stark Co.), for some years before moving to Hamilton County, Indiana. He bought land in Hamilton County from Henry Adolf (see entry), another coverlet weaver. Forrer was assisted in his weaving for a time by John Klein (see entry) before Klein moved on to set up his own shop. 4, 1856–1857.

FORRY, Rudolph (1827–1914). He appears in Reinert as weaving in Windsor Township, Pennsylvania (York Co.), in 1847. Tax records give his primary occupation as a farmer rather than a weaver. He is buried in the Mennonite cemetery in Springettsbury Township (York Co.). 2, both 1847.

FORSTER, William. He is listed by the O.H.S. as weaving in Marion County, Ohio, in 1857. 1, 1857.

FOUTH, Jacob. Fouth is described in W. W. Reilly & Co. as a coverlet weaver in Piketon, Ohio (Pike Co.). *

FOX, John. According to W. W. Reilly & Co., he was a coverlet weaver in McCutchenville, Ohio (Wyandot Co.). *

FRAILEY, Michael (ca. 1799– ). Born in Pennsylvania, he appears in the 1850 and 1860 U. S. censuses as a coverlet weaver in Hummelstown, Derry Township, Pennsylvania (Dauphin Co.). The borders of his coverlets often had the word "PATENT" woven in and included eagles and trees. 7, 1835–1839.

FRANCE, Joseph. He is listed by the C.C.G.A. and Safford and Bishop as weaving in Rhode Island in 1814. *

FRANCES, ———. Listed by Rabb as weaving in Switzerland County, Indiana, in 1850, Montgomery states that no weaver by this name was found in the 1850 U. S. census of Indiana. Frances is also listed by the C.C.G.A., Safford and Bishop, and Kovel and Kovel as weaving in Indiana; the dates are unknown. *

FRANKLIN WOOLEN FACTORY. See entry for George Cosley.

FRANZ, Michael. He appears as a weaver in Miami County, Ohio, in 1839 in the C.C.G.A., Safford and Bishop, and Kovel and Kovel. 6, 1839–1851.

FRAZIE, J. He is listed by the C.C.G.A., Kovel and Kovel, and Madden as weaving in Casey, Illinois (Clark Co.), in 1860, and by Safford and Bishop as a weaver there in 1861. *

FREDERICK, Henry T. (ca. 1813– ). He was born in Pennsylvania and is included in the tax lists for South Middleton Township, Pennsylvania (Cumberland Co.), as a coverlet weaver from 1847 to 1852. The 1850 U. S. census for South Middleton Township describes him as a weaver. 1, 1846.

FRENCH, B. French worked as a weaver in Waterville and Clinton, New York (Oneida Co.). He is listed in French as a carpet weaver in Cazenovia, New York (Madison Co.). The borders of his coverlets often contain lions, and occasionally "Lion" is inscribed above. 12, 1835–1840.

FRENCH, P. One coverlet bearing this name, Bethany, New York (Genesee Co.), and 1832 has been recorded; it has not been determined if P. French was the weaver or the client.

FREY, Abraham ( –ca. 1860). The tax lists of Mount Joy Township, Pennsylvania (Lancaster Co.), include Frey as a peddler in 1855, as a "coverlid pedlar" in 1857, and as a weaver in 1859. 4, 1858.

FREY, Christian (1811–1888). Born and trained as a weaver in Germany, he came to America and worked as a weaver for a short time in Baltimore, Maryland.

[61]

He then moved near Fairfield, Hamiltonban Township, Pennsylvania (Adams Co.), where he lived the rest of his life, farming and weaving. Frey's account book for the period 1844 to 1852, which lists the sale of over forty coverlets, is in the collection of the Historical Society of York County, Pa. His pattern book (privately owned) lists the names of designs he used; these same names also appear in the account book. It is believed that he used a drawloom rather than a Jacquard-equipped loom. *

FREY, Samuel B. ( –ca. 1871). He appears in tax records of Mount Joy Township, Pennsylvania (Lancaster Co.), in 1855 and 1856 as a "pedlar, Coverlet Factory," and as a coverlet peddler in 1857. His estate inventory, 1871, includes a peddler's wagon valued at $35. It has not been determined if there was a connection between Samuel B. and Abraham Frey (see entry). *

FRIDLEY, Abraham. Born in Pennsylvania, he is listed by Montgomery as a weaver in Steuben County, Indiana, in 1850, when he was working in the household of Enos Michael (see entry), also a coverlet weaver. *

FRIEDEL, Robert (ca. 1827– ). Born in Saxony, Germany, he appears in the 1870 U. S. census of Mount Joy, Pennsylvania (Lancaster Co.), as a coverlet weaver. *

FRITZINGER, Jerret (ca. 1819– ). Fritzinger was born in Pennsylvania. Reinert says that he was weaving in Allentown, Pennsylvania (Lehigh Co.), in 1844. The 1850 U. S. census locates him in Allentown, where a young German-born weaver, John Seidenspinner, was working in his household. An estate inventory for a "Jared" Fritzinger was taken in Allentown in October 1900. 4, 1844–1845.

Coverlet border design featuring spread eagles and stars; double weave in blue wool and white cotton. Attributed to James Alexander, Orange Co., N. Y., 1822. Collection of Mr. and Mrs. Foster McCarl, Jr.

[ 62 ]

## G

GABRIEL, Henry (1812–1887). Born at Herborn in the duchy of Nassau, Germany, Gabriel came to America in 1836 and established a woolen mill at Millerstown (now Macungie), Pennsylvania (Lehigh Co.). He is reported to have introduced the Jacquard-type loom for weaving figured goods and coverlets to the area, and is said to be the "great-grandfather of all similar industries in this part of Pennsylvania," according to Roberts. In 1850 he moved his business to Allentown, in Lehigh County, where it became the "Allentown Woolen Mill." The factory burned in 1873 but was rebuilt. An inventory of his estate mentions a mansion house in Allentown and the Henry Gabriel Woolen Mill. March 29, 1887, Lehigh County Courthouse. (See also entry for George P. Weil.) 4, 1 dated 1845.

GALLEY, Jacob (1803–1829). In 1827 he advertised in the Uniontown, Pennsylvania, *Genius of Liberty* that he was starting to weave coverlets at his residence in Tyrone Township (Fayette Co.), on the road leading from the Broad Ford on the Youghiogheny River to Hurst's Mill on Jacob's Creek. Galley was killed in an accident while young and probably never had a Jacquard-equipped loom because the apparatus was not introduced to the United States until the mid-1820s. *

GAMBEL, J. He is listed by Safford and Bishop as weaving in 1834; the location is unknown. *

GAMBER, M. G. Recorded coverlets show that he was weaving in 1840 and 1844; the locations are unknown, and there is no other information about this weaver. 2, 1840 and 1844.

GAMBLE, J. A John Gamble who was born in Scotland is listed in the 1850 U. S. census as a weaver in Mifflin County, Pennsylvania. In 1860 J. Gamble is included in *Boyd's Business Directory, Adams–York*, as weaving in Edgemont, Pennsylvania (Delaware Co.). 3, 1833–1835.

GAMBLE, Sam. He is listed by Hall as weaving near Glasgow, Kentucky (Barren Co.), between 1830 and 1844. The only known coverlet attributed to Sam Gamble is an overshot weave and is undated.

GARBER, C. According to Safford and Bishop and a recorded coverlet, he was weaving at Ruff's Creek, Pennsylvania (Greene Co.), in 1840. In 1851 he was weaving in Washington County, Pennsylvania. 2, 1840–1851.

GARBER, Jonathan. He was weaving at Beaver Dams, Maryland (Frederick Co.), from 1839 to 1843. An 1839 coverlet has the inscription "No man can better it." 4, 1839–1843.

GARBRY, M. Y. From coverlets recorded to date, it has been learned that Garbry was weaving at Piqua, Ohio (Miami Co.), in 1847 and 1852. 2, 1847–1852.

Garet, Jacob. One coverlet has been recorded with this name, the letters "T. T.," and 1837; it is not known if Garet was the weaver or the client.

Garis, John (ca. 1810– ). He was weaving in Valparaiso, Indiana (Porter Co.), between 1849 and 1852, according to Montgomery. The corner blocks on the two coverlets recorded by Montgomery contain the inscriptions "Industry Leads to Virtue" and "This is a Part of the Work of Art." 2, 1849–1852.

Garner, Jacob. He is listed by the O.H.S. as weaving in Strasburg, Ohio (Tuscarawas Co.), in 1850. One coverlet with the name Jacob Garver on it has been recorded. 1, 1848.

Garret, Thomas. Reinert cites this weaver's advertisement in the *Maryland Herald and Hagerstown Weekly Advertiser*, October 31, 1804: "Coverlet, Carpet, and Table Linen Weaving. Thomas Garret." *

Gauss, George. Identified as a German-born weaver who settled in Belleville, Illinois (St. Clair Co.), in 1847, Madden states that Gauss was a tapestry weaver until the Civil War, when he began to weave carpets. 2, undated.

Geb, L. R. He is listed by Reinert as weaving in Maytown, East Donegal Township, Pennsylvania (Lancaster Co.), in 1846. Geb is probably the John R. Gebhart (see entry) who was weaving there at that time. No coverlets bearing the name L. R. Geb have been recorded.

Gebhart, John R. (ca. 1808– ). Born in Pennsylvania, he was a weaver in Maytown, East Donegal Township, Pennsylvania (Lancaster Co.). The 1850 U. S. census describes him as a weaver in Maytown and spells his name "Gephart"; at that time his son John, also a weaver, was living at home. *Boyd's Business Directory, Adams–York*, lists them as "J. R. & J. F. Gebhart, coverlid manufacturer" in Maytown. 6, 1840–1849.

Geller, Adam (ca. 1804– ). He may have been weaving in Somerset or Bedford County, Pennsylvania, in 1856, when he is said to have been working near the woolen mill operated by John Keagy (see entry). He appears in the 1850 U. S. census as an innkeeper in Harrison Township, Pennsylvania (Bedford Co.). *

Gepfert, A. Dated 1846, one coverlet by this weaver has been recorded.

Gernand, Jacob B. He was a weaver at Graceham, Maryland (Frederick Co.), in 1836 and probably for several years later. 13; 2 in 1836, but most undated.

Gernand, W. H. Weaving at Westminster, Maryland (Carroll Co.), he called himself a "Damask Coverlet Manufacturer" on his coverlets. 13; 1855–1879.

Gerthner, Xavier. Probably born in Germany, he was weaving in the Mohawk Valley area of New York. Later his name was spelled "Gardner." Written in German, a surviving pattern book of 1807 that Gerthner owned contains one hundred drafts and directions for weaving coverlets. *

Getty, A. This weaver is listed by the C.C.G.A., Kovel and Kovel, and Safford and Bishop as weaving in Lockport, New York (Niagara Co.); the dates are unknown. Montgomery suggests that A. Getty is Ann Hay Getty, but states that members of the Getty family say she was not a coverlet weaver. *

Getty, J. A. He is listed by Hall and Safford and Bishop as weaving in Indiana; the dates are unknown. Hall illustrates a coverlet attributed to this weaver, dated 1839, and said to have been woven in Indiana. A similar photograph in Jessie Farrall Peck, "Weavers of New York's Historical Coverlets," *Antiques*, XVIII (July 1930), pp. 22–25, shows a coverlet dated 1839 attributed to the same weaver. Employing patriotic elements and the legend "American Independence Declared July 4, 1776, Wove in 1839," the coverlet is of a pattern usually associated with New York state weavers. 1 (with this name), 1839.

Getty, James. He is listed by Hall as weaving at Lockport, New York (Niagara Co.), dates unknown. *

Getty, John. Montgomery identifies him as a weaver at Lockport, New York (Niagara Co.); the dates are unknown. *

Gibbs, John. Born in County Antrim, Ireland, he learned weaving before coming to America. In 1818 he worked briefly for James Alexander in Newburgh, New York (Orange Co.), weaving coverlets for $4 each. Alexander Account Book, New York State Historical Association, Cooperstown. He moved to Balmville (apparently in New York) where he was a linen weaver, and then went to Canada for a time but returned to Newburgh; he died there at age 66. *

Gilbert, C. A coverlet with this name, Bethany, New York (Genesee Co.), and 1838 has been recorded. It is not known if Gilbert was the weaver or the client.

Gilbert, Samuel (ca. 1802– ). He is listed by Kovel and Kovel and Reinert as weaving in Trappe, Pennsylvania (Montgomery Co.). 9, 1843–1860.

Gilchrist, Hugh (ca. 1806–1857). Born in Kilmarnock, Ayrshire, Scotland, Gilchrist came to America in 1828. Montgomery states that he worked as a weaver in Massachusetts, Connecticut, Ohio, and Kentucky before settling in Franklin County, Indiana. Later he moved to Decatur County, Indiana, for the remainder of his life. The 1850 U. S. census lists him as a weaver. See also entry for William Gilchrist. 3, undated.

Gilchrist, William (1803– ). Born in Kilmarnock, Ayrshire, Scotland, he was a brother of Hugh Gilchrist (see entry) and had settled in Mount Carmel, Indiana (Franklin Co.), by 1832. Montgomery states that he owned a farm jointly with William

[ 63 ]

Craig, Sr. (see entry), a coverlet weaver. It appears that William Gilchrist devoted his time to farming rather than weaving; the 1850 U. S. census describes him as a farmer and Hugh as a weaver.

GILMOUR, Gabriel (1800–1843). Montgomery states that he was born in Kilmarnock, Ayrshire, Scotland, learned weaving there, and settled in Decatur County, Indiana. In 1836 he was weaving in Dunlapsville, Indiana (Union Co.). Like his brothers, he used a sailboat trademark instead of signing his name on coverlets, and it is not possible to estimate how many coverlets were made by Gabriel Gilmour alone. According to Montgomery, Gabriel married a sister of William Craig, Sr., also a coverlet weaver (see entry). Gabriel probably did not weave after 1838 because he was ill. 21 (Gilmour family), 1838–1842.

GILMOUR, Joseph (ca. 1805– ). Like his brothers, Gabriel, Thomas, and William Gilmour, Joseph was born in Scotland and trained as a weaver before coming to America in 1831. In 1836 he was in Union County, Indiana, and by 1839 he had located near Dunlapsville in Union County. He used the sailboat trademark, too. Montgomery states that he did no weaving after 1845, when he moved to Missouri. 21 (Gilmour family), 1838–1842.

GILMOUR, Thomas (ca. 1813– ). Thomas Gilmour was also born in Scotland, where he was trained as a weaver. Montgomery believes that he did not do any weaving in America, concentrating on farming in Franklin County, Indiana, instead. *

GILMOUR, William (ca. 1807– ). Born in Scotland like his brothers, Gabriel, Joseph, and Thomas, William was trained there as a weaver. William moved to Union County, Indiana, in 1836 from Connecticut, where he had been working with Joseph and Gabriel. According to Montgomery, he was the only one of the four brothers to continue weaving after 1845; he was listed in the 1850 U. S. census as a weaver. He used the sailboat trademark also. Safford and Bishop state that William moved to Oskaloosa, Iowa (Mahaska Co.), in 1858. 21 (Gilmour family), 1838–1842.

GINN, Robert (1805– ). Born in Ireland, he learned weaving there and came to America at the age of 17. Ginn stopped first in Philadelphia, moved on to Steubenville, Ohio (Jefferson Co.), and finally settled in Piqua, Ohio (Miami Co.), in 1839. One coverlet dated 1846 is attributed to him.

GISH, S. M. One coverlet has been recorded with this name and the date 1852; it is not known if Gish was the weaver or the client.

GLASSLEY, John (ca. 1831– ). Born in Pennsylvania, he was a weaver in Mount Joy, Pennsylvania (Lancaster Co.). In the 1870 U. S. census he appears as a day laborer in Mount Joy. Although Glassley lived in Indiana between 1858 and 1867, he could not be traced as a weaver there. A woven inscription along

*Eagles grasp the American flag under one wing in this coverlet border design; blue weave in blue wool and white cotton. Woven by "W. K.," Knox Co., Ohio, ca. 1835. Collection of Mr. and Mrs. Foster McCarl, Jr.*

[64]

the bottom of his coverlets reads "Latest Stile Warranted Made by John Glassley Mount Joy Lan Co Pa." 3, undated.

GLASSLEY, Joseph (ca. 1839– ). A native of Pennsylvania, he is listed in the 1870 U. S. census as working in a coverlet factory in Mount Joy, Pennsylvania (Lancaster Co.). *

GLEN, Hugh. According to records of the New York State Historical Association at Cooperstown, he advertised on January 1, 1832, that he was from Scotland and that he had commenced weaving in the town of Middlefield. He was prepared to weave "carpets, double carpet coverlets, single carpet coverlets, cotton bedspreads, and damask drapes." *

GLOBE FACTORY. See entry for John Keagy.

GOEBELL, Henry. He is listed by Reinert and Kovel and Kovel as weaving in 1841; the location is unknown, but it may have been Berks County, Pennsylvania. *

GOOD, Jacob (ca. 1800– ). Good was supposedly weaving at Leitersburg, Maryland (Washington Co.), until he moved to Ohio about 1867, turned to carpenter work, and abandoned weaving. His coverlets are said to have had "traditional," presumably overshot, designs, and he apparently did not use a Jacquard-equipped loom. 2, undated.

GOOD INTENT WOOLEN FACTORY. This factory was located on Bermudian Creek in Huntington Township, Pennsylvania (Adams Co.), and was operated in 1847 by Jacob A. Myers. It was also known as the Heikes Woolen Factory and operated until at least 1872. *

GOODMAN, Daniel (ca. 1800– ). Born in Pennsylvania, he is included by Reinert as weaving in Nescopeck, Pennsylvania (Luzerne Co.), in 1842. The 1850 U. S. census lists him as a weaver in Black Creek Township, Luzerne Co. 10, 1841–1844.

GOODMAN, John S. A native of Pennsylvania, he is listed by the C.C.G.A., Safford and Bishop, and Kovel and Kovel as weaving in Black Creek, Pennsylvania (Luzerne Co.), in 1830. The 1850 U. S. census locates him in Black Creek, Luzerne Co., as a weaver. 8, 1830–1851.

GOODMAN, Peter (ca. 1783– ). A Pennsylvania native, he appears in Reinert as weaving in Black Creek Township, Pennsylvania (Luzerne Co.), in 1852. The 1850 U. S. census describes him as a weaver in Delaware Township, Mercer Co. He may be the Peter Goodman who was weaving in Danville, Pennsylvania (Montour Co.), about 1831. 10, 1832–1854.

GOODWIN, Harmon. He is listed by Hall, the C.C.G.A., Safford and Bishop, and Kovel and Kovel as weaving in Maine; the dates are unknown. *

GORDON, L. He was a weaver at the Keagy Factory, Bedford County, Pennsylvania, in 1840. (See entry for John Keagy.) 1, 1840.

GOTWALS, M. The name Gotwals, New Britain Township, Pennsylvania (Bucks Co.), and 1841 appear on one recorded coverlet; it is not known if Gotwals was the weaver or the client.

GRAHAM, John (ca. 1798– ). Born in Derry County, Ireland, he was weaving in Mount Vernon, Ohio (Knox Co.), where the 1850 U. S. census locates him as a weaver. 2, 1853 and 1855.

GRAHAM, Samuel (1805–1871). Born in Manchester, England, he came to America at the age of eighteen and settled in New Castle, Indiana (Henry Co.). He used an eagle alighting on a leafy branch as a trademark on his coverlets. According to Montgomery, he used this motif until 1850, when he usually replaced it with a potted rose. 26, 1843–1860.

GRAMLYG, John (ca. 1805– ). Born in Prussia, his name also appears as "Kramlich," "Granalich," and "Gramlic" in tax lists over the years. The 1850 U. S. census describes him as a weaver in Allentown, Pennsylvania (Lehigh Co.), where he was employed by Charles Wiand (see entry). He is included in tax lists from 1853 to 1888 as a self-employed weaver in Anthony Township, Pennsylvania (Montour Co.). He marked his coverlets with the name White Hall, a village in Anthony Township. Tax lists for 1888–1889 show that his property was sold to J. Kreamer. 3, 1863–1868.

GRANOLD, J. George. He was weaving at Sidney, Ohio (Shelby Co.), in 1852 and 1853. 2, 1852 and 1853.

GRAPE, ———. See entry for John Henry March.

GRAVE, David Isaac (ca. 1803–1864). Born in Pennsylvania, he is listed by the C.C.G.A. and Kovel and Kovel as weaving in Ohio in 1836; according to Safford and Bishop, he was working in Morgan County, Indiana, in 1836 and 1839. Montgomery states that he and his family settled near Richmond, Indiana (Wayne Co.), in 1816. Grave occasionally used his entire name when he signed a coverlet, but more often used the abbreviation "D. I. G." 9, 1836–1849.

GREENWALD, John W. (ca. 1812–1865). Pennsylvania-born Greenwald was weaving in Greenwich Township, Pennsylvania (Berks Co.), in 1845, when his name was spelled "Grunewald." The 1850 census of manufacturers for Maxatawny Township, Berks County, describes him as a coverlet and carpet weaver whose factory "using flying machines produced 100 coverlets annually at value of $450." By 1858 he was weaving in Lobachsville, Berks Co. The 1860 U. S. census of Pike Township, Berks Co., includes a "Greenwalt" who had a wool factory. An inventory taken a short time after his death gives his residence as Albany Township, Berks Co., and includes a "weaver loom and fixtures" valued at $1, along with large amounts of cotton yarn, linen spinning wheels, and one bundle of dyed yarn. December 8, 1865, Berks County Courthouse. *

GRIEST FULLING MILL. Located in northeastern Adams

[ 65 ]

County, Pennsylvania, this mill was erected by David Griest, who operated it until he died in 1851. His son then managed it. The mill produced woolen cloth and also made blankets during the Civil War. A few coverlets are reported to have been made there, but none has been located.

GRIMM, Peter (1832–1914). Born in Ohio, he was weaving in Loudonville, Ohio (Ashland Co.), where he is said to have bought land from F. Yearous (see entry), also a coverlet weaver. Mohican Historical Society, Loudonville, Ohio. The 1860 U. S. census lists him as a carpet weaver in Loudonville. 20, 1840–1867.

GRUBE, Emanuel (1813–1890). Born in Pennsylvania, he was weaving in Warwick Township, Pennsylvania (Lancaster Co.). The 1850 and 1860 U. S. censuses for Lancaster County include him as a weaver. Grube's woven inscriptions sometimes read "Emanuel Grube, Warwick T. L. A. C. P." He is buried in the Salem Lutheran cemetery, Kissel Hill, Lancaster Co. 8, 1835–1848.

## H

HAAG, Jacob (ca. 1812–   ). Born in Germany, he was working as a weaver in Emmaus, Pennsylvania (Lehigh Co.), by 1847. The 1850 U. S. census of Salisbury Township, Lehigh Co., describes him as a weaver, and he appears in the 1860 U. S. census as a coverlet weaver in Emmaus. His birthplace is given as Bavaria. A deed of December 2, 1863, lists Haag as then living in Stephenson County, Illinois, and selling property in Emmaus, Pennsylvania. Northampton County Courthouse, Easton, Pa. 4, 1847–1857.

HAAG, Jonathan. One coverlet with this name and February 10, 1842, but lacking a location of manufacture has been recorded. It is not known if Jonathan Haag was the weaver or the client.

HABECKER, David (1800–1889). Data gathered from one recorded coverlet indicate that he may have been weaving in Pekin, New York (Niagara Co.), in 1846.

HACKMAN, L. This name and the date 1845 have been found on one recorded coverlet; the location where the coverlet was woven and whether Hackman was its weaver or owner are not known.

HADSELL, Ira (ca. 1813–   ). Born in New York, he was weaving at Palmyra, New York (Wayne Co.), by 1849, according to the C.C.G.A. and Safford and Bishop. The 1850 U. S. census lists him as a coverlet weaver there. He made double woven coverlets without center seams, often using a design of American eagles with the motto "E Pluribus Unum" as well as American flags and the word "Liberty." (See also entry for James Van Ness.) 17, 1851–1866.

HAESELER, H. Recorded coverlets indicate that he was weaving at Orwigsburg, Pennsylvania (Schuylkill Co.), from 1841 to 1843. 4, 1841–1843.

HAIN, Peter L. (1834–1882). He appears in Reinert as weaving at his woolen mill in Heidelberg Township, Pennsylvania (Berks Co.), about 1860. 1, undated.

HALDEMAN, John M. He was weaving in New Britain Township, Pennsylvania (Bucks Co.), in 1844 and is probably the weaver who in 1840 signed his work "J. M. H. & Co." 1, 1844.

HALL, ———. Although listed by the C.C.G.A., Safford and Bishop, and Kovel and Kovel as weaving in 1869, this name, mistaken for that of a weaver, is thought to be a misreading of part of the legend "Washington Hail, 1869," incorporated in the coverlet pattern.

HAMAS, Elias. According to the O.H.S., he was weaving in Cleveland, Ohio (Cuyahoga Co.), in 1848. *

HAMELTON, John. From recorded coverlets, it has been learned that Hamelton was weaving in Machenoy, Pennsylvania (Northumberland Co.), in 1836 and in Jackson Township, Northumberland Co., from 1839 to 1844. Reinert locates him, as John Hamilton, in Jackson Township (Northumberland Co.), in 1841. He made single woven coverlets and usually added the letters "P. A. N." at the end of his inscriptions. Their meaning is not known, but may have something to do with a statement of patent. Hamelton may be the Hamilton who was weaving in Lanark, Illinois (Carroll Co.), in 1850 (see entry). 11, 1836–1844.

HAMILTON, John. He is listed by the C.C.G.A., Safford and Bishop, Kovel and Kovel, and Madden as weaving in Lanark, Illinois (Carroll Co.), in 1850. He may have worked earlier in Northumberland County, Pennsylvania (see entry for Hamelton).

HAMMOND, Denton (   –1850). He was weaving in Johnsville, Maryland (Frederick Co.); the dates are unknown. *

HAMMOND, John (1823–1871). A son of Denton Hammond (see entry), he was a weaver in Johnsville, Maryland (Frederick Co.), in 1857. He is buried in the Beaver Dam cemetery there. 1, 1857.

HARCH, J. He is listed by the C.C.G.A., Safford and Bishop, and Kovel and Kovel as weaving with Andrew Kump (see entry); the dates and location are unknown. Kump was weaving in Hanover, Pennsylvania (York Co.), but no weaver named Harch has been located. *

HARING, David D. (   –1889). He was weaving in Norwood, New Jersey (Bergen Co.), from at least 1830 to 1842, according to the information gathered from recorded coverlets. Elvehjem Art Center, *American Coverlets of the Nineteenth Century from the Helen Louise Allen Textile Collection* (Madison, Wis., 1974), states that Haring wove in Bergen County from 1800 to 1835. According to the Art Institute of Chicago, Haring had his shop in West Norwood,

[ 66 ]

Bergen Co., where he installed and operated a loom with a Jacquard-type attachment shortly after the mechanism was introduced into the United States. Many of the coverlets signed by or attributed to Haring have a small white rose with several leaves in the corners. It may be a trademark, but the design also appears on coverlets made by I. Christie (see entry). Some of Haring's coverlets show his full name, while others have only the initials "D. D. H." Many include the full date and the name of the owner woven in a cartouche in a border rather than in the corners. 18, 1830–1842.

HARING, James A. The Newark Museum, Newark, New Jersey, lists him as a weaver in Norwood, New Jersey (Bergen Co.), about 1825. *

HARPER, William. According to the C.C.G.A., Kovel and Kovel, and Safford and Bishop, he was weaving at Bridgeport, Virginia (Harrison Co., now in West Virginia), in 1839. In 1850 he is said to have woven a coverlet in the Hemfield Railroad pattern, but it is not signed and no other coverlet by Harper has been recorded.

HART, J. From recorded coverlets it has been learned that Hart wove from at least 1845 to 1851. In 1847 he gave his location as Ohio; in 1851 he was in Wilmington, Ohio (Clinton Co.). He incorporated as a woven inscription a version of the Golden Rule that was also employed by Abram Allen (see entry): "Be ye to others kind and true as you'd have others be to you and neither say nor do to them what e'er you would not take again." A coverlet dated 1851 has the legend, "If good we plant not, vice will fill the place and rankest weeds the richest soils deface." 4, 1845–1851.

HARTING, Peter (1799–1864). His name is spelled "Hartung" on one of his coverlets. Harting is listed by Reinert as weaving in Vera Cruz, Pennsylvania (Lancaster Co.), in 1832; it is known that he was weaving from 1832 to 1834, but no location appears on his coverlets. Harting wove the legend, "Der Depig W" ("The Coverlet Weaver") on one coverlet dated 1834. He is buried in the Swamp graveyard, West Cocalico Township, Lancaster Co. The inventory of Harting's estate includes one coverlet and a "Lot of Linen" valued at $29. November 10, 1864, Lancaster County Courthouse. 6, 1832–1834.

HARTMAN, John (ca. 1805– ). Born in Germany, he was weaving with his brother Peter (see entry) in Wooster, Ohio (Wayne Co.), in 1837. From 1837 to 1844 he wove by himself in Milton Township, Ohio (Richland Co.), and the 1850 U. S. census for Richland County describes Hartman as a weaver. By 1851 he had moved to La Fayette, Ohio (Allen Co.); he was still there in 1857. 20 (John Hartman alone), 1837–1857; 3 (John and Peter Hartman in partnership), 1837–1838.

HARTMAN, Peter. Born in Germany, he moved to Ohio from Pennsylvania in 1831 and settled north of Wooster (Wayne Co.), where he was a coverlet weaver and minister. In 1837 he and his brother John (see entry) were weaving together in Wooster; he worked alone from 1840 to 1845. Hartman is listed by the C.C.G.A., Safford and Bishop, and Kovel and Kovel as weaving at La Fayette, Ohio

Eagles with "Liberty" inscribed above their heads alternate with fruit trees in this coverlet border design; double weave in blue wool and white cotton. Woven by J. Stiff, Stillwater (possibly N. Y.), 1836. Collection of Mr. and Mrs. Foster McCarl, Jr.

(Allen Co.), in 1843. 11 (Peter Hartman alone), 1840–1845; 3 (Peter and John Hartman in partnership, 1837–1838.

HARTMANN, Charles G. He is listed by Madden as a coverlet weaver in Shelbyville, Illinois (Shelby Co.), and in Effingham, Illinois (Effingham Co.); the dates are unknown. *

HARTZ, Daniel. One coverlet has been recorded with this name and the date 1836; it is not known if Hartz was the weaver or the client.

HAUSMAN, Allen B. He was weaving in Groveland, New York (Livingston Co.), in 1839, according to Safford and Bishop. *

HAUSMAN, Benjamin (ca. 1799– ). Born in Pennsylvania, he is included in Kovel and Kovel as weaving in Allentown, Pennsylvania (Lehigh Co.), in 1836. Reinert shows him there in 1839, Safford and Bishop in 1858. The 1850 census of manufacturers for York County, Pennsylvania, lists Hausman as a coverlet weaver who used hand power and two looms and employed two other weavers. He produced 300 blankets annually, valued at $1,350. On April 30, 1852, Hausman advertised in the *People's Advocate* of York that he was moving his weaving establishment to a new location at the corner of South Duke and East Main (now Market) streets in York, where he planned to weave "Coverlets Better and Cheaper than Ever" and "summer and winter spreads or coverlets." The prices ranged from $3 to $7.50. 12, 1838–1843 (Allentown location), 1845–1848 (York location).

HAUSMAN, Ephraim (ca. 1813–1901). A Pennsylvania-born son of Jacob Hausman, Sr. (see entry), he was weaving in Trexlertown, Pennsylvania (Lehigh Co.). He is listed in the 1850 U. S. census for Lehigh County as a coverlet weaver; in the 1860 census he is described as a weaver and dyer. Ephraim is buried in the Trexlertown cemetery. 8, 1850–1872.

HAUSMAN, G. He was weaving at Trexlertown, Pennsylvania (Lehigh Co.), in 1836. 1, 1836.

HAUSMAN, Jacob, Jr. (ca. 1808– ). Born in Pennsylvania, a son of Jacob Hausman, Sr. (see entry), he is identified as weaving in Friedensburg, Lobachsville, and Rockland, Pennsylvania (Berks Co.), in 1842 by Kovel and Kovel, in the same locations in 1846 by Safford and Bishop, and in Friedensburg alone in 1849. The 1850 U. S. census describes him as a weaver in Oley Township, Berks Co. According to Reinert, he was weaving in Friedensburg and Rockland in 1859. 1, 1849.

HAUSMAN, Jacob, Sr. (1788–1863). Born in Pennsylvania, Safford and Bishop locate him in Lobachsville, Pennsylvania (Berks Co.), in 1838. The 1850 U. S. census lists him as a weaver in Oley Township, Pennsylvania (Berks Co.). From his coverlets it is known that he was weaving in Trexlertown in 1834 and in Lobachsville from 1839 to 1857. Hausman had a fulling mill in Lobachsville, where he is buried. 29, 1834–1857.

HAUSMAN, Joel (ca. 1826– ). Hausman was born in Pennsylvania. He appears as a coverlet weaver in Upper Macungie Township, Pennsylvania (Lehigh Co.), in the 1850 U. S. census, when he was living in the household of Solomon Hausman (see entry), who may have been his father. *

HAUSMAN, Solomon (ca. 1794–1866). Born in Pennsylvania, Reinert lists him as a weaver in Trexlertown, Pennsylvania (Lehigh Co.), in 1832; Safford and Bishop also locate him there in 1848. The 1850 U. S. census places him without an occupation in Upper Macungie Township, Lehigh County. Living with him were Ephraim and Joel Hausman (see entries), who are listed as coverlet weavers. 16, 1836–1848.

HAUSMAN, Tilghman (1832–1917). A son of Jacob Hausman, Jr. (see entry), he was born in Pennsyl-

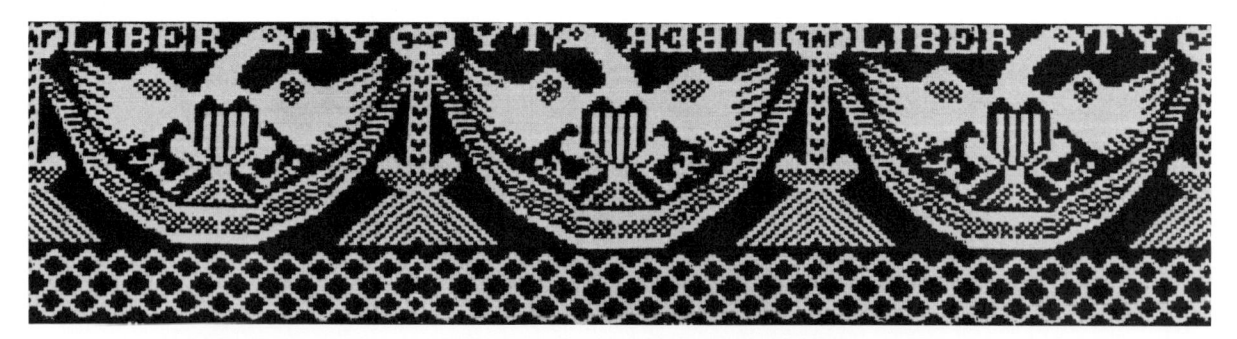

Coverlet border design of eagles above swags with "Liberty" inscribed above their heads; double weave in blue wool and white cotton. Woven by Garret Van Doren, Millstone, N. J., 1838. Collection of Mr. and Mrs. Foster McCarl, Jr.

vania. Tilghman Hausman appears in the 1850 U. S. census as a weaver in Oley Township, Pennsylvania (Berks Co.), where he was living in his father's household. Reinert states that for many years Tilghman was the weaving foreman at the Berks County prison. He is buried in the cemetery at Lobachsville. 1, 1868.

Hay, Ann. Hall lists Ann Hay as a coverlet weaver, attributing a coverlet she illustrates to her. However, the coverlet bears the trademark of the Craig family, and Montgomery states that Ann Hay's family said she was never a coverlet weaver. See entry for A. Getty.

Hay Weaving Shop. This shop was in operation around 1845 at Second and Spring streets, Batavia, Ohio (Clermont Co.), according to the Clermont County Historical Society, Batavia. The weavers working there are not known. 1 (attributed); undated.

Hechler, Samuel. Several of his handwritten drafts for coverlets, dated 1826 and 1828, are in the Berks County Historical Society, Reading, Pennsylvania. The drafts are marked with his name, but they are not for a Jacquard-equipped loom. *

Hecht, Abslam. He is listed by the C.C.G.A., Safford and Bishop, and Kovel and Kovel as weaving in Maryland in 1849. *

Hefner, George (ca. 1806–1878). Born in Pennsylvania, he was weaving in Greentown, Ohio (Stark Co.), in 1844 and 1845. The 1850 U. S. census describes him as a coverlet weaver in Lake Township, Ohio (Stark Co.); in his household was George Petna, a young Ohio-born coverlet weaver. The 1850 U. S. census of manufacturers indicates that Hefner had a coverlet factory in Plain Township, Stark Co. Using hand-powered looms, Hefner employed two men and produced 180 coverlets, valued at $1,260, annually. 3, 1844–1845.

Heifner, J. Philip. He was weaving in Perry Township, Ohio (Wayne Co.), in 1844, and in Hayesville, Ohio (Ashland Co.), in 1847. By 1860 he was weaving in Olney, Ohio (Richland Co.). 3, 1844 and 1860.

Heikes Woolen Factory. See entry for the Good Intent Woolen Factory.

Heilbronn, George. He is listed by Reinert as weaving in Pennsylvania, probably in Berks County; the dates are unknown. Safford and Bishop locate him in Basil, Ohio (Fairfield Co.), in 1839 and 1850, the C.C.G.A,. in Lancaster, Ohio (Fairfield Co.), in 1850. In 1857 he had a shop in Lancaster on Columbus Street, south of Main Street. He advertised on December 31, 1857, in the Lancaster *Ohio Eagle* that he had received a variety of new patterns from the East, and that he would make coverlets, requiring twenty cuts of woolen yarn for each. 6 (Basil, Ohio), 1843–1845; 25 (Lancaster, Ohio), 1847–1855.

Heilbronn, J. He was weaving at Adelphi, Ohio (Ross

*Coverlet border design of spread eagles with stars and the U. S. Capitol; double weave in blue wool and white cotton. Attributed to James Alexander, Orange Co., N. Y., 1822. Collection of Mr. and Mrs. Foster McCarl, Jr.*

[69]

Co.), from 1839 to 1842, and at Lancaster, Ohio (Fairfield Co.), in 1849, although only one recorded coverlet by Heilbronn shows the latter location. 8, 1839–1849.

HEILBRONN, J. J. ( –ca. 1842). Heilbronn was weaving at Basil, Ohio (Fairfield Co.), from 1838 to 1842, and used the term "Fancy Coverlet" in his woven inscriptions. He operated a woolen mill along the canal in Basil and may be the John J. Heilbronn who died on December 8, 1842, at the age of 33, being buried in Basil. 25, 1838–1842.

HEISER, William L. He is listed in W. W. Reilly & Co. as a coverlet weaver in Chillicothe, Ohio (Ross Co.). *

HEMON, James. He is listed in W. W. Reilly & Co. as a coverlet weaver in Circleville, Ohio (Pickaway Co.). *

HENDERSON, George, Jr. (ca. 1804– ). Born in Pennsylvania, he appears in the 1850 U. S. census as a weaver in Green Township, Pennsylvania (Franklin Co.). He advertised that he had moved to Chambersburg, Pennsylvania (Franklin Co.), where he would continue to weave coverlets, diaper, and carpets at his new shop on the west side of Market Street. Henderson offered to accept country produce of all sorts as payment. He also advertised for a young apprentice to learn the weaver's trade. *Chambersburg Whig*, May 13, 1836. *

HERMAN, John. Montgomery says that he may be a coverlet weaver who moved from Butler County, Ohio, to Ripley County, Indiana, in 1855. *

HERRETER, ———. See entry for Kepner's Woolen Mill.

HERRMANN, Charles A. Madden lists him as a weaver in Champaign County, Illinois; the dates are unknown. *

HERSH, Henry (1808–1882). Born in Pennsylvania, he is identified as a weaver in Leacock Township, Pennsylvania (Lancaster Co.), by the 1850 U. S. census; in his household was Rudolph Ressler, also a weaver (see entry). His will was written in Strasburg, Lancaster Co., but he died in the city of Lancaster. An inventory of his estate taken shortly after he died includes a carpet loom and fixtures valued at $2.50. He is buried in the Zion Reformed cemetery in New Providence, Lancaster Co. 4, 1846–1849.

HESHE, Henry. He is listed in W. W. Reilly & Co. as a coverlet weaver in Poplar, Ohio (Crawford Co.). *

HESSE, D. One coverlet has been recorded with this name, Logan, Ohio (Hocking Co.), and 1860.

HESSE, F. E. (ca. 1827– ). Born in Germany, he is included as a weaver in the 1860 U. S. census of Logan Village, Logan Township, Ohio (Hocking Co.). 2, 1860–1862.

HESSE, L. (ca. 1809– ). A native of Germany, L. Hesse is located by Safford and Bishop in Somerset, Ohio (Perry Co.), in 1847, where he was weaving from at least 1840 to 1860. The 1850 U. S. census also lists him as a weaver in Somerset. 20, 1838–1860.

HICKS, Samuel (1804–1888). Born in Lebanon County, Pennsylvania, according to Montgomery he was a weaver in Millerstown (now Annville), Lebanon Co., before he moved to Chambersburg, Ohio (Montgomery Co.), in 1835. He moved on to Indiana in 1838, settling in Adams Township, Madison Co. During the Civil War, he moved to Ovid, Indiana (Madison Co.), where he died; he is buried in the Gilmore cemetery, Adams Township, Madison Co. 2 dated 1834; 5 undated.

HICKS, William (1821–1903). In 1850 he was weaving in Madison County, Indiana, according to the C.C.G.A., Safford and Bishop, and Kovel and Kovel. His relationship to Samuel Hicks (see entry) has not been established; Montgomery believes that he was not a son of Samuel, while the *Commemorative Biographical Record of Prominent and Representative Men of Indianapolis and Vicinity* (Chicago, 1908), states that he was. Hicks made single woven coverlets, often using a trademark consisting of a peacock and a flower in addition to his name. 6, undated.

HILLIARD, Philip. One recorded coverlet indicates that Hilliard was weaving in Lower Mount Bethel Township, Pennsylvania (Northampton Co.), in 1839; he is included as a weaver in the 1840 tax list in Upper Mount Bethel Township. Instead of signing his full name on coverlets, he used the initials "P. H." 6, 1835–1846.

HINKEL, Christian K. (ca. 1813–1899). Safford and Bishop state that Hinkel, a native of Pennsylvania, was weaving in Shippensburg, Pennsylvania (Cumberland Co.), in 1841. The 1850 U. S. census identifies him as a weaver in Shippensburg, *Boyd's Business Directory, Adams–York*, as a carpet weaver on King Street. 5, 1840–1852.

HINSHILLWOOD, Robert (ca. 1798– ). Born in Scotland, he is recorded by the O.H.S. as weaving in Salem, Ohio (Columbiana Co.), in 1848. He appears without an occupation in Franklin Township, Ohio (Portage Co.), in the 1850 U. S. census. *

HIPP, Sebastian (ca. 1830– ). He is identified by Kovel and Kovel as weaving in Mount Joy, Pennsylvania (Lancaster Co.); the dates are not known. Mount Joy tax records, 1831–1846, do not include Hipp. The 1850 U. S. census lists him as a German-born weaver in Mifflin Township, Ohio (Richland Co.), where he was living with Henry Shearer (see entry), another German-born weaver. 3, 1853–1854.

HIPPERT, Samuel. He is listed by Reinert as weaving in Mount Joy, Pennsylvania (Lancaster Co.), in 1833. Hippert is included in the 1837 and 1838 tax

Coverlet border design of baskets of pears and flowers; double weave in red and blue wool. Woven by John Klein, Hamilton Co., Ind., 1868. Collection of Mr. and Mrs. Foster McCarl, Jr.

Coverlet corner block showing a turkey perched in a tree and a rooster at the base of the trunk; Beiderwand weave in red wool and white cotton. Woven by Henry Oberly, Womelsdorf, Pa., ca. 1840. Collection of Mr. and Mrs. Foster McCarl, Jr.

lists of Elizabethtown, Pennsylvania (Lancaster Co.), where he bought property in 1840. There is no record of its sale. On coverlets he used the initials "S. H." instead of his full name. 11, 1834–1837.

HOAGLAND, James S. (ca. 1820–    ). This weaver's name is also spelled "Hogeland." According to Montgomery, he was born in Virginia and went to Lafayette, Indiana (Tippecanoe Co.), in 1842. He appears as a farmer in Morgan County, Indiana, in the 1850 U. S. census. Hoagland advertised in the September 28, 1854, *Lafayette American* that he was weaving. The C.C.G.A., Safford and Bishop, and Kovel and Kovel include him as weaving in Lafayette in 1856. Coverlet inscriptions reading "J. S. Hogeland's (or Hoagland's) Sons" indicate that he was joined in business by at least some of his offspring. Also see entry for Thomas Jackson. 2, 1855 and 1857.

HOERR, Adam (ca. 1812–    ). Born in Germany, he is described as a weaver in the 1850 U. S. census for Harmony (now Old Economy), Pennsylvania (Butler Co.). It has been determined from recorded coverlets that Hoerr was weaving at Harmony from 1848 to 1856. 3, 1848–1856.

HOFFMAN, ———. He was weaving in 1848. The location is unknown, but it may have been in western Pennsylvania, possibly Somerset County. It is believed that Hoffman was working with Aaron Casebeer (see entry); they signed their work "made by Casebeer and Hoffman." 4 (Hoffman and Casebeer), all 1848.

HOHULIN, Gottlich. He is listed by the C.C.G.A., Safford and Bishop, and Kovel and Kovel as weaving in 1861; the location is unknown. Madden gives his name as "Gottlieb Huhulin" and claims that he was weaving in Goodfield, Illinois (Woodford Co.), but the dates are unknown. *

HOKE, George. He appears in W. W. Reilly & Co. as a coverlet weaver in West Brookfield, Ohio (Stark Co.). *

HOKE, Martin (1815–1893). Hoke was born in Germany. The C.C.G.A. and Kovel and Kovel say that he was weaving in 1842, location unknown, while Safford and Bishop locate him in Dover, Pennsylvania (York Co.), in 1842 and 1847, where he was in fact weaving continuously from 1833 to at least 1842. Information from recorded coverlets indicates that he was weaving in both Dover and York boroughs, York County, from 1842 to at least 1847. The 1850 U. S. census shows him as a coverlet maker in the south ward, York. "Patent" and "Lady's Fancy" are incorporated in the inscriptions of some of Hoke's coverlets. Hoke is buried in the Prospect Hill cemetery, York. 54, 1833–1847.

HOLLAND, James. See entry for Abel White.

HOLLER, J. One coverlet with this name and 1839 has been recorded; it is not known if Holler was the weaver or the client.

HOLMES, John. He is listed by the New York State Historical Association, Cooperstown, as weaving coverlets at Delhi, New York (Delaware Co.). He came to America from Scotland in 1817 and wove cloth at Delhi for many years. 1, 1841.

HOOVER, Andrew (ca. 1802–1877). Born in Pennsylvania, he was weaving from 1837 to 1849 at Hanover. The county and state are not identified on his coverlets. The 1850 U. S. census lists him as a weaver in East Hanover Township, Pennsylvania (Dauphin Co.). 3, 1837–1849.

HOOVER, John. Montgomery believes that he may have been weaving in Hagerstown, Indiana (Wayne Co.), in the Test Woolen Mills (see entry). *

HOOVER, M. He is listed in Hawes as a coverlet weaver in Canton, Ohio (Stark Co.). *

HOPEMAN, ———. The C.C.G.A., Safford and Bishop, and Kovel and Kovel believe that he was weaving in New York state; the dates are unknown. *

HORNBREAKER, Henry. According to the O.H.S., he was a weaver in St. Clairsville, Ohio (Belmont Co.), in 1830. *

*Coverlet border design featuring eagles and stars above eagles with hearts on their breasts; double weave in blue wool and white cotton. Woven by David D. Haring, Bergen Co., N. J., 1833. Collection of Mr. and Mrs. Foster McCarl, Jr.*

[71]

Horsfall, Henry. He appears in W. W. Reilly & Co. as a coverlet weaver in New Lisbon, Ohio (Columbiana Co.). *

Hosfeld, F. Reinert includes Hosfeld as weaving in Allentown, Pennsylvania (Lehigh Co.); the dates are unknown. *

Housman, ———. He is listed by the C.C.G.A., Safford and Bishop, and Kovel and Kovel as weaving between 1839 and 1845; the location is unknown. These entries may refer to one of the Hausmans (see entries). *

Huber, Damus (1811– ). Born in Germany, he appears in the C.C.G.A., Safford and Bishop, and Kovel and Kovel as weaving in Dearborn County, Indiana, from 1840 to 1850. Montgomery states that he owned land on which a loom house was erected in Jackson Township, Indiana (Dearborn Co.), but that there is no indication Damus Huber was ever a weaver. His brother John (see entry) was a coverlet weaver.

Huber, John (ca. 1807– ). German-born, Montgomery indicates that he came to America with his brother Damus. He is listed by the C.C.G.A., Safford and Bishop, and Kovel and Kovel as weaving in Jackson Township, Indiana (Dearborn Co.), from 1840 to 1850. The 1850 U. S. census describes him as a weaver in Kelso Township, Dearborn Co. 5, all undated.

Hudders, J. S. Safford and Bishop indicate that he was weaving in Bucks County, Pennsylvania, in 1849. 1, 1849.

Hull, Lewis. He is listed by Reinert and Kovel and Kovel as weaving in New Holland, Pennsylvania (Lancaster Co.), in 1831, but Hull's name does not appear in tax lists for that location or in Lancaster County deeds or estate settlements. 1, 1831.

Hull, Mathias. According to the C.C.G.A., Safford and Bishop, and Kovel and Kovel, he was a weaver; the dates and location are unknown. *

Humphreys, S. Safford and Bishop believe that he was a weaver in Bethany, New York (Genesee Co.), in 1835. *

Huntington, Edwin (ca. 1829– ). The 1850 U. S. census for Wolcott, New York (Wayne Co.), lists him as a New York-born weaver living in the household of Daniel Conger (see entry). *

Hunter, William J. (ca. 1839– ). Born and trained as a weaver in the United States, he moved to Canada during the Civil War and wove coverlets there, according to Burnham and Burnham. No coverlets woven by Hunter in the United States have been recorded.

I

Impson, Jacob. He is described by the C.C.G.A., Safford and Bishop, and Kovel and Kovel as weaving in Cortland County, New York, in 1845. Recorded coverlets show that he was there as early as 1833. 14, 1832–1845.

Imsweller, Henry. The 1804 and 1805 tax records of York, Pennsylvania (York Co.), list Imsweller as a coverlet weaver. *

Inger, J. Fritz. This name is given by Kovel and Kovel to a weaver in Allentown, Pennsylvania (Lehigh Co.), in 1845, but it is a misreading of J. Fritzinger, who was a coverlet weaver there (see entry).

Ingham, David (1800–ca. 1891). Born in Batley, York-

*Coverlet border design of eagles and stars flanked by willow and fruit trees; double weave in blue wool and white cotton. Woven by Harry Tyler, Jefferson Co., N. Y., 1843. Collection of Mr. F. James McCarl.*

shire, England, he came to America around 1828 and settled in Bradford County, Pennsylvania, where he and his brother Joseph (see entry) wove coverlets in the Monroeton Woolen Factory between 1841 and 1845. David Ingham was a weaver and farmer in LeRoy Township, Bradford Co. from 1848 to 1868. He retired in 1868 and moved to Tioga County, Pennsylvania, where he died. 3 (D. Ingham alone), 1848–1868; 3 (J. and D. Ingham), 1841–1845.

INGHAM, Joseph. He was weaving with his brother David at the Monroeton Woolen Factory, Bradford County, Pennsylvania, between 1841 and 1845. He is also listed by the C.C.G.A. as weaving in 1847, but the location is unknown. 3 (J. and D. Ingham), 1841–1845.

IRVIN, James. He is listed by the C.C.G.A., Safford and Bishop, and Kovel and Kovel as weaving in Pulaski, New York (Oswego Co.), in 1859, his name being spelled "Irwin." According to the Oswego County Historical Society, information derived from issues of *Pulaski Democrat* in the 1850s shows that Irvin purchased a carpet loom that had been operated on a seasonal basis for at least two years by Charles S. Mayo (see entry). In December 1850 Irvin advertised that he had moved his shop just north of the printing office on Jefferson Street, where he offered a wide variety of goods: "Coverlets Figured, Striped, and Rag Carpets, Shoals [Shawls], Blankets, Flannels, Full Cloth, Diapers, and Grain Bags," in addition to any other type of weaving that the public would expect to find at a fine custom shop. 2, 1848 (or 1838?) and 1854.

IRWIN, L. See entry for James Irvin.

## J

JACKSON, John Hamelton. Although identified by the C.C.G.A., Safford and Bishop, and Kovel and Kovel as weaving in Pennsylvania in 1840, this is a misreading of the inscription(s). (See the entry for John Hamelton, who worked in Jackson Township, Pennsylvania [Northumberland Co.])

JACKSON, Thomas (ca. 1815– ). Born in England, he appears in the 1850 U. S. census as a weaver living in the household of James S. Hogeland (see entry), a weaver in Lafayette, Indiana (Tippecanoe Co.). *

JENISON, J. He is listed in W. W. Reilly & Co. as a coverlet weaver in Stark County, Ohio. *

JESSUP, James. Madden identifies Jessup as a weaver in Fairfield, Illinois (Wayne Co.), in the nineteenth century. *

JOHNSON, D. P. One coverlet with this weaver's name, Orleans County, New York, and 1848 has been recorded.

JONES, L. According to the O.H.S., Jones was a weaver in Cornersburg (now Marshallville), Ohio (Wayne Co.), in 1849. *

JORDAN, Thomas (ca. 1825– ). Born in Ohio, he is listed in the 1850 U. S. census as a coverlet weaver in Hagerstown, Indiana (Wayne Co.). Montgomery believes that he may have worked in the Test Woolen Mills (see entry). *

JOTTER, Jacob. He is listed in W. W. Reilly & Co. as a coverlet weaver in Monroe, Ohio (Butler Co.). *

JUKES, Benjamin. Two coverlets woven in 1837, whose locations of manufacture are not indicated, have been recorded.

JUNE, Benjamin (ca. 1790– ). Born in Massachusetts, he is described as a coverlet weaver in the 1850 U. S. census for Brunswick, Ohio (Medina Co.). 2, both 1846.

## K

K———, M———. A weaver using only these initials as a signature on his coverlets was working in Springfield Township, Pennsylvania (Bucks Co.), in 1841 and 1842. 4, 1841–1842.

K———, W———. A weaver using only these initials on his coverlets was working in Knox County, Ohio; the dates are unknown. 1, undated.

KACHEL, John (1809–1889). Born in Pennsylvania, he was a weaver in Robeson Township, Pennsylvania (Berks Co.), being listed as such in the 1850 U. S. census. His name, however, is spelled "Cochel." 12, 1838–1857.

KALEY, John. He was weaving in 1836 and 1840; the location is unknown. 2, 1836–1840.

KAPP, Christof. Reinert identifies him as weaving in Warwick Township, Pennsylvania (Lancaster Co.), in 1839. *

KAPPEL, Gottfried. According to Safford and Bishop, he was weaving in Zoar, Ohio (Tuscarawas Co.), in 1845 and 1871, where he is located in 1871 by the C.C.G.A. and Kovel and Kovel. A weaving house was built in Zoar in 1825; a larger woolen mill in 1830. Kappel appears as manager in 1830, and he and his sons were in charge throughout its career. John Ramsay, "Zoar and Its Industries," *Antiques*, XLVI (December 1944), p. 335. The mill sold coverlets and yard goods from 1845 to 1873. Some of the coverlets are signed with only the word "Zoar," while others are inscribed with "Zoar, G. Kappel & Co." and the date. 6, 1845–1850.

KAUFMAN, John. Reinert indicates that he was a weaver in Bucks County, Pennsylvania. On his earliest dated recorded coverlets, which he numbered, he used his initials as a signature. By 1839 Kaufman was signing his full name, and he no longer used a numbering system. 10, 1837–1846.

KEAGY, Abraham (1786–1867). Born in Pennsylvania,

[73]

in 1813 he arrived in Morrison's Cove, Pennsylvania (Bedford Co.), where he built and operated a woolen mill that his son John (see entry) later operated. According to a 1972 informant, Keagy was known locally as "Machine Abe" because of his mechanical ability. The 1850 U. S. census describes him as a machinist in Woodberry, Bedford Co. *

KEAGY, Abraham. He was the son of John Keagy (see entry).

KEAGY, I. In 1849 he was weaving at Woodberry, Pennsylvania (Bedford Co.), and may be John Keagy. Only one coverlet with this name is known—"Manuf. by I. Keagy."

KEAGY, John (1811–1890). Born in Pennsylvania, the son of Abraham Keagy (see entry), he was weaving in Woodberry, Bedford Co., as early as 1849 and owned and operated a woolen mill, called the Globe Factory, at Morrison's Cove, Pennsylvania (Bedford Co.). John Keagy appears in the 1850 U. S. census of Middle Woodberry Township, Bedford Co., as a manufacturer, and he and Peter Longenecker (see entry) were listed in the 1850 census of manufacturers as having a woolen factory, presumably the Globe Factory, there. Using water power, they had three power looms, one hand loom, and employed five men and two women. The mill produced 150 coverlets annually, which were valued at $600. During the Civil War the mill made blankets for the Union Army. In 1868 a new mill that had six power looms and employed thirteen men was built. John's sons, Samuel and Abraham (see entries), took over its operation in 1879. 11 (Globe Factory), 1 dated 1855; 1 (Keagy and Longenecker), 1850.

KEAGY, Samuel (1837– ). He was the son of John Keagy (see entry). In 1879 he and his brother Abraham (see entry) took over the operations of their father's woolen mill.

KEAN, Carl Lewis. Born in Germany, he came to America and settled in Louisville, Kentucky (Jefferson Co.). He is listed by the C.C.G.A. and Safford and Bishop as weaving in Scott County, Kentucky, from 1850 to 1860. Montgomery states that he and his brother Frederick (see entry) were weaving together in Kentucky. 1 (C. L. Kean), undated; 1 (F. A. and C. L. Kean), 1840.

KEAN, Frederick A. (ca. 1811–1893). He came to America from Germany, applied for citizenship in Jefferson County, Ohio, in 1836, and received it eight years later in Louisville, Kentucky (Jefferson Co.). According to Montgomery, he wove with his brother Carl (see entry) when they lived in Louisville. The 1850 U. S. census lists Frederick Kean in Harrison Township, Indiana (Vigo Co.), but does not indicate his occupation. He is listed by the C.C.G.A., Safford and Bishop, and Kovel and Kovel as weaving in Terre Haute, Indiana (Vigo Co.). "Mr. Kean was the only weaver known identified with Terre Haute." *Leaves of Thyme,* VII (December 1956), pp. 1–2. 8, 1843–1847 (locations where woven not noted); 1 (woven with C. L. Kean), 1840.

KECK, ———. See entry for Fehr & Keck.

KEEFER, William. One coverlet has been recorded with this name and the date 1848.

KEENER, Henry. According to Reinert, he was weaving in Womelsdorf, Pennsylvania (Berks Co.), in 1841. 6, 1839–1844.

KEENER, Jacob. Reinert says that he was weaving in Lancaster, Pennsylvania (Lancaster Co.), in 1857; the 1857 city directory locates him as a "coverlid" weaver on Dorwart Street near West King Street. *

KEENER, John (ca. 1808– ). He is included as a weaver in Mount Joy, Pennsylvania (Lancaster Co.), tax lists for 1854, which is how he is described in the 1860 U. S. census. Mount Joy tax lists for 1864 show "John Keener—weaver employed by Manning &

*Eagles on "stilts" with stars overhead repeat in this coverlet border design; double weave in blue wool and white cotton. Weaver unidentified, probably New York or Ohio, 1835. Courtesy of Mrs. Elizabeth C. Prescott.*

Wantz," while an inventory of 1866 includes "about 50 yds. carpet" valued at $25. June 11, 1866, Lancaster County Courthouse. *

KEIFER, Louis. He is listed by the O.H.S. as weaving in Canton, Ohio (Stark Co.), in 1835. *

KELL, D. He was weaving in Jackson County, Ohio, dates unknown. 3, undated.

KENNEDY, David. The O.H.S. says that he was a weaver in Steubenville, Ohio (Jefferson Co.), from 1829 to 1832. He advertised in the June 6, 1829, issue of the Steubenville *Western Herald and Steubenville Gazette* that he was weaving. (See n. 20, p. 12, and n. 23, p. 14.) *

KEPNER, Absalom B. He was weaving in 1833, according to the O.H.S. Kepner advertised in the July 1, 1833, issue of a local newspaper that he was beginning coverlet weaving in Covington, Newberry Township, Ohio (Miami Co.), that he planned to start by September 1, and that he would make both single and double woven coverlets, plus carpets. *

KEPNER, Isaac. He appears in Reinert, Safford and Bishop, and Kovel and Kovel as weaving in Montgomery County, Pennsylvania. In 1836 he was weaving in North Hanover Township, Montgomery Co.; by 1838 he was in Pottstown, Pennsylvania (Montgomery Co.). 5, 1836–1843.

KEPNER'S WOOLEN MILL. Located on Little Marsh Creek, Highland Township, Pennsylvania (Adams Co.), this mill was operated in 1872 by "Herreter and Sweitzer," about whom nothing more is known. 1 (attributed), undated.

KERNS, William (1807–   ). Born in Pennsylvania, Montgomery lists him as a weaver in Wabash Township, Indiana (Parke Co.), as early as 1847, and indicates that in 1858 he bought land with a "coverlet shop" on it. 4, 3 undated, 1 1852.

KIEHL, Benjamin (1807–1895). He was born in Berks County, Pennsylvania, and moved to Lancaster County in 1822, where he worked as a weaver at a location four miles outside of Lancaster along the Lancaster–New Holland Pike. He stopped weaving in 1846 and moved into Lancaster, was appointed a railroad repairman, and worked for the Pennsylvania Railroad until he retired in 1888. *Lancaster Intelligencer*, September 13, 1895. 6, 1834–1837.

G. W. KIMBLE WOOLEN FACTORY. See entries for Gottlieb Eckert, August Vogel, and Jacob Walter.

KING, Daniel (ca. 1828–1888). He was weaving in Stark County, Ohio, and may be the Daniel King who died on February 23, 1888, at age 60 and was buried in the Welty cemetery, Sugar Creek Township, Ohio (Stark Co.). 2, 1856 and 1859.

KING, Joseph. According to the O.H.S., he was weaving in Morristown, Ohio (Belmont Co.), from 1839 to 1855. *

KIRST, John. Reinert lists him as a weaver in Centre Township, Pennsylvania (Berks Co.), in 1848. *

KISNER, Benedict. Kisner was weaving at No. 93 Bank Street, Baltimore, Maryland; the 1860 city directory describes him as part of Kisner and Company (see John A. Kisner entry), which was in operation at the southwest corner of Warren and Bethel streets. Kisner's recorded coverlets are signed "Manufactured by B. Kisner No. 93 Bank Street, Baltimore, Md." 5, undated.

KISNER, John A. City directories for the period 1856 to 1860 show this weaver as part of Kisner and Company (see Benedict Kisner entry), located at the

Coverlet border pattern of eagles and flowering bushes, with "Eagle" inscribed along the border edge; Beiderwand weave in red, green, and blue wool and natural cotton. Woven by Martin Breneman, York Co., Pa., 1839. Courtesy of Mr. and Mrs. H. F. Riffle, Jr.

southwest corner of Warren and Bethel streets, Baltimore, Maryland. *

KITSON, Nathan. He is listed by Montgomery as having advertised in the April 23, 1848, issue of the *Richmond Palladium* (Richmond, Ind.) that he was ready to weave double woven coverlets and other goods. *

KITTINGER, John. He was weaving at Springfield, Ohio (Portage Co.). 5, 1838–1840.

KLAR, Francis Joseph. According to Safford and Bishop, Kovel and Kovel, and Reinert, Klar was weaving in Reading, Pennsylvania (Berks Co.). 4, 1838–1843.

KLEHL, J. He is listed by Safford and Bishop as weaving in Hamilton County, Indiana, in 1868, but Montgomery does not mention Klehl. *

KLEIN, Andrew. Montgomery states that he was born in Germany and settled with his family (see entries) in Shelbyville, Indiana (Shelby Co.). Andrew was one of four sons who wove with their father, Michael, until his death in 1851. The sons tried to keep the business going until 1854 when the father's estate was settled. Then the family scattered, Andrew moving to Dearborn County, Indiana, between 1854 and 1855. In 1857 he joined his brother John in Noblesville, Indiana (Hamilton Co.), where they purchased an old woolen mill and operated it as a loom house and shop. The Kleins used a large rose for a trademark and usually incorporated the date of manufacture. The use of a trademark rather than individual names makes it impossible to distinguish which family member wove a particular piece. 3, (Klein family), 1850–1854.

KLEIN, Francis (ca. 1829–   ). According to Montgomery, Francis, who was born in Germany, was weaving with his family (see entries) in Shelbyville, Indiana (Shelby Co.), from the late 1840s to 1854. He moved to Ripley County, Indiana, in 1855. The Kleins used a trademark of a large rose, usually incorporating the date of manufacture. 2 (Klein family), 1850 and 1854.

KLEIN, Fredoline (ca. 1831–   ). He was born in Germany and, according to Montgomery, was weaving with his father and three brothers (see entries) in Shelbyville, Indiana (Shelby Co.). Fredoline Klein moved to Rush County, Indiana, in 1855. 3 (Klein family), 1850–1854.

KLEIN, John (ca. 1834–1901). He came to America from Germany with his family (see entries) and, according to Montgomery, was weaving with his father and three brothers in Shelbyville, Indiana (Shelby Co.). After 1854 he moved to Hamilton County, Indiana, where he worked with Henry Adolf and Martin Forrer (see entries). By 1857 John and his brother Andrew opened a weaving shop in Noblesville (Hamilton Co.). After the Civil War, John became a sewing machine salesman. His later coverlets do not have the Klein trademark of a rose, but they are signed with the location of manufacture (Hamilton County) and the date. Montgomery believes that John usually included the full name and age of the person for whom the piece was woven. 3 (Klein family), 1850–1854; 6, 1857–1868.

KLEIN, Mathias. According to recorded coverlets, he was weaving in Montgomery County, Ohio, from 1839 to at least 1842. W. W. Reilly & Co. lists him as a coverlet weaver in Montgomery County, spelling his name "Clein." 12, 1839–1850.

KLEIN, Michael (   –1851). Montgomery states he was born in Germany and came to America with his family, which included his sons Andrew, Francis, Fredoline, and John (see entries). They settled in Shelbyville, Indiana (Shelby Co.), where he worked from the late 1840s until his death in 1851. The 1850 census of manufacturers describes him as a property owner with a weaving shop that made carpets and coverlets. His capital inventory was $1,000.

*Coverlet border design of eagles and stylized willow trees; double weave in red wool and white cotton. Weaver unidentified, Scipio, N. Y., 1834. Courtesy of Cynthia and William Lanford.*

Michael Klein and his sons used a rose trademark and the date of manufacture. The use of a trademark rather than individual names makes it impossible to distinguish which family member wove a particular piece. 3 (Klein family), 1850–1854.

KLINGER, Absalom (1817–1901). Born in Pennsylvania, "in his younger years he came to Millersburg, Berks [now Bethel] Co. (Pa.) to learn the weaver's trade . . . he liked Millersburg and settled down there." Morton L. Montgomery, comp., *Historical and Biographical Annuals of Berks County, Pennsylvania* (Chicago, 1909). He learned to weave from Daniel Bordner (see entry), a coverlet weaver in Millersburg. The 1850 U. S. census includes Klinger as a coverlet weaver in Bethel Township, Berks Co. Klinger numbered his coverlets: the earliest recorded coverlet is number 1499, woven in 1843; the latest, number 2003, was woven in 1855. 11, 1843–1864.

KLINHINZ, John. He was weaving in Ohio, but the exact location is unknown. He may be the John Kleinhans who was in Ottawa County, Ohio, in 1840. 4, 1848–1854.

KLIPPERT, Henry. One coverlet with this name and 1840 has been recorded. It is not known whether Klippert was the weaver or the client.

KNIRIM, A. D. He was weaving in Dixon, Illinois (Lee Co.), in 1868, and is also described as a professional weaver by Madden. 1, 1868.

KOCH, Valentine. See entry for Valentine Cook.

KOSTNER, J. M. He was weaving in Lewisville, Ohio (Coshocton Co.), in 1846. 1, 1846.

KRAMLICH, John. See entry for John Gramlyg.

KREBS, Philip (ca. 1780– ). Records of the Lebanon County, Pennsylvania, Historical Society list him as weaving "in Reamstown Street" in Fredericksburg, Pennsylvania (Lebanon Co.), in 1810. The 1850 U. S. census lists him as a Pennsylvania-born weaver in Fredericksburg; living with him was his son Philip. He was weaving in 1848, but the location is not indicated. However, according to the Lebanon County Courthouse records, he may have been in Fredericksburg as late as 1862. *

KUDER, Solomon (ca. 1806–1866). Born in Pennsylvania, his name is often spelled "Kuter" on his coverlets. From 1835 to 1855 he was weaving in Trexlertown, Pennsylvania (Lehigh Co.); the 1850 U. S. census lists him as a coverlet weaver in Upper Macungie Township, Lehigh Co. In his household at the time was Hiram Backer, a young Pennsylvania-born coverlet weaver. Roberts states that Kuder had spent some time in New Jersey as a young man, where he learned enough English to teach school when he returned to Trexlertown; that he had a store in Reading, Pennsylvania (Berks Co.), for a time; and that he then was the weigher of iron ore mined at Trexlertown. Kuder wrote a book, *Der Praktische Familien-Fäber (The Practical Family-Dyer)* (Allentown, Pa., 1858), on dyeing yarn and cloth. His single woven coverlets usually had a different inscription in each of the two bottom corners—in one corner, "Manufactored by S. Kuter Trexlertown Lehigh County," in the other, "Sold by S. Kuter and Manufactored for [name]." 21, 1835–1855.

KUDER, William. Kovel and Kovel believe that William, the son of Solomon Kuder (see entry), was weaving in Norristown, Pennsylvania (Montgomery Co.), dates unknown. Reinert locates him in Trexlertown, Pennsylvania (Lehigh Co.), in 1849. 4, 1849–1850.

KUMP, Andrew (1811–1868). He first appears in the 1835–1836 tax lists for Hanover, Pennsylvania (York Co.), as a coverlet weaver. In an advertisement

*Coverlet border design of eagles, churches, and trees, "Monroe" being inscribed above; Beiderwand weave in blue wool and white cotton. Weaver unidentified, possibly Pennsylvania or Ohio, 1843. Courtesy of Elizabeth L. Williams.*

placed in the August 13, 1845, issue of the *Hanover Spectator*, Kump announced that he was continuing "the DAMASK COVERLET WEAVING" at his old stand in Baltimore Street, Hanover. Furthermore, "He has lately added to his establishment, entirely new machinery of the latest eastern inventions, . . . He is now prepared to weave Coverlets for $2 and will furnish the necessary Cotton Yarn for each coverlet for $1.62½." An article was written in praise of Kump's work citing "specimens . . . of various colors and patterns executed in the best style, affording evidence of no ordinary degree of taste and skill," which would be displayed at the National Fair in Washington, D. C., on May 20, 1846. *Hanover Spectator*, May 13, 1846. Kump included "Damask Coverlet Manufacturer" and his name, location, and date on his later coverlets. He is listed as a coverlet weaver in the 1850 U. S. census; Valentine Cook (see entry), another coverlet weaver, was working for him. The 1850 census of manufacturers for Hanover describes Kump as a coverlet weaver who, "using hand power and one man, produces annually 250 coverlets at a value of $1,600." 77, 1834–1853.

# L

LAGET, A. He is listed by W. W. Reilly & Co. as a coverlet weaver in Middletown, Ohio (Butler Co.). *

LAKE, Salmon (ca. 1794– ). Born in Connecticut, Lake moved to New York state, where he advertised that he was weaving coverlets and ingrain carpet between Fredonia and Dunkirk (Chautauqua Co.). *Fredonia Censor*, December 5, 1832. One coverlet, dated 1847 and woven in Fredonia, has been recorded. Lake appears in the 1850 U. S. census as a weaver in Pomfret, New York (Chautauqua Co.). 1, 1847.

LANDES, John. He is listed by the C.C.G.A. as weaving in 1756, and by Safford and Bishop in 1805; the location is not known. Because of the early date, his products obviously were not woven with the aid of a Jacquard-type attachment. Landes's book of coverlet designs is now in the library of the Historical Society of Pennsylvania, Philadelphia. He should not be confused with John Landis. *

LANDIS, John. Reinert indicates that he was weaving in 1840, possibly in Berks or Lancaster County, Pennsylvania. 1, 1840.

LANTZ, J. Reinert locates him in Bethlehem, Pennsylvania (Northampton Co.), in 1837; Safford and Bishop in East Hempfield Township, Pennsylvania (Lancaster Co.), the same year. 2 (East Hempfield Township), 1 dated 1837.

LASHELL, L. M. The O.H.S. says that he was weaving in Sullivan, Ohio (Ashland Co.). *

LASHELS, George W. (ca. 1806– ). Born in New Jersey, he lived in New York state between 1833 and 1839 and had moved to Ohio by 1840. From the coverlets recorded, it is known that Lashels was weaving in Huntington Township, Ohio (Lorain Co.), from at least 1848–1850, where the 1850 U. S. census locates him. W. W. Reilly & Co. also describes him as a weaver in Huntington Township. 6, 1848–1850.

LATOURETTE, Henry (ca. 1832–1892). He was born in Indiana, the son of John LaTourette (see entry), also a coverlet weaver. He appears in the 1850 U. S. census as a coverlet weaver in Wabash Township, Indiana (Fountain Co.), where Montgomery states that he wove coverlets until 1871. LaTourette died in Colorado but was buried in Covington, Indiana (Fountain Co.). The family trademark is a flower with laterally placed vines and the date. After their father's death in 1849, the LaTourettes included the word "Year" in all of their weaver's blocks. Since Henry and his sister Sarah used the same trademark rather than their names, it is impossible to say how many of the coverlets recorded were woven by Henry himself. 16 (Henry or Sarah LaTourette), 1849–1858.

LATOURETTE, John (1793–1849). He was born in New Jersey. Montgomery states that he lived in Germantown, Ohio (Montgomery Co.), before moving to Indiana in 1828, where he wove coverlets in Fountain County. After John's death, his family carried on the weaving business. The coverlets woven by the LaTourette family all have a trademark instead of the weaver's name. John used a flower with laterally placed vines; the date the piece was woven appears beneath the flower. "Frenchman's Fancy," "Connecticut Beauty," and "Texas Star" are some of his patterns. 7, 1841–1849.

LATOURETTE, Sarah (1822–1914). She was born in Germantown, Ohio (Montgomery Co.), the daughter of John LaTourette (see entry), also a coverlet weaver, and moved to Fountain County, Indiana, with her family in 1828. Sarah assisted her father and continued weaving with her brother Henry after their father's death in 1849. She is described as a weaver in the 1850 U. S. census; the census of manufacturers for that year says that she had a coverlet weaving business in Fountain County. Employing two men and one woman and using hand looms, the La Tourettes annually produced 200 coverlets valued at $500. Madden believes that she was weaving in Vermilion County, Illinois, in 1858. For a discussion of the family trademark, see the entry for Henry LaTourette. See also the entry for Sarah Van Sickle. 16 (Henry or Sarah LaTourette), 1849–1858.

LAUGHLIN, M. According to the O.H.S., he was weaving in Logan County, Ohio, in 1845; he may be the James McLaughlin (see entry) who was a weaver in Steubenville, Ohio (Jefferson Co.), in 1844. *

Coverlet whose interior pattern features eagle medallion repeats, while the borders are composed of confronting birds with rose bushes; Beiderwand weave in blue and red wool and white cotton. Weaver unidentified, Bucks Co., Pa., 1842. Abby Aldrich Rockefeller Folk Art Center, bequest of Margaret H. Davies.

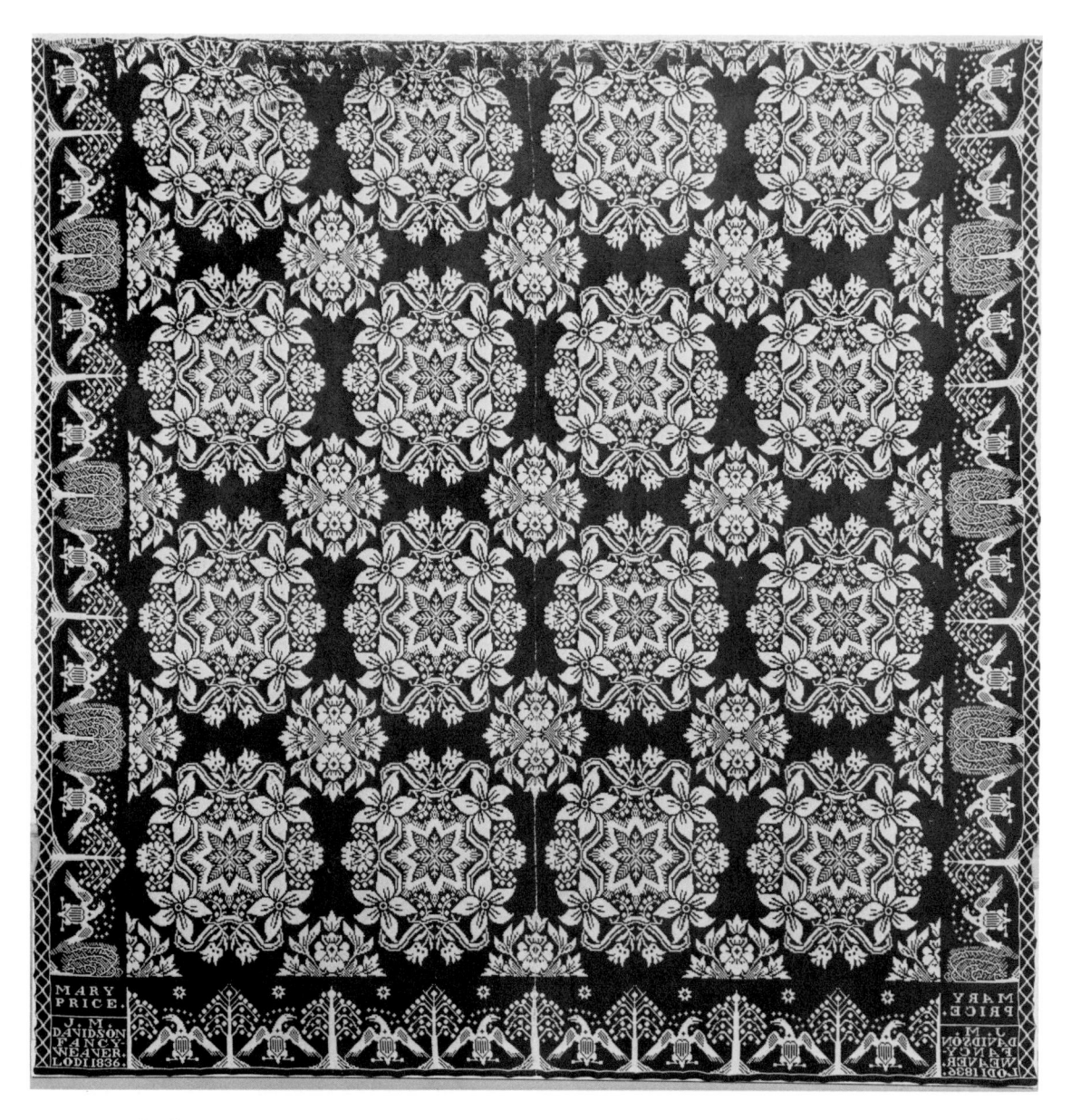

"Lilies of France" interior design and borders composed of eagles alternating with willow and fruit trees; double weave in blue wool and white cotton. Woven by J. M. Davidson, Lodi, N. Y., 1836. Collection of Mr. and Mrs. Foster McCarl, Jr.

LAWRENCE, David. He is listed by W. W. Reilly & Co. as a coverlet weaver at the mouth of Yellow Creek, Ohio (Jefferson Co.). *

LAWSON, David (ca. 1790– ). Born in Ireland, he is described as a weaver in the 1860 U. S. census for Pike Township, Ohio (Coshocton Co.). Lawson signed his coverlets with the initials "D. L." and added the location beneath, but did not date them. 2, undated.

LAWYER, James (ca. 1810– ). Montgomery states that he was born in New Jersey and moved to Washington County, Indiana, sometime before 1838. Lawyer advertised in the August 29, 1838, issue of the *Washington Republican* that he was starting a weaving business in his home and would weave coverlets and table linen. He is known to have been in Washington County as late as 1855. *

LEBAR, Pamela. She was a weaver in Northampton County, Pennsylvania, in 1843, according to the C.C.G.A. and Safford and Bishop. *

LEDERMAN, Henry (ca. 1819– ). Born in France, he was in America by 1852, and Montgomery states that he settled in Adams Township, Indiana (Hamilton Co.), where he was weaving in 1859. The 1860 U. S. census locates him there. 1, 1859.

LEE, John (ca. 1788– ). Born in England, he was in Galena, Indiana (Floyd Co.), by 1848, according to Montgomery. The 1850 U. S. census shows him there. It is likely that he wove overshot coverlets. *

LEEHMAN, Joseph (ca. 1813– ). Born in Pennsylvania, he appears in the 1870 U. S. census of Mount Joy, Pennsylvania (Lancaster Co.), as a coverlet manufacturer; in his household was his son Joseph, also a coverlet weaver. *

LEHR, Daniel. Possibly the son of weaver George Lehr (see supplement), three signed and dated coverlets indicate that Daniel was weaving in Wayne County, Ohio, in 1848. One of them locates him in Dalton. 3, 1848.

LEIDIG, Peter. From recorded coverlets it is known that Leidig was weaving in Schaefferstown, Pennsylvania (Lebanon Co.), from 1837 to 1841 with a partner, George Renner (see entry). Their coverlets are signed "Renner & Leidig," and include the date and occasionally the name of the town woven into the corner blocks. 7, 1837–1841.

LEISEY, Peter (ca. 1803– ). He was born in Pennsylvania. The 1850 U. S. census describes him as a farmer in West Cocalico Township, Pennsylvania (Lancaster Co.). He was weaving in Denver, Cocalico Township; the full dates of his activity are unknown. The 1859–1860 Lancaster city directory locates him in Reinholdsville, Lancaster Co., as does *Boyd's Business Directory, Adams–York.* 6, all undated.

LEITZ, ———. He is listed by Safford and Bishop as weaving in Milwaukee, Wisconsin (Milwaukee Co.), in 1850. *

LEITZ, J. Reinert locates him in East Hempfield Township, Pennsylvania (Lancaster Co.), in 1849. It is not known if he is related to, or is the same, Leitz who was weaving in Wisconsin (see entry). *

LENTZ, Cornelius (ca. 1836– ). He appears in the 1860 U. S. census for the second ward of Allentown, Pennsylvania (Lehigh Co.), as a "coverlid weaver" who was born in Pennsylvania. *

LEOPOLD, Valentine. The O.H.S. lists him as weaving in Canton, Ohio (Stark Co.), in 1823 and 1833. *

LEWIS, Harvey. He is listed by the O.H.S. as weaving in Ohio in 1831. *

LEYKAUFF, Michael. See William Eichner entry.

LICHTY, Benjamin (1811–1882). Born in Lancaster County, Pennsylvania, his name is also spelled "Leighty" and "Lighty." Apprenticed as a weaver at the age of 17, he went to Ohio in 1832 and settled in Stark County. From 1836 to 1854 Lichty was weaving in Bristol, Ohio (Wayne Co.). In 1854 he moved to Jackson Township, and in 1860 to New Berlin (now North Canton), both in Stark County, Ohio. Later he returned to Lancaster County, Pennsylvania, where he died. 24, 1838–1854.

LINDERMAN, Jacob. Reinert locates him in Union Township, Pennsylvania (Berks Co.), in 1841 and in 1845. *

LOCHMAN, Christian L. (1790–1864). He was born in Pennsylvania and was weaving in Hamburg, Pennsylvania (Berks Co.), at least between 1838 and 1842, where Christian and his son William (see entry) appear in the 1850 U. S. census as weavers. Christian Lochman is buried in the Greenwood cemetery, Hamburg. 7, 1838–1842.

LOCHMAN, William (1818–1900). Born in Pennsylvania, he was weaving with his father, Christian (see entry), in Hamburg, Pennsylvania (Berks Co.). He is included in the 1850 U. S. census as a weaver in his father's household. *

LOGAN, Patrick (ca. 1752– ). Montgomery identifies Logan as a weaver in Franklin County, Indiana, in 1820, and states that his coverlets would have been in the overshot weave. *

LONG, C. He is listed by the O.H.S. as a weaver in Jefferson County, Ohio, in 1845 and 1846. 1, 1846.

LONG, David. He was weaving in 1846 and 1848, but the locations are not on his coverlets. Reinert says that he was working near Chambersburg, Pennsylvania (Franklin Co.), in 1848. He may be the David N. Long who died in 1904 in Buffalo, New York (Erie Co.). His will, probated in February 1904, mentions that he had formerly lived in Waynesboro, Pennsylvania (Franklin Co.), and had been a resident of Buffalo about forty years. 2, 1846–1848.

LONG, Jacob. He was weaving in Knox County, Ohio, in 1843. 2, 1843.

LONG, John. Reinert locates him in Haycock Township, Pennsylvania (Bucks Co.), in 1815. *

LONG, John. The O. H. S. lists John Long as weaving in Holmes County, Ohio, in 1840–1855. 2, 1846–1855.

LONG, M. A. This name, New Britain Township, Pennsylvania (Bucks Co.), and 1835 have been found on a single recorded coverlet; it is not known whether Long was the weaver or the client.

LONGENECKER, Peter (ca. 1821–    ). Born in Pennsylvania, he is described as a manufacturer in the 1850 U. S. census for Woodberry, Pennsylvania (Bedford Co.). He is probably the weaver who worked with John Keagy (see entry) in Bedford County in 1850; they signed their work "Made by Keagy and Longenecker." One such coverlet has been recorded; no coverlets made by Longenecker alone have been identified.

LORENZ, Peter (ca. 1801–    ). He was born in France. The signature blocks on his coverlets also show his name spelled "Lorentz." The C.C.G.A. locates him in Wayne County, Indiana, in 1838; however, Montgomery states that Lorenz has not been found in any Indiana records. The O.H.S. says that he was weaving in Xenia, Ohio (Greene Co.), in 1843, and that he later moved from Warren County, Ohio, to Illinois. The 1850 U. S. census includes Lorenz as a weaver in German Township, Ohio (Montgomery Co.). 19, 1836–1846.

LOVETT, Rodman (1809–1895). Born in Pennsylvania, he is identified by the O.H.S. as weaving in Canton, Ohio (Stark Co.), in 1832; the 1850 U. S. census says that he was a farmer in Plain Township (Stark Co.). Hawes lists him as having a grocery store in Canton. He is buried in the West Lawn cemetery, Canton. *

LOWMILLER, William (1809–1879). He was born in Pennsylvania. From recorded coverlets, it is known that he wove in Level Corners, Pennsylvania (Lycoming Co.), from 1836 to 1838, and in Muncy borough (Lycoming Co.) from 1840 to 1852, where the 1850 U. S. census also locates him. In his household was Charles Roberts, a young Pennsylvania-born weaver. Parts of two sets of punched pattern cards for a Jacquard-type attachment are in the collection of the Muncy Historical Society, Muncy, Pa. One partial set, dated 1835, is for an interior design and is marked "Star Pattern," the other, marked "Rose Pattern," is for a border. 19, 1836–1845.

LUNN, William. From 1832 to 1835, Lunn was weaving in Utica, Ohio (Licking Co.), as indicated by the inscriptions on his coverlets. He was still weaving in 1836, but he no longer included the locations. 8, 1832–1836.

LUTZ, E. He is listed by Reinert as weaving in East Hempfield Township, Pennsylvania (Lancaster Co.), in 1847. *

LUTZ, Jacob (ca. 1806–1861). Born in Pennsylvania, he appears in the 1830 tax records of East Hempfield Township. No occupation is indicated; however, from 1831 to 1846 he is recorded in the tax lists there as a weaver. An inventory taken shortly after Lutz's death mentions "three weaving looms and apparatus thereto belonging," valued at $15. 17, 1838–1857.

## Mc

M———, I———. The Allen County Historical Society, Lima, Ohio, states that this weaver was working in Bellefontaine, Ohio (Logan Co.). Inscriptions on recorded coverlets indicate that "I. M." was weaving in Logan County between 1847 and 1850. There is a possibility that a coverlet woven by a "J. M." in Logan County in 1853 is by this same weaver. 5, 1847–1850.

M———, J———. See entry for "I. M."

MCCANN, George. He is listed by Madden as a weaver in Aurora, Illinois (Kane Co.), dates unknown.

MCCLELLAN, J. The O.H.S. says that he was weaving in Orange (now Nankin), Ohio (Ashland Co.), in 1842. *

MCCLELLAN, William. He was weaving in Ashland and Orange, Ohio (Ashland Co.); his name is also spelled "McClelland" on some coverlets. 5, 1840–1847.

MCGURK, Andrew. One coverlet with this name and Somerville, Ohio (Butler Co.), the date undetermined, has been recorded. It is not known whether McGurk was the weaver or the individual for whom the coverlet was woven.

MACINTYRE, A. One recorded coverlet bears the inscription "Wove by A. MacIntyre"; the date and location are not indicated.

MCKENNA, ———. One coverlet bearing the inscription "McKenna/Weaver" has been recorded; the date and location of manufacture do not appear.

MACKEON, Abraham B. He is listed by the C.C.G.A. as weaving in 1841, location unknown. 1, 1841.

MCKINNEY, James. The C.C.G.A. locates McKinney in Brookville, Indiana (Franklin Co.), in 1813, but Montgomery states that he is not listed in any of the Indiana census reports or other state records. *

MCLAUGHLIN, James. He was a weaver in Steubenville, Ohio (Jefferson Co.), in 1844, according to the O.H.S. *

MCLERAN, James (ca. 1799–    ). Born in Scotland, he immigrated to America and had settled in Pennsylvania by 1825. The O.H.S. locates McLeran in Salem, Ohio (Columbiana Co.), in 1848, where he was weaving coverlets and ingrain carpeting. The 1850 U. S. census places McLeran in Perry Township, Ohio (Columbiana Co.). His name is spelled "MacLeran" on one coverlet. 5, undated.

Coverlet with medallions composed of birds holding "Liberty" banners in their beaks and alternating with floral designs; double weave in blue wool and white cotton. Weaver unidentified, possibly New York or New Jersey, ca. 1840–1845. Collection of Mr. and Mrs. Foster McCarl, Jr.

McMillen, Samuel (ca. 1822– ). According to the O.H.S., he was a weaver in Steubenville, Ohio (Jefferson Co.), in 1837, where he appears in the 1850 U. S. census as a Virginia-born coverlet weaver, and in W. W. Reilly & Co. as a coverlet weaver. *

McNall, John. W. W. Reilly & Co. identifies McNall as a coverlet weaver. *

## M

Maddhes, C. According to an inscription on one recorded coverlet, Maddhes was weaving in Davenport, Iowa (Scott Co.), in 1855.

Mann, Mathias (1803–1893). Born in Württemberg, Germany, he was a weaver in Hanover, Pennsylvania (York Co.), where he first appears in the tax lists in 1834. *Boyd's Business Directory, Adams–York,* lists him as a weaver in Hanover, as does the 1860 U. S. census. He is buried in the Mount Olivet cemetery, Hanover. 13, undated.

Manning, ———. See entry for John Keener.

March, John Henry ( –1847). He was weaving in Salona, Pennsylvania (Centre, later Clinton, Co.), between 1838 and 1847. He appears as a coverlet weaver in the tax lists of Lamar Township (Clinton Co.), and when he died, his residence was in Bald Eagle Township, Clinton Co. Two of March's recorded coverlets dated 1838 and 1839 are signed "J. H. March & Grape"; three, dating from 1840–1841, are signed "J. H. March & Co." Nothing more is known about the other weavers who worked with him. 18, 1838–1847.

Marion, Edward. According to the O.H.S., he was a weaver in Steubenville, Ohio (Jefferson Co.), in 1837. *

Mark, Matthew W. He is listed by the O.H.S. as weaving in Fayette County, Ohio, in 1843. *

Marr, John. Safford and Bishop locate him in Milton, Indiana (Wayne Co.), in 1843; Montgomery states that he was working there for John Wissler (see entry), but that nothing else is known about him. *

Marsh, J. The C.C.G.A. lists him as a weaver in 1840; the location is not known. *

Marshall, Edward W. From a single recorded coverlet, it is known that Marshall was weaving in Steubenville, Ohio (Jefferson Co.), in 1840.

Marsteller, A. He was weaving in 1854 in "L. S.," probably Lower Saucon Township, Pennsylvania (Northampton Co.). 1, 1854.

Marsteller, Thomas (ca. 1812– ). Born in Pennsylvania, he appears in the 1850 U. S. census as a weaver in Saucon Township, Pennsylvania (Northampton Co.), where Reinert locates him as early as 1842. Inscriptions on his coverlets indicate that he was weaving in Lower Saucon Township, Northampton Co., from 1845 to 1860. *Boyd's Business Directory, Berks–Schuylkill,* lists him as weaving in Hellertown (Northampton Co.). It has not been determined if there was a connection between Thomas and A. Marsteller (see entry). 13, 1845–1860.

Martin, Robert. An Irish-born farmer and weaver, the O.H.S. places him in Jefferson County, Ohio, dates unknown. *

Masters, Margaret. She is listed in W. W. Reilly & Co. as a weaver in Belleville, Ohio (Richland Co.). *

Mater, William Henry (ca. 1794– ). He is described by the 1850 U. S. census as a weaver in Washington Township, Ohio (Sandusky Co.), and by the O.H.S. as weaving in Fremont, Ohio (Sandusky Co.), in 1851. *

Matteson, H. A. This name, Bethany, New York (Genesee Co.), and 1837 occur on one coverlet; it is not known whether Matteson was the weaver or the client.

Maurer, Johannes (1784–1856). Maurer is listed by Reinert as weaving in the Mahantango Valley of Schuylkill County, Pennsylvania, dates unknown, and he is buried in the Union cemetery, Schuylkill Haven, Pennsylvania (Schuylkill Co.). It is not known if he is related to John Maurer (see entry). *

Maurer, John (1809– ). Born in Württemberg, Germany, he emigrated to Baltimore, Maryland, in 1832. According to Montgomery, he traveled to the Mahantango Valley in Schuylkill County, Pennsylvania, where he worked as a weaver, later moved on to Ohio, and settled in Franklin County, Indiana, in 1835. Maurer advertised that he was ready to weave coverlets and other materials at his home on Blue Creek near Brookville, Indiana (Franklin Co.). *Indiana American,* November 23, 1838. It is not known if he is related to Johannes Maurer (see entry). *

Maus, Philip ( –1880). Born in Germany, he immigrated to Pennsylvania. The 1850 and 1860 U. S. censuses for Lower Nazareth Township (Northampton Co.) describe him as a weaver. A deed dated 1865 locates Maus there, where he was working as a weaver. 3, 1845–1848.

Maxwell, William. He is listed in W. W. Reilly & Co. as a coverlet weaver in Belmont County, Ohio. *

Mayo, Charles S. In early 1849, he advertised in the *Pulaski Democrat* (Pulaski, New York) that he would weave coverlets and carpets on Jefferson Street in Pulaski, Oswego Co. *

Mealy, ———. He appears in Safford and Bishop as weaving in Milwaukee, Wisconsin (Milwaukee Co.), in 1850. *

Meckel, J. S. He is listed in W. W. Reilly & Co. as a coverlet weaver in Stark County, Ohio. *

Meeks, Josiah (ca. 1815– ). Born in Virginia, the O.H.S. locates Meeks in Trumbull County, Ohio, in 1838. He advertised in the April 12, 1838, issue of

"Lilies of France" interior with eagle and "Liberty" borders; double weave in blue wool and white cotton. Woven by Garret Van Doren, Millstone, N. J., 1838. Collection of Mr. and Mrs. Foster McCarl, Jr.

the *Western Reserve Chronicle* (Warren, Ohio) that he was weaving coverlets in Howland, Ohio (Trumbull Co.). (See n. 23, p. 14.) The 1850 U. S. census describes him as a farmer in Vienna Township, Trumbull Co. *

MEILY, Charles. He is included in the records of the O.H.S. as a weaver in 1830, and the C.C.G.A., Safford and Bishop, and Kovel and Kovel locate him in Mansfield, Ohio (Wayne Co.), in 1837. It has been determined from recorded coverlets that Meily was weaving in Wayne County, Ohio, between 1835 and 1848. 16, 1830–1848.

MEILY, Emanuel, Jr. (ca. 1805–1869). Born in Pennsylvania, he is listed by the Lebanon County Historical Society, Lebanon, Pennsylvania, as weaving in Fredericksburg, Lebanon Co., around 1810. On March 1, 1834, Emanuel Meily, Jr., and John and Samuel Mellinger (see entries) received a U. S. patent for a "weaving machine" to weave coverlets, diaper, carpets, and so forth, which was described as a type of machine never before used in America. Meily appears in the 1842 Lebanon borough tax records as a weaver; in his household were two other weavers, Henry Bellman and David Yingst (see entries). David Yingst later married Emanuel's daughter Christianna. Meily is included in the 1850 U. S. census for Lebanon as a blue-dyer, while the 1860 city directory describes him as a weaver at the corner of Market and Hill streets. 24, 1833–1848.

MEILY, John Henry (1817–1883). The O.H.S. says that he was born in Lebanon, Pennsylvania (Lebanon Co.), where he learned to weave from his father, Emanuel Meily, Jr. (see entry). John Henry Meily worked in Canton, Ohio (Stark Co.), for ten years, and then moved to Lima, Ohio (Allen Co.), where he had a coverlet and carpet factory from at least 1842 to 1850, and perhaps later. Meily used a trademark of two small cornucopias within his signature block, which contained the words "Lima, Ohio." 5, undated.

MEILY, Samuel (ca. 1806–   ). Born in Pennsylvania, he was weaving in West Lebanon, Ohio (Wayne Co.), in 1837, and it has been determined from inscribed coverlets that Meily was weaving in Mansfield, Ohio (Richland Co.), from at least 1839 to 1857. The 1850 U. S. census locates him as a weaver in Madison Township, Richland Co. His shop in Mansfield was at the corner of East Fourth and South Adams streets. 28, 1837–1857.

MELLINGER, Daniel. He was weaving in 1848, location unknown. 1, 1848.

MELLINGER, John (ca. 1800–1888). He was born in Pennsylvania and was weaving in 1834 in Millerstown (now Annville) in Lebanon Co. From at least 1834 to 1839 his coverlets were inscribed "John Mellinger & Son," but the son has not been identified; Safford and Bishop list John Mellinger & Sons as working in Seneca County, Pennsylvania, in 1836. He was weaving alone from 1839 to 1853. On March 1, 1834, John and Samuel Mellinger and Emanuel Meily, Jr. (see entries), received a U. S. patent for a "weaving machine" to produce coverlets, carpets, diaper, and other materials. Apparently the machine was of a type never before used in America. In late 1834 they sold a part interest in it to Daniel Bordner (see entry), another coverlet weaver. The 1850 U. S. census locates John Mellinger as a weaver in Warwick Township, Pennsylvania (Lancaster Co.), living in the household of Henry Moh, a laborer. Mellinger died in Lebanon. 11, 1834–1853.

MELLINGER, Samuel (ca. 1787–   ). A native of Pennsylvania, Mellinger was in Lebanon borough, Pennsylvania (Lebanon Co.), in 1834 when he, Emanuel Meily, Jr., and John Mellinger (see entries) received a U. S. patent for a "weaving machine" of a type never before used in America to weave coverlets and other goods. Later in 1834, a part interest was sold to another coverlet weaver, Daniel Bordner (see entry). The 1850 U. S. census describes Samuel Mellinger as a weaver in Ephrata Township, Pennsylvania (Lancaster Co.). 3, 1838–1839.

*Coverlet interior design of confronting peacocks perched in trees; Beiderwand weave in dark blue, light blue, and red wool and natural cotton. Woven by James Pearson, Chippewa (probably Ohio), ca. 1835. Collection of Mr. and Mrs. Foster McCarl, Jr.*

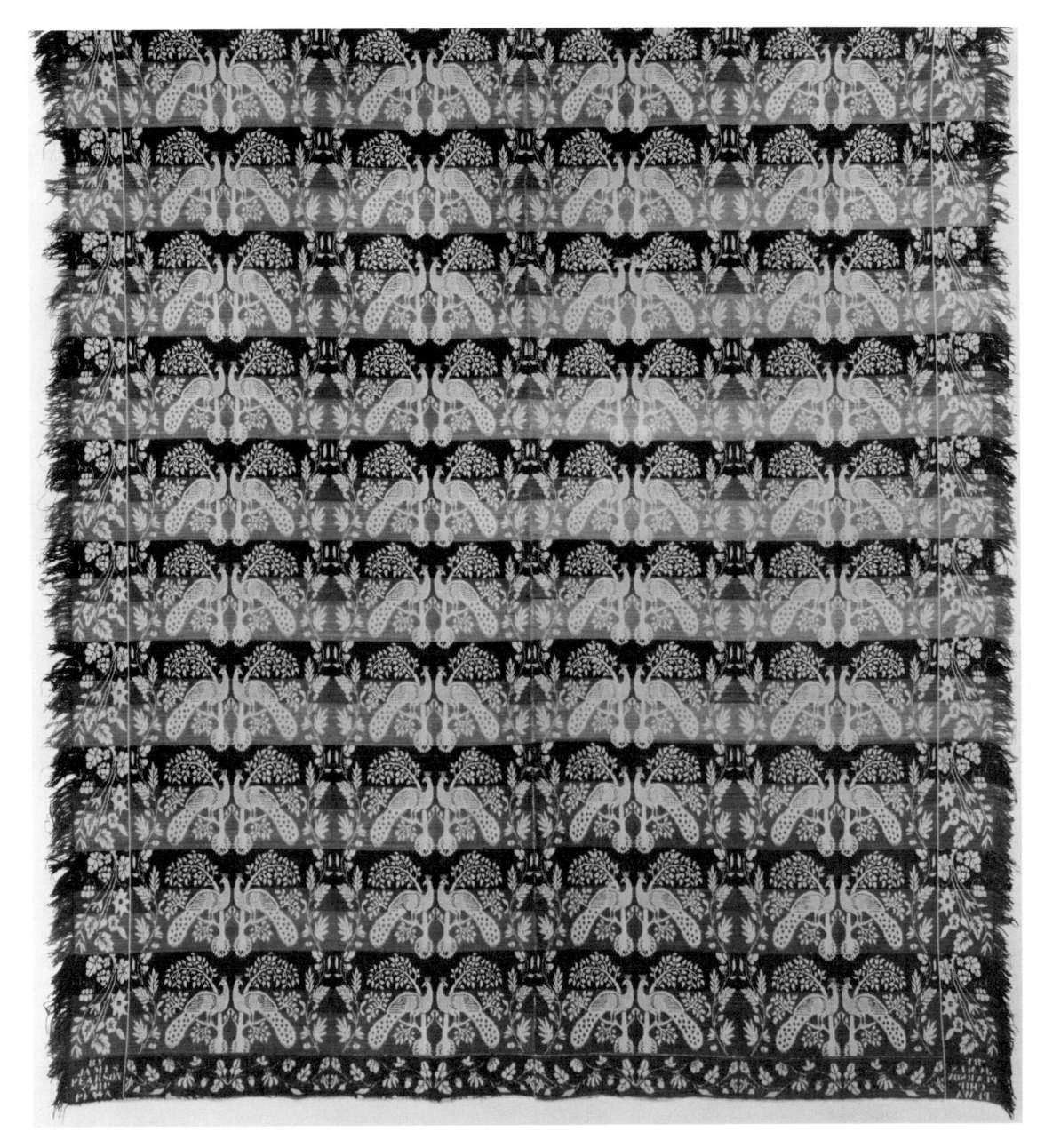

Coverlet with a pattern of confronting peacocks perched in trees and a flowering vine border; Beiderwand weave in dark blue, light blue, and red wool and natural cotton. Woven by James Pearson, Chippewa (probably Ohio), ca. 1835. Collection of Mr. and Mrs. Foster McCarl, Jr.

MELLINGER, W. S. Two coverlets woven by this individual in 1838 and 1842 have been recorded; the locations are not indicated.

MENCH, E. He is listed by the C.C.G.A. as weaving in 1840; the location is unknown. *

MENSER, David (ca. 1830– ). He appears in the 1850 census for Somerset Township, Pennsylvania (Somerset Co.), as a Pennsylvania-born weaver living in the household of Aaron Casebeer (see entry). *

MERKLE, Alexander (ca. 1816– ). Born in Scotland, the O.H.S. locates him in Steubenville, Ohio (Jefferson Co.), in 1837; the 1850 U. S. census describes him as a woolen manufacturer there. In his household was his son James, also a weaver. *

MERKLE, James. See entry for Alexander Merkle. *

METZ, L. Two coverlets by Metz, woven in Montgomery County, Pennsylvania, in 1841 and 1842, have been recorded.

METZGER, F. He is listed by the C.C.G.A. as weaving in Pennsylvania; the date is unknown. *

MEYER, Johann Philip. Reinert says that Meyer was weaving at Kutztown, Pennsylvania (Berks Co.), in 1794; he would not have been using a Jacquard-type attachment at that early date. *

MICHAEL, Enos (ca. 1824–1890). He was born in Dauphin County, Pennsylvania, the son of Philip Michael (see entry), a coverlet weaver. Montgomery states that the family moved from Dauphin County, Pennsylvania, to Brockville (now Fremont), Indiana (Steuben Co.), in 1849. The 1850 U. S. census indicates that another Pennsylvania weaver, Abraham Fridley, was living with Enos Michael and his wife. Michael made coverlets in the 1850s, but he appears in the 1860 U. S. census as a farmer and in 1880 as a real estate and loan agent. He died in Fremont and is buried there. 3 (Indiana), 1849–1852; 2 (Kinderhook, Michigan [Branch Co.]), 1859 and 1870. Fremont is on the Indiana–Michigan state line.

MICHAEL, Philip. Born in Dauphin County, Pennsylvania, he was the son of a German immigrant. From recorded coverlets, it is evident that Michael was weaving in Susquehanna Township, Dauphin Co., from 1837 to 1846. Montgomery states that in 1849 Michael moved his family to Brockville (now Fremont), Indiana (Steuben Co.), and stopped weaving, although his son Enos (see entry) continued the trade. Philip Michael died in Brockville. 5, 1837–1846.

MICHAELS, ———. He is listed by Madden as weaving in Albion, Illinois (Edwards Co.). *

MILLER, Ambrose (1812–ca. 1891). Born in Althaus, Alsace–Lorraine, France, he was trained as a weaver in Europe. He had emigrated to Kentucky by 1847, then moved to Blair County, Pennsylvania, where he worked as a weaver. Tax lists for Newry (Blair Co.) indicate that he resided there from 1879 to 1887; in 1887–1888 he is identified as a carpet weaver in Blair Township (Blair Co.). 13, 1849–1868. Several 1868 coverlets spell his last name "Muller."

MILLER, Gabriel (ca. 1823– ). Born in Pennsylvania, he is listed by the C.C.G.A. as weaving there in 1820. Hall states that he worked in Bethlehem, Pennsylvania (Northampton Co.); the dates are unknown. The 1850 U. S. census describes him as a weaver in Heidelberg Township, Pennsylvania (Lehigh Co.). Two unsigned, undated coverlets have been attributed to Miller.

MILLER, Henry. He was a weaver at McCutchenville, Ohio (Seneca Co.). 6, 1846–1851.

MILLER, Levi M. S. Safford and Bishop locate him in Jackson Township, Ohio (Hancock Co.), in 1860. 2, 1838 and 1858.

MILLER, Maximilian (ca. 1823– ). Born in Württemberg, Germany, he is identified as a "master coverlid weaver" in Emmaus, Pennsylvania (Lehigh Co.), in the 1860 U. S. census. *

Coverlet corner block showing a turkey perched in a tree and a rooster at the base of the trunk; Beiderwand weave in red wool and white cotton. Woven by Henry Oberly, Womelsdorf, Pa., ca. 1840. Collection of Mr. and Mrs. Foster McCarl, Jr. See color plate facing page 71.

[ 88 ]

MILLER, Robert (ca. 1832– ). Born in England, he is listed by the C.C.G.A. and Safford and Bishop as weaving in Salem, Indiana (Washington Co.), in 1857 and 1858; Montgomery believes that he came to America in 1853 and settled in Washington Township, Indiana (Washington Co.). The Washington Township Enrollment for Volunteers and Militia, 1862, also includes him as a weaver. *

MILLER, Theodore H. (ca. 1823– ). A native of Germany, Miller was weaving in Lafayette, Indiana (Tippecanoe Co.). Montgomery states that the 1858 Lafayette city directory lists Miller as a weaver and dyer who was working for Henry Neely; he still appears as a weaver in the 1870 U. S. census. 2, 1857.

MILLER, Tobias. The C.C.G.A. and Safford and Bishop locate him in LaGrange County, Indiana, in 1867, but Montgomery claims that there is no proof of this and that no coverlets woven by Tobias Miller have been found in Indiana. *

MILROY, ———. Although he appears in the C.C.G.A. and Safford and Bishop as weaving in Mifflin County, Pennsylvania, in 1851, no such weaver has been found in Mifflin County records or in the 1850 U. S. census. There is a town named Milroy in Mifflin County, and presumably the error in previous lists has resulted from a misreading of a woven inscription. *

MOLL, David. A single coverlet with this name and 1841 has been recorded; it is not known whether Moll was the weaver or the client.

MONCRIFF, A. B. (ca. 1818– ). Born in Scotland, he is included in the 1850 U. S. census as a weaver in Richland Township, Ohio (Fairfield Co.). He appears in W. W. Reilly & Co. as a coverlet weaver in West Rushville, Ohio (Fairfield Co.). *

MONROETON WOOLEN FACTORY. See entries for David and Joseph Ingham.

MOON, Robert (ca. 1801–1887). Born in England, the O.H.S. locates him as weaving in Columbus, Ohio (Franklin Co.), in 1843 and 1844, while the 1850 U. S. census for Columbus identifies him as a "carder," and the 1850–1851 Columbus city directory lists him as a weaver on Fourth Street between North and Spring streets. At the time of his death he was living in Montgomery Township, Ohio (Franklin Co.). *

MOORE, Robert. An advertisement placed by G. Stich (see entry) states, in part, that Stich had purchased the establishment of Robert Moore in Newark, Ohio (Licking Co.). *Advocate*, February 27, 1836. It is assumed that Moore was a weaver in Newark, although no other data about him or his work have been recorded. *

MOREHOUSE, P. M. This name and the date 1837 have been recorded on one coverlet; it is not known whether Morehouse was the weaver or the client.

MORREY, ———. Morrey is listed by the C.C.G.A., Safford and Bishop, and Kovel and Kovel as weaving in Ohio; the dates of his activity are unknown. This may be the weaver identified by Hall as "Mowry," who is believed to have worked in Ohio. *

MOSER, Jacob. He was weaving at Pine Grove, Pennsylvania (Centre Co.). 3, 1836–1839.

MOSSER, John (ca. 1811– ). Born in Germany, he appears in the 1850 U. S. census as a weaver in Mifflin Township, Ohio (Richland Co.), and in W. W. Reilly & Co. as a coverlet weaver in West Windsor, Richland Co. *

MOUNT PLEASANT MILLS. See entries for Joseph and William Schnee and Benjamin Angstad.

MOWRY, ———. See entry for Morrey.

MOYALL, James. He is listed in W. W. Reilly & Co. as a coverlet weaver in New Carlisle, Ohio (Clark Co.). *

MOYER'S WOOLEN MILL. Reinert believes that it operated between Schartelsville and Hamburg, Pennsylvania (Berks Co.), in 1862. *

MUEHLENHOFF, Heinrich. Possibly born in Germany, he was weaving in Duboistown, Pennsylvania (Lycoming Co.), in 1850. His coverlet pattern book is now in the Lycoming County Historical Society, Williamsport, Pa. Written in German, the book contains 44 coverlet patterns, a few drafts, over 100 folk medicine recipes and remedies, and some financial data; lengthy German prayers make up the rest of the book. *

MUIR, John (1815–1892). Montgomery states that he was born in Kilmarnock, Ayrshire, Scotland, and came to America in 1841. In the February 23, 1843, issue of the *Greencastle Visitor* (Greencastle, Ind.), he advertised that he was starting a weaving business and would weave ingrain carpeting and double woven coverlets. In the 1850 U. S. census he appears as a weaver in Greencastle Township, Indiana (Putnam Co.). Muir moved to Fillmore (Putnam Co.) in 1855 and died in Jackson Township, Indiana (Parke Co.), being buried in the Union cemetery there. John Muir and his brothers Robert, Thomas, and William (see entries) used the same trademark (see illustration, p. 128). 27 (Muir family), 1840–1858.

MUIR, Robert (ca. 1808– ). According to Montgomery, Robert Muir was born in Kilmarnock, Ayrshire, Scotland, and came to America in 1835 with his wife, Agnes, a sister of the Gilmour brothers, Gabriel, Joseph, Thomas, and William (see entries), who were coverlet weavers in Indiana. Robert Muir first settled in New Haven, Connecticut (New Haven Co.), then moved to Germantown, Indiana (Wayne Co.), in 1837. In 1840 he was joined by his brother William (see entry), with whom he worked until 1842. Robert moved to a farm in Lib-

Coverlet interior composed of clusters of large flowers with elaborate foliate borders; Beiderwand weave in red wool and white cotton. Woven by Henry Oberly, Womelsdorf, Pa., ca. 1840. Collection of Mr. and Mrs. Foster McCarl, Jr.

[ 90 ]

erty Township, Indiana (Delaware Co.), in 1844. He joined his wife's brother, Joseph Gilmour (see entry), in Missouri in 1853. Like his brothers, Robert used the Muir family trademark. 27 (Muir family), 1840–1858.

Muir, Thomas (ca. 1810–    ). He was born in Kilmarnock, Ayrshire, Scotland and came to Germantown, Indiana (Wayne Co.), where he worked with his brother Robert (see entry), until 1842. By 1850 he was weaving in Indianapolis, Indiana (Marion Co.), with his brother William (see entry). Thomas is said to have died near Indianapolis. He used the Muir family trademark. 22 (Muir family), 1840–1858.

Muir, William (1818–1888). Montgomery states that he was born in Scotland and worked in Germantown, Indiana (Wayne Co.), with his brothers Robert and Thomas from 1840 to 1842, after which he settled in West Indianapolis, Indiana (Marion Co.). He is listed there in the 1850 U.S. census, and the 1850 census of manufacturers says that he was operating a weaving business that used hand-powered looms, employed three men, and had an annual production of 40 coverlets valued at $400. William was working with his brother Thomas and with Irish-born weavers Jonathan Wilson and Robert Shaw. He moved to Clay County, Indiana, in 1858, where he farmed and gradually gave up weaving. Like his brothers, he used the Muir family trademark. 27 (Muir family), 1840–1858.

Mundwiler, Samuel. From recorded coverlets it is known that he was weaving in Hopewell Township, Ohio (Seneca Co.), from 1848 to 1851. His name is also spelled "Mundweiler." 5, 1848–1851.

Murphy, Richard. Murphy advertised in an 1827 issue of the *Washington Whig* that he had started a weaving business in Dorchester, New Jersey (Cumberland Co.), and would make single and double woven coverlets, diaper, and other materials. *

Murr, Lewis (ca. 1812–    ). Reinert locates Murr in New Holland, Pennsylvania (Lancaster Co.), in 1831, and he appears in the 1830 U.S. census as a Pennsylvania-born weaver in New Holland, Earl Township, Pennsylvania (Lancaster Co.). H. F. Bridgen, *Atlas of Lancaster County, Pennsylvania* (Lancaster, Pa., 1864), lists him as a "coverlid and carpet maker and dyer" in New Holland. *

Musselman, Samuel B. (1799–1871). From recorded coverlets it is known that he was weaving in Milford, Pennsylvania (Bucks Co.), from 1837 to 1847 and in Hilltown, Pennsylvania (Bucks Co.), from 1847 to 1859. On his earlier coverlets Musselman sometimes used the abbreviation "S. B. M. M." rather than his full name; he also numbered his work. The inscription on his earliest recorded coverlet is "Milfor Bucks County S.B.M.M. Pat. W. 1837 No. 23," that on his latest recorded coverlet, "S. B. Musselman Coverlet Weaver Hiltaun Bucks Co. 1859." Musselman stopped numbering his coverlets sometime between 1853 and 1859, and No. 873, dated 1853, is the highest recorded coverlet. "This coverlet belongs to" followed by the name of the owner and the date occurs on some of Musselman's coverlets. 27, 1837–1859.

Myer, I. Two coverlets by this weaver, dated 1836 and 1838, have been recorded; the location has not been

*Border detail with confronting birds in a flowering tree; double weave in light and dark blue wool. Attributed to David D. Haring, Bergen Co., N. J., 1835. Collection of Mr. and Mrs. Foster McCarl, Jr. See half-title page.*

[ 91 ]

firmly established, although he may have worked near Millersville, Pennsylvania (Lancaster Co.).

MYER, P. He is included in the C.C.G.A. and Safford and Bishop as weaving in 1841, location unknown. This weaver and I. Myer (see entry) may be related—the phraseology used in their inscription blocks is identical: "Property of ———, Wove by ———." 1, 1838.

MYERS, Charles D. According to Montgomery, Myers was a native of Ohio who first moved to Wayne County, Indiana, and then to Hamilton County, where he is described as a farmer and weaver. One coverlet in a geometric doublecloth weave has been recorded; according to family tradition, it was woven by Myers.

MYERS, D. One coverlet woven in East Hempfield Township, Pennsylvania (Lancaster Co.), in 1836 by this weaver has been recorded. A relationship between D. Myers and Daniel L. Myers (see entry) has not been verified.

MYERS, Daniel L. He was weaving in Bethel Township, Ohio (Clark Co.), from at least 1839 to 1852, according to recorded coverlets. The 1850 census of manufacturers shows him as having a coverlet weaving business in either Bethel, Pike, or Madison Township, Ohio (Clark Co.). At that time he employed one man and produced 50 coverlets annually valued at $450; his business also produced 300 yards of carpet per year at a value of $225. Madden erroneously located Daniel L. Myers in Bethel Township, Illinois. 26, 1839–1852.

MYERS, Elizabeth (1828–1917). Reinert believes that she was weaving in Streetsboro, Ohio (Portage Co.), dates unknown. *

MYERS, James. He is listed in W. W. Reilly & Co. as a coverlet weaver in Clark County, Ohio. *

# N

NAGEL, Philip. He appears as a weaver in the Dover Township, Pennsylvania (York Co.), tax records from 1834 to 1836. 2, 1834–1837.

NASH, Matilda. She is identified by Safford and Bishop as an Irish-born weaver working in Switzerland County, Indiana, in 1838. *

NEELY, Henry. See entry for Theodore Miller.

NETZLY, Jacob. The 1847 tax list for Warwick Township, Pennsylvania (Lancaster Co.), lists Jacob Netzly as a weaver. He signed the coverlets he made after 1846 with his initials, "J. N.," instead of his full name. 9, 1836–1850.

NETZLEY, Uriah. Madden locates Netzley in Naperville, Illinois (Du Page Co.); the dates of his activity are unknown. *

NEVEL, Frederick (1838–1923). Nevel was born in Württemberg, Germany, and, according to the O.H.S., he was weaving coverlets and carpets in Dundee, Ohio (Tuscarawas Co.), in the mid-nineteenth century. He dated but did not sign his work. *

NEY, William (ca. 1811–1892). Born in Pennsylvania, he is described in the 1850 U. S. census as a weaver in Myerstown, Pennsylvania (Lebanon Co.). Living in his household was Andrew Deitsch, a German-born weaver. Ney's location and occupation were unchanged in 1860, when he was listed in *Boyd's Business Directory, Berks–Schuylkill*. He died in Jackson Township (Lebanon Co.), his name being spelled "Nye." 31, 3 dated 1850, the remainder undated.

NICHOLS, Richard (ca. 1785–1860). Born in Maryland, he first traveled to Tennessee and later settled in Metamora, Indiana (Franklin Co.), sometime be-

*Coverlet border design featuring rows of birds and flowering bushes; Beiderwand weave in blue and red wool and light blue cotton. Weaver unidentified, possibly Pennsylvania or Ohio, 1845. Abby Aldrich Rockefeller Folk Art Center, bequest of Margaret H. Davies.*

[ 92 ]

fore 1816. According to Montgomery, Nichols stayed in Metamora until he moved to Illinois in 1850, dying there. He made overshot coverlets and does not appear to have used a Jacquard-type attachment. *

NICKLAS, George (ca. 1820–1860). Born in Germany, he immigrated to Pennsylvania and is listed in the 1850 U. S. census as a carpet weaver in Chambersburg, Pennsylvania (Franklin Co.). A young German-born weaver by the name of George Henry Nicklas (possibly a relative) was living in his household at that time. Nicklas is also described as a carpet weaver in *Boyd's Business Directory, Adams–York*, being located on Main Street near Catherine Street in Chambersburg. In his will, he requested that the "Looms and fixtures of my weaver shop including dye kettles shall be sold to my nephew Peter Nicklas for the sum of $200." January 24, 1860, Franklin County Courthouse. 16, 1840–1860.

NICKLAS, George Henry (ca. 1827– ). See entry for George Nicklas. *

NICKLAS, Peter. See entry for George Nicklas. 1 (Chambersburg), 1862.

NURRE, Joseph. Nurre is located by Safford and Bishop in Dearborn County, Indiana, in 1839; Rabb states that he was there about 1850. Montgomery says that he does not appear in any of the records of Dearborn County, but that he did work in Cincinnati, Ohio (Hamilton Co.). *

O

OBERHOLTZER, A. It has been determined from recorded coverlets that Oberholtzer wove in Zieglersville, Lower Frederick Township, Pennsylvania (Montgomery Co.), from at least 1836 to 1838. 5, 1836–1838.

OBERLY, Henry (ca. 1805–1874). Oberly was born in Pennsylvania and wove coverlets in Berks County, Pennsylvania; Safford and Bishop locate him weaving in Wormelsdorf, Pennsylvania (Berks Co.). In his corner blocks, Oberly often used a turkey perched on a tree limb with a small rooster standing on the ground below the tree. A few of his Jacquard coverlet designs that were drawn on paper are in the collection of the Berks County Historical Society, Reading, Pa. 12, 2 dated 1838.

OERTLE, Joseph. He appears in Madden as weaving in Peoria, Illinois (Peoria Co.), dates unknown. *

OPPEL, C. & Co. Although listed by Safford and Bishop as weaving in Zoar, Ohio (Tuscarawas Co.), in 1850, this is probably a misreading of an inscription used by the weaver Gottfried Kappel (see entry). *

ORMS,———. He is described by the C.C.G.A. and Safford and Bishop as weaving in Malaga, Ohio (Monroe Co.), dates unknown. *

OSBON, Aaron C. (ca. 1840– ). He was living in Jackson Township, Indiana (De Kalb Co.), when Jacob Snyder (see entry) moved there from Ohio in the late 1850s; Osbon was trained as a weaver by Snyder. He is listed as a weaver in the 1862 Enrollmen for Volunteers and Militia of Indiana. Montgomery states that Osbon's name is sometimes spelled "Osburn," "Osborn," or "Osborne." 1, 1861.

OTT, C. He is listed by Safford and Bishop as weaving in Franklin Township, Ohio (Richland Co.), in 1844. *

OVERHOLT, Henry O. (ca. 1813– ). Born in Penn-

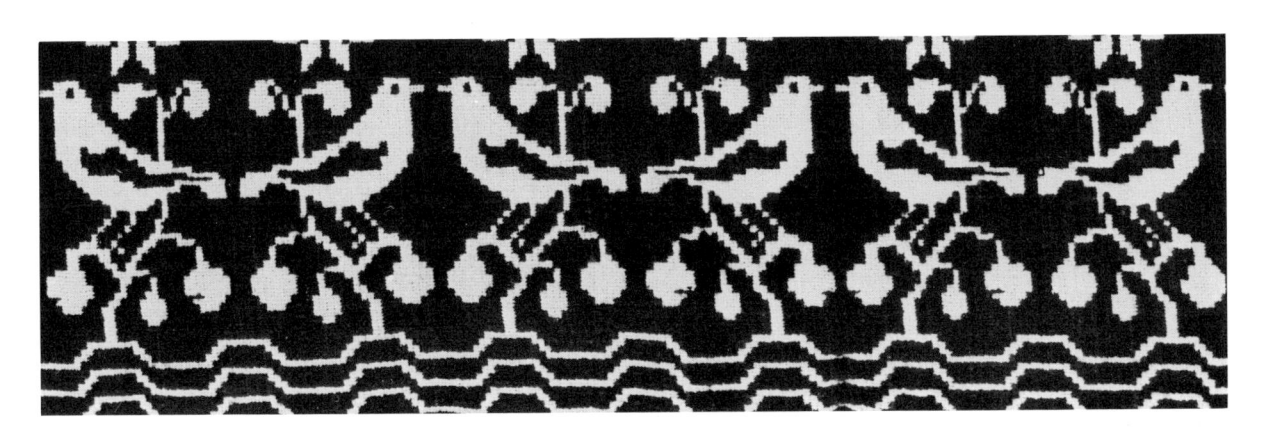

*Coverlet border design with rows of birds balanced on cherry sprigs; double weave in blue wool and natural cotton. Attributed to Abram Allen, Clinton Co., Ohio, 1839. Art Institute of Chicago.*

[93]

sylvania, he is included in the C.C.G.A. and Safford and Bishop as a weaver in 1842, location unknown. Overholt is described in the 1850 U. S. census as a weaver in East Huntingdon Township, Pennsylvania (Westmoreland Co.). Two recorded coverlets indicate that he was in Westmoreland County in 1844 and 1846. 4, 1842–1846.

OXLEY, Joseph (ca. 1813–    ). He appears in the O.H.S. records as weaving near Cambridge and Winterset, Ohio (Guernsey Co.), about 1843. The 1850 U. S. census describes him as a "carder" (wool carder) in Madison Township, Ohio (Guernsey Co.), stating that he was born in Ohio. The O.H.S. has attributed one coverlet, woven about 1843, to Oxley; no other coverlets have been recorded.

P

PACKER, J. He is located by Safford and Bishop as weaving in Brownsville, Pennsylvania (Fayette Co.), in 1839, by the C.C.G.A. in Pennsylvania in 1839. 1 signed by J. Packer and C. Douglass (see entry), 1838; 4 signed by Packer alone, 1839–1841.

PATTEN, P. C. Although he is listed by Reinert as weaving in Strinestown, Pennsylvania (York Co.), dates unknown, no such person has been found in the York County records. The word "patent" was sometimes included in the inscription blocks and border inscriptions used by some weavers, and Reinert's listing may be a misreading of such an inscription. *

PATTERSON, Thomas (ca. 1781–    ). See entry for Benjamin Yordy.

PEARSON, James. He appears in the C.C.G.A. and Safford and Bishop as weaving in Chippeway, with the date and state of manufacture not indicated. According to recorded coverlets, Pearson was weaving in Chippewa and Chatham Center, Ohio (Medina Co.); the O.H.S. locates him as weaving at Chatham in 1840. 8, undated.

PECK, ———. The O.H.S. places Peck in Nova, Ohio (Ashland Co.), in 1840. *

PEDEN, Joseph. According to Montgomery, he advertised in the August 23, 1828, issue of the *Farmers' and Mechanics' Advocate* (Charlestown, Ind.) that he was ready to weave coverlets and other goods at his home in Clark County, Indiana, "in the newest fashion." However, Montgomery also states that Peden was working a full decade before the Jacquard attachment was in use in Indiana and that his coverlets were probably in geometric weaves. *

PETER, H. P. One coverlet with the legend "1839 H. P. Peter HE EL" has been recorded. No other documentation for a weaver by this name has been found.

PETER, Reuben (ca. 1821–    ). He was born in Pennsylvania and is described as a weaver in the 1850 U. S. census. The signature blocks of Peter's coverlets indicate that he was weaving in Heidelberg Township, Pennsylvania (Lehigh Co.). An estate inventory dated March 9, 1857, taken in Washington Township (Lehigh Co.), for a Reuben Peter, includes "1 blanket weaving machine" valued at $1.50. Lehigh County Courthouse. The 1860 U. S. census includes an individual who must be a second

*Coverlet border design of stylized pine trees, birds, and flowering plants; double weave in blue wool and white cotton. Woven by Phillip Hilliard, Northampton Co., Pa., 1841. Private Collection.*

[ 94 ]

Reuben Peter as a carpet weaver in the fifth ward, Allentown, Pennsylvania (Lehigh Co.). 3, 1841–1850.

PETERMAN, Casper (ca. 1780– ). Born in Germany, he immigrated to the United States about 1806, later settling in Brandywine, Pennsylvania (Chester Co.). He appears in the 1850 U. S. census as a coverlet weaver in West Caln Township, Pennsylvania (Chester Co.), Peterman's pattern book is in the collection of the Metropolitan Museum of Art, New York City. 3, 1841–1843.

PETNA, George (ca. 1833– ). See entry for George Hefner.

PETRIE, ———. He is listed by the C.C.G.A. and Safford and Bishop as weaving near Albany, New York (Albany Co.); the dates are unknown. *

PETRY, Henry (ca. 1816– ). Born in Pennsylvania, the O.H.S. locates him in Canton, Ohio (Stark Co.), in 1839, and possibly as early as 1827. The C.C.G.A. and Safford and Bishop list Petry as weaving in Canton in 1842; the 1850 U. S. census places him in Canton Township, Ohio (Stark Co.), as a coverlet weaver. 5, 1840–1843.

PETRY, Peter (ca. 1809– ). According to the records at the O.H.S., Petry was born in Washington County, Maryland, and was raised by his uncle, Jacob Summers, who instructed him in the arts of "figured weaving." The O.H.S. says that he was weaving in London, Ohio (Madison Co.), in 1835. The 1850 U. S. census lists him as a weaver in Union Township, Ohio (Madison Co.). *

PHLEGAN, Henry (ca. 1810– ). Born in Waldeck, Germany, his name is spelled "Pflagger" in the 1850 U. S. census of Lithopolis, Bloom Township, Ohio (Fairfield Co.). W. W. Reilly & Co. includes him as a coverlet weaver. *

PHILLIPS, M. E. One coverlet has been recorded bearing this name, the date 1848, and "Ohio." It is not known whether Phillips was the weaver or the client.

PIERCE, Merrily. She appears in the C.C.G.A. and Safford and Bishop as weaving in 1834, but the location is not indicated. *

POMPEY, L. W. Pompey is included as a weaver in 1831 by the C.C.G.A. and Safford and Bishop, but the location is unknown. There is a town of that name in Onondaga County, New York, so perhaps "Pompey" refers to the location of manufacture and not to a weaver. One coverlet with the inscription "1831 Pompey" has been recorded.

PORTER, C. C. According to recorded coverlets, C. C. Porter was weaving at "Porter's Factory," Virginia (Jefferson Co.); the dates are unknown. Since Jefferson County is now in West Virginia, Porter must have been working there before 1863. 2, undated.

POWDER VALLEY WOOLEN MILL. Reinert believes that this mill was in operation in Lower Milford Township, Pennsylvania (Lehigh Co.), but gives no dates. *

PRIMROSE, Jacob. According to records at the New York State Historical Association, Cooperstown, Primrose moved from Sussex County, New Jersey, in 1803 and settled in West Dryden, New York (Tompkins Co.), where he wove coverlets. *

PROBST, Henry (ca. 1805– ). Born in Pennsylvania, Probst was weaving "Near Allentown," according to an inscribed coverlet dated 1846. In 1847 he was weaving with another individual; they signed their work "Probst & Seip." Coverlets recorded after 1847 were presumably woven by Probst alone. The 1850 U. S. census locates him in South Whitehall Township, Pennsylvania (Lehigh Co.), as a weaver. 4, 1846–1857.

*Border design featuring birds perched on tree limbs, while smaller birds underneath alternate with churches; double weave in blue wool and white cotton. Attributed to David D. Haring, Bergen Co., N. J., 1831. Courtesy of Gretchen S. Truslow.*

PURSELL, Daniel (ca. 1815–    ). Born in Ohio, he appears in Safford and Bishop as weaving in Portsmouth, Ohio (Scioto Co.), in 1840 and 1850. The 1850 U. S. census includes him as a weaver in Portsmouth district, Scioto County. 10, 1 dated 1840.

R

RANDEL, Martin. He is listed by the O.H.S. as weaving in Chardon, Ohio (Geauga Co.), in 1848. 1, 1848.

RASSWEILER, H. Reinert locates him in Allentown, Pennsylvania (Lehigh Co.), in 1843. He inscribed his work "Manufactory of H. Rassweiler, Allentown." 3, 1843–1846.

RASSWEILER, Philip (ca. 1822–    ). Born in Germany, he appears in Reinert, Safford and Bishop, and Kovel and Kovel as weaving in Orwigsburg, Pennsylvania (Schuylkill Co.), in 1844. Between 1848 and 1851 he was weaving in Millersburg, Pennsylvania (Dauphin Co.); the 1850 U. S. census locates him as a coverlet weaver in Upper Paxton Township, Dauphin Co. In 1867 he was weaving in Cedarville, with the state not indicated on the coverlet. 7, 1844–1867.

RATTRAY, Matthew (1796–1872). Born in Paisley, Scotland, he was apprenticed as a weaver before coming to the United States in 1818. He moved to Richmond, Indiana (Wayne Co.), in 1822, where he established a weaving shop. Rattray advertised in an 1831 issue of the Richmond *Palladium* that he was "prepared to weave common carpeting"; in an 1841 issue he offered to weave "any kind of a FIGURE on COVERLETS and CARPETS." (See n. 27, p. 21, and p. 17.) He is listed in the 1850 U. S. census as a manufacturer; in 1865 his occupation was still "weaver," according to Montgomery. Rattray used an eagle under an arc of stars of varying number as a trademark. 9, 1846–1853.

RAUCH, M. The O.H.S. describes this weaver as working in the Miami Valley of Ohio between 1850 and 1860. He used a floral design that he called "Peace & Plenty." *

RAUSER, Gabriel (ca. 1803–    ). Born in Germany, he sometimes spelled his name "Rausher." He appears in the 1850 U. S. census as a weaver in Delaware County, Ohio, where recorded coverlets locate him as early as 1842. Reinert includes a Gabriel Rauscher who was weaving in Lehigh County, Pennsylvania, dates unknown. The C.C.G.A. and Kovel and Kovel place Rausher in Ohio in 1840 and 1853; Safford and Bishop locate him in Ohio and Pennsylvania in 1840 and 1853 respectively. 17, 1842–1858.

REDICK, John. Four coverlets by John Redick have been recorded; two woven in Troy Township, Ohio (Richland Co.), in 1852, and two in Tamaroa, Illinois (Perry Co.), in 1869.

REED, V. R. The C.C.G.A., Safford and Bishop, and Kovel and Kovel include Reed as weaving at Benton, New York (Yates Co.), in 1883. *

REED, William. He is listed by W. W. Reilly & Co. as a coverlet weaver in Stark County, Ohio. *

REEVE, Joseph H. In an 1817 *New Jersey Mirror*, Reeve "advised the public he had a loom in readiness for weaving double and figure work, huckabuck [huckaback], broad cloths, blanketings, etc., figure work, Venetian and rag carpeting, and fancy and plain weaving in general." He was working in Mount Holly, New Jersey (Burlington Co.). *

REICHERT, H. He appears in W. W. Reilly & Co. as a coverlet weaver in Bucyrus, Ohio (Crawford Co.). *

REINER, Georg. Reinert says that he was weaving in Lower Milford Township, Pennsylvania (Lehigh Co.), in 1810. *

REITER, Nicholas. Born in Germany, Montgomery de-

*Bird perched in a flowering tree border design; double weave in blue wool and white cotton. Weaver unidentified, possibly New York or New Jersey, 1856. Collection of Theo Van De Polder, Lawton, Mich.*

The coverlet interior has a row of alternating clusters of roses and tulips which together with a row of birds in flight flank a center strip of eagles alternating with floral medallions. The side borders contain pots of flowers and a fox and hound by a flowering bush in which a bird is perched, while eagles and stars and roosters appear in the bottom border; double weave in blue wool and white cotton. Woven by David D. Haring, Bergen Co., N. J., 1833. Collection of Mr. and Mrs. Foster McCarl, Jr.

scribes him as an assistant to Samuel Stinger (see entry), working in Carthage, Indiana (Rush Co.), in the 1850s. *

REMY, James. According to Montgomery, Remy advertised that he was going to weave coverlets and other materials near Hubbell's Crossroads, Logan Township, Indiana (Dearborn Co.). *Richmond Palladium*, August 2, 1834. He does not appear in the 1840 U. S. census and his later whereabouts are unknown. *

RENNER, George. Reinert locates him in Schaefferstown, Pennsylvania (Lebanon Co.), in 1838, where he was weaving with Peter Leidig (see entry). Renner is described as a "blue dyer" in Heidelberg Township, Pennsylvania (Lebanon Co.), in the 1842 and 1843 tax lists. 7 (Renner and Leidig), 1837–1841.

RENNER, P. Kovel and Kovel say that he probably was weaving in Lebanon County, Pennsylvania, dates unknown, but this may be a misreading of an inscribed coverlet by George Renner (see entry). *

RESSLER, Rudolph (ca. 1822– ). The 1850 U. S. census counts Ressler as a Pennsylvania-born weaver who was living in the household of another weaver, Henry Hersh (see entry), in Leacock Township, Pennsylvania (Lancaster Co.). 3, 1851–1857.

REZINOR, John. He is described as a weaver in the 1850 U. S. census, having been born in New York and working in Clinton Township, Ohio (Knox Co.). *

RICH, John (1786–1871). Born in Wiltshire, England, he came to America and settled in Clinton County, Pennsylvania. Rich built a woolen mill on Larry's Creek in Clinton County, where local farmers helped him weave in the winter. The mill was destroyed by a flood in 1849 and Rich then worked at Chatham's Run Factory, also in Clinton County; a county map of 1862 identifies his factory as "J. Rich and Son." The factory was moved to Woolrich and was the beginning of the Woolrich Woolen Mills. Michael Bond Rich, *History of the First 100 Years in Woolrich* (Williamsport, Pa., 1930). Rich is buried in the Old Crawford cemetery, Dunstable Township, Clinton Co. 5, one dated 1853.

RICHARDSON, ———. He is identified by the C.C.G.A., Safford and Bishop, and Kovel and Kovel as weaving in 1835, location unknown. *

RIEGEL, Simon (ca. 1807– ). Born in Pennsylvania, the O.H.S. locates Riegel in Tremont City, Ohio (Clark Co.), dates unknown. He was in German Township, Clark Co., by 1847, where the 1870 U. S. census lists him as a carpet weaver. German Township was often misspelled "Germin" in Riegel's woven inscriptions. 8, 1847–1872.

RINGER, Peter (ca. 1829– ). The 1850 U. S. census includes him as a coverlet weaver in Chester Township, Ohio (Wayne Co.). 2, 1852 and 1858.

RISSER, L. D. Reinert and Kovel and Kovel locate Risser as weaving in Pennsylvania; Reinert suggests that he worked in Berks County. The dates of his activity are unknown. *

ROBERTS, Charles. See entry for William Lowmiller.

ROBINSON, Anson. One coverlet with this name and 1842 has been recorded; it is not known whether Robinson was the weaver or the client.

ROBINSON, James. He was working for James Alexander near Newburgh, New York (Orange Co.), in 1806. According to Alexander's account book, Robinson wove coverlets, blankets, cloth, ticking, and so forth. New York State Historical Association, Cooperstown. *

ROGERS, John (ca. 1807– ). Born in Ireland, he settled in Washington Township, Indiana (Wayne Co.), where he is described as a weaver in the 1850 U. S. census. According to Montgomery, Rogers was involved in a thriving weaving business in Wayne County from 1848 to 1856. Besides Rogers, the weaver, there was a "colourer," a carder, and a spinner. Roger's trademark was an "X" formed from

*Border design of a two-story frame house; double weave in blue wool and white cotton. Woven by the Gilmour brothers, Indiana, 1839. Collection of Mr. and Mrs. Foster McCarl, Jr.*

A tilelike arrangement of floral motifs forms the center design, the side borders contain lilies, and the bottom border shows houses and a picket fence; double weave in blue wool and white cotton. The sailboat in the corner block is the weaver's trademark. Woven by the Gilmour brothers, Indiana, 1839. Collection of Mr. and Mrs. Foster McCarl, Jr. See frontispiece.

[ 99 ]

four sprays of leaves that radiated from a central flower; underneath was the date of manufacture. 8, 1849–1870.

Rose, William Henry Harrison (1839–1913). He appears in Hall as weaving in Rhode Island, dates unknown; Safford and Bishop locate him there in 1860. Rose lived near Kingston, Rhode Island (Washington Co.), where he wove coverlets and other items. He did not use a Jacquard-type attachment but did overshot weaving. Samples of his work still exist, and one of his looms is at the University of Rhode Island, Kingston.

Rossvilles, ———. Although he is listed by the C.C.G.A., Safford and Bishop, and Kovel and Kovel as weaving in New York state in 1851, this name is probably a misreading of the location, Rossville, New York (Richmond Co.). *

Rottman, G. Four undated coverlets with this name have been recorded. A large eagle, possibly a trademark, appears in the corner of each.

Rotzel, Mathias. He was weaving in Columbiana County, Ohio, in 1848. 1, 1848.

Routt, Daniel. According to the O.H.S., he wove coverlets and wool blankets in Ohio in 1838. *

Royer, John. Reinert indicates that Royer was weaving in New Holland, Pennsylvania (Lancaster Co.), in 1836, but he cannot be found in any tax records, deeds, or estate settlements of that county. 3, 1836–1837.

## S

S———, D———. A coverlet with these initials, woven in Bethany, New York (Genesee Co.), in 1835 has been recorded; it is not known if the initials refer to the weaver or the client.

S———, G———. This individual was weaving between 1840 and 1844, probably in Ohio; the full identity has not been determined. 5, 1840–1844.

S———, J———. Woven in 1839, 1840, and 1843, three coverlets with these initials have been recorded; the location is not indicated on the coverlets, and the full identity of the weaver has not been determined.

Saeger, Martin (ca. 1827–   ). He is identified as a coverlet weaver in the second ward of Allentown, Pennsylvania (Lehigh Co.), in the 1860 U. S. census. Saeger's birthplace is given as Württemberg, Germany. *

Salisbury, Henry. A coverlet with this name and 1849 has been recorded; Salisbury also appears in Safford and Bishop as weaving in 1849, location unknown. 1, 1849.

Salisbury, J. A coverlet with this name, woven in 1838 in Bethany, New York (Genesee Co.), has been recorded; it is not known whether Salisbury was the weaver or the client.

Salisbury, Mary. She is listed by Safford and Bishop as weaving in Jefferson County, New York, in 1842. *

Satler, J. Recorded coverlets reveal that Satler was weaving in Leacock Township, Pennsylvania (Lancaster Co.). 5, 1845–1846.

Satler, Lewis. Reinert believes that he was weaving in Leacock Township, Pennsylvania (Lancaster Co.), in 1842, where the tax rolls first record him in 1841 as a weaver, his name being spelled "Saddler." Satler is last mentioned in the 1843 tax lists. A firm connection with J. Satler (see entry) has not yet been proven. 2, 1841 and 1843.

Saurly, Nicholas (ca. 1824–   ). The 1860 U. S. census records him in the second ward of Allentown, Pennsylvania (Lehigh Co.), as a coverlet weaver born in Holland. *

Sayles, C. One coverlet with this name, woven in 1836 in New York, has been recorded; it is not known whether Sayles was the weaver or the client.

Sayles, J. M. He appears in the C.C.G.A. and Kovel and Kovel as a weaver in Knox County, Illinois, in 1851, and in Safford and Bishop as weaving in Clinton County, Illinois, in 1851. 1, 1851.

Saylor, Jacob. Williams brothers, *History of Franklin and Pickaway Counties, Ohio, with illustrations and biographical sketches of some of the prominent men and pioneers* (Cleveland, 1880), state that Saylor came to Ohio from Somerset County, Pennsylvania, during the War of 1812, settled in Tarlton, Saltcreek Township, Pickaway Co., and became one of the area's pioneer merchants. 1, 1857.

Scheelin, Conrad. Reinert identifies him as weaving in 1849, location unknown. *

Schipper, Jacob. He is located by Madden in Quincy, Illinois (Adams Co.), dates unknown. *

Schmeck, John. Reinert says that Schmeck was a weaver in Berks County, Pennsylvania, in 1842. *

Schnee, Joseph (1792–1838). He appears in the C.C.G.A., Safford and Bishop, Kovel and Kovel, and Reinert as weaving in Freeburg, Pennsylvania (Union Co.), in 1835 and 1836. He worked in the Mount Pleasant Mills in Snyder (now Union) County, where he taught Benjamin Angstad (see entry) how to weave. When Joseph left the mill, his son William (see entry) took it over. Joseph Schnee and Benjamin Angstad were weaving in Lewisburg (Union Co.) in 1836 and 1838, signing their work "Angstad and Schnee Lewisburg." In 1836 he was appointed a justice of the peace for part of Washington Township (Union, now Snyder, Co.). An inventory of Schnee's estate taken after his death in 1838 includes 2 "machine looms" valued at $55, "a lot of weaving gears" worth $1.20, "sundry weaving gears" valued at 50¢, and "shuddles" at 50¢. Inventory, November 28, 1838, Union County Courthouse, Lewisburg, Pa. At the time of his death, Schnee lived in

[ 100 ]

Crib or sample coverlet whose interior design features a double repeat of floral medallions. The side borders are composed of potted flowers and buildings, while the bottom border contains confronting eagles; Beiderwand weave in light blue, dark blue, green, red, and gold wool and natural cotton. Weaver unidentified, probably Pennsylvania, ca. 1850. Collection of Mr. and Mrs. Foster McCarl, Jr.

Freeburg (Snyder Co.). 23 (Schnee alone), 1835; 4 (Angstad and Schnee), 1836–1838.

SCHNEE, Joseph F. Schnee advertised in the March 10, 1841, issue of the *Lewistown Republican* (Lewistown, Pennsylvania), that he was going to start a weaving business at Strunk's Mills (formerly Forsythe's), where he would make patent coverlets and carpets. This location was within three miles of Lewistown. Samples of his work would be on display at the public house of Jacob Lotz in Brown Township and at Strunk's Mills. Later that year, he advertised that he was in business at Strunk's Mills. Because he did not use his middle initial in signing his coverlets, it is difficult to determine which pieces were by him and which were by Joseph Schnee (see entry). 2, 1840.

SCHNEE, William. A son of Joseph Schnee (see entry), he took over his father's factory, the Mount Pleasant Mills, in Snyder County, Pennsylvania. 4, 1838–1842.

SCHNEIDER, Johann Adam. From recorded coverlets, it has been learned that Schneider was weaving in Adams Township, Ohio (Washington Co.). In 1830 his coverlets bore the legend, "I. A. Schnider Adams Taunschip Washington C. Ohio," while some read "J. A. Schneider" or "Johann Adam Schneider," with no location indicated. 5, 1830–1856.

SCHNEIDER, John E. He was a weaver in Hamburg, Missouri (St. Charles Co.). Otto Charles Thieme, University of Wisconsin, has been conducting research into the career of Schneider, and has located nineteen whole or fragmented coverlets attributable to him which date from 1850 to 1872.

SCHNELL, Jacob (1815–1902). Born in Pennsylvania, Reinert locates him near Shrewsbury, Pennsylvania (York Co.), in 1848, where he appears in the tax records from 1840 to 1860. Taken shortly after his death, an inventory of his estate includes 4 woolen coverlets valued at $7.50, 130 yards of "homemade and ingrain carpeting" valued at $23.40, and a carpet loom and fixtures worth $2.50. Schnell is buried in the Lutheran cemetery, Shrewsbury Township. 22, 1844–1870.

SCHOCH, Charles. Recorded coverlets indicate that Schoch was weaving in Thompson Township, Ohio (Seneca Co.), from 1840 to 1848. Montgomery believes that he moved to Fulton County, Indiana, where he is described as a farmer in the 1850 and 1860 U. S. censuses for Aubbeenaubbee. Some of his coverlet inscriptions read "G. Schoch" or "Schock" rather than "C. Schoch." 7 (Ohio), 1840–1848; 3 (Indiana), 1859–1862.

SCHOONMAKER, James. According to White, Schoonmaker was a weaver of carpets and coverlets in Paterson, New Jersey (Passaic Co.); in 1825 he had a shop with two looms on Ward Street. *

SCHRACK, Joseph. He appears in Reinert as weaving in Heidelberg Township, Pennsylvania (Berks Co.), in 1797. *

SCHRADER, H. Two coverlets by Schrader have been re-

*This pattern, which has houses with smoke rising from their chimneys, churches, and pagodalike structures, is sometimes referred to as the "Boston Town Border"; double weave in blue wool and white cotton. Weaver unidentified, probably Ohio, ca. 1840. Collection of Mr. and Mrs. Foster McCarl, Jr.*

A row of half-timbered buildings with pennants, cupolas, and chimneys is featured in this coverlet border design; Beiderwand weave in red, blue, and green wool and natural cotton. Woven by Henry K. Frederick, Cumberland Co., Pa., 1846. Courtesy of E. T. Wilson.

Coverlet border design composed of classical style houses with picket fences and large trees; double weave in red wool and white cotton. Woven by D. Shamp, Wyoming Co., N.Y., 1847. Margaret Woodbury Strong Museum, Rochester, N.Y.

Large public buildings alternate with smaller houses that are tucked behind trees; double weave in red and blue wool and white cotton. Weaver unidentified, possibly Ohio, ca. 1840–1850. Courtesy of Mrs. Henry B. Wilson.

The "Hemfield Railroad" pattern features a locomotive and engineer; double weave in red and blue wool and natural cotton. Weavers believed to have produced coverlets in this pattern include Daniel Campbell, William Harper, Martin Burns, George Coulter, and Harvey Cook. Weaver unidentified, possibly West Virginia or Pennsylvania, ca. 1840–1850. Collection of Mr. and Mrs. Foster McCarl, Jr.

corded, one woven in Canal Winchester, Ohio (Franklin Co.), in 1849, and the other in Jefferson County, Ohio, date unknown.

SCHREFFLER, Henry (1814–1881). Reinert believes that Schreffler was weaving in Salona, Pennsylvania (Clinton Co.), in 1851. He appears as a weaver in tax lists for Lamar Township (Clinton Co.) between 1841 and 1856, but he is not included in the 1850 U. S. census for Clinton County. *

SCHREFFLER, Isaac (ca. 1826– ). Born in Pennsylvania, he is described as a weaver in the Lamar Township, Pennsylvania (Clinton Co.), tax records between 1847 and 1856, and as a carpet weaver in 1857 and 1858. Schreffler was a "coverlid weaver" in the 1850 U. S. census for Salona (Clinton Co.). *

SCHREFFLER, Samuel (ca. 1804– ). Schreffler was born in Pennsylvania and is included in the 1845 tax lists for Mifflinburg, Pennsylvania (Union Co.). The 1850 U. S. census locates him as a "coverlid weaver" in Salona, Lamar Township, Pennsylvania (Clinton Co.). 4 (Salona), 1849–1853.

SCHRIVER, Jacob (1816–1896). *History of Cumberland and Adams Counties, Pennsylvania* (Chicago, 1886) states that Schriver was born in Pennsylvania, the son of John Schriver, also a weaver, from whom he learned to weave, making "that his principal occupation in connection with farming." Jacob served as school director and registrar and recorder of Adams County, and as postmaster of Hampton (Adams Co.) from 1851 to 1860. He is buried in the Evergreen cemetery, Gettysburg, Pennsylvania (Adams Co.). 23, 1841–1858.

SCHRIVER, John. See entry for Jacob Schriver.

SCHRONTZ, ———. He is described by Rabb as a coverlet weaver in Indiana and by Safford and Bishop as a weaver in Dearborn County, Indiana; the dates are unknown. Montgomery states that the name Schrontz has not been found in any Indiana records. *

SCHULTZ, John N. (ca. 1812– ). Born in Germany, he appears in the 1850 U. S. census as a carpet weaver in Peters Township, Pennsylvania (Franklin Co.). 4 (Mercersburg, Pa.), 1847–1867.

SCHUM, Joseph. One coverlet with this name and Lancaster, Pennsylvania (Lancaster Co.), date unknown, has been recorded; it is not known whether Schum is the name of the weaver or the client.

SCHUM, Peter. One coverlet by this weaver, made in Lancaster, Pennsylvania (Lancaster Co.), has been recorded. The coverlet is undated and nothing more has been discovered about Schum.

SCHUM, Philip (1814–1880). Born in the grand duchy of Hesse–Darmstadt, Germany, he settled in Lancaster, Pennsylvania (Lancaster Co.), sometime after 1844, and is recorded as weaving there by the C.C.G.A., Safford and Bishop, Reinert, and Kovel and Kovel. By 1856 he had established a weaving business known as the Lancaster Carpet, Coverlet, Quilt, and Yarn Manufactory. At first it was in a small building on Dorwart Street; a larger factory was erected in 1862 at the corner of Strawberry and South Water streets. Beginning with four men and one or two looms, Schum progressed to four looms employing eight men, and later the establishment had at least twenty looms that required forty men. In 1875 Schum's production per week was about 400 "quilts," about 500 yards of carpets, plus quantities of blankets, yarns, and flannels. An inventory of his estate includes a carpet shop, a weaving shop, a dyehouse, a store, a coalyard, and another store. Also listed were 390 "half-wool coverlets" valued at $920, along with numerous counterpanes, "cradle quilts," and other bed coverings. (See p. 15.) 17, 1855–1869.

SCHWARTZ, John, Jr. (ca. 1856– ). He appears in the 1880 U. S. census for York, Pennsylvania (York Co.), as a carpet weaver living with his father (see entry). According to the York city directories for 1882–1888, he and his father were carpet weavers on South George Street. *

A tavern, a church or courthouse, and palm trees alternate in this border design; double weave in blue wool and white cotton. Weaver unidentified, probably Ohio, ca. 1840. Collection of Mr. and Mrs. Foster McCarl, Jr.

SCHWARTZ, John, Sr. (ca. 1811–1892). Born in Pennsylvania, he lived in York, Pennsylvania (York Co.), where he is described as a weaver in the south ward in the 1850 U. S. census. The York city directories from 1856 to 1871 list Schwartz as a weaver on South George Street, while the 1880 U. S. census and the York city directories from 1882 through 1888 include him as a carpet weaver living with his son John, also a carpet weaver. An article in the *Hanover Herald* (York Co.), dated October 7, 1882, states that he had "manufactured 200 yards of silk from his own cocoons in 1848, from which his wife and daughter made dresses." According to the article, Schwartz's was the first silk manufactured in the United States. John Schwartz, Sr., is buried in the Prospect Hill cemetery in York. 5, 1837–1854.

SCHWARTZ, Michael (ca. 1810–1904). A native of Pennsylvania, the 1860 U. S. census locates Schwartz as a weaver in Manheim, Pennsylvania (Lancaster Co.). An inventory taken shortly after his death includes a loom, 83 yards of rag and chain carpet valued at $11.25, and a "lot of sundries in [the] weaving shop." Inscriptions on his coverlets read "Mate by M. Schwartz in Manheim." 10, 1842–1858.

SEEWALD, John Philip. He was born in Germany and, according to Madden, about 1828 came to Philadelphia, where he learned the weaver's trade. In 1834 he settled at Ridge Prairie near the present town of O'Fallon, Illinois (St. Clair Co.), where he began weaving household linens and coverlets for residents of the area. 5, 1842–1849.

SEIBERT, John, Jr. Born in Pennsylvania, the son of a weaver, Seibert is listed in the 1850 U. S. census for Lowhill Township, Pennsylvania (Lehigh Co.), as a weaver living with his father and brother Owen (see entry). 15 (by either John, Jr., or John, Sr.), 1844–1849; 2 (woven in Reading, Pennsylvania, Berks Co.), undated.

SEIBERT, John, Sr. (1796–1854). A native of Pennsylvania, he is listed by Reinert, Safford and Bishop, and Kovel and Kovel as weaving in Lowhill Township, Pennsylvania (Lehigh Co.), in 1846. The 1850 U. S. census describes Seibert as a weaver in Lowhill Township; in his household were his sons, John and Owen (see entries), both weavers. He had a third son, Peter (see entry), who was also a weaver. 15 (by either John, Jr., or John, Sr.), 1844–1849.

SEIBERT, Owen (ca. 1828–    ). The son of weaver John Seibert, Sr. (see entry), Owen was born in Pennsylvania. He is listed in the 1850 U. S. census for Lowhill Township, Pennsylvania (Lehigh Co.), as a weaver living with his father and brother, John, Jr. (see entry). *

SEIBERT, Peter (1821–    ). Peter Seibert was born in Lowhill Township, Pennsylvania (Lehigh Co.), the son of a weaver, John Seibert, Sr. (see entry). The 1850 U. S. census locates him as a weaver in the Lehigh ward of Easton, Pennsylvania (Northampton Co.); *Boyd's Business Directory, Berks–Schuylkill*, describes him as a coverlet manufacturer at 196 Northampton Street in Easton. According to Roberts, Seibert built a weaving shop during the Civil War, but ill health forced him to retire in 1867, when he moved to Allentown, Pennsylvania (Lehigh Co.). 8, 1846–1847.

SEIDENSPINNER, John (ca. 1831–    ). Born in Württemberg, Germany, he was weaving in Allentown, Pennsylvania (Lehigh Co.), with Woodring (see entry), another weaver. They signed their work as being woven by "Woodring and Seidenspinner." The 1860 U. S. census gives Seidenspinner as a "cov-

*On this border birds in trees alternate with churches and pine trees; double weave in blue wool and white cotton. Weaver unidentified, probably New York, 1839. Courtesy of Mr. and Mrs. Robert C. Kelley.*

erlid weaver" in Allentown's second ward. 1 (Woodring and Seidenspinner), undated.

SEIFERT, Andrew (ca. 1820–1900). Born in York County, Pennsylvania, he was weaving with his brother Henry (see entry) in Mechanicsburg, Pennsylvania (Cumberland Co.), where the 1850 U. S. census locates him. In Seifert's household was his brother Emanuel (see entry), also a weaver. Mechanicsburg tax records show that he was a weaver there from 1847 to 1887. A deed of April 1844 indicates that Andrew and Henry Seifert purchased a lot on the south side of Main Street in Mechanicsburg on which stood a two-story brick house and possibly a weaving shop; they bought the lot from Charles Young (see entry), a coverlet weaver. The 1850–1852 tax lists show that in addition to the brick house, there was a frame weaving shop on the lot. See also entry for Seifert & Co. Andrew Seifert is buried in the Chestnut Hill cemetery just outside Mechanicsburg. 4 (woven by Henry and Andrew), 1843–1850; none recorded by Andrew alone.

SEIFERT, Emanuel (ca. 1830–    ). A native of York County, Pennsylvania, he was living in Mechanicsburg, Pennsylvania (Cumberland Co.), with his brothers Andrew and Henry. The 1850 U. S. census shows that Emanuel was a weaver living in his brother Andrew's home. Mechanicsburg tax records for 1856–1859 and 1865–1867 describe him as a weaver; from 1859 to 1861 he appears as a "spiritualist," and from 1862 to 1864 as a laborer. (See also entry for Seifert & Co.) *

SEIFERT, Henry (ca. 1823–1905). Henry Seifert was born in York County, Pennsylvania. Mechanicsburg, Pennsylvania (Cumberland Co.), tax records for 1847–1852 show that Henry was weaving with his brother Andrew; the 1852 tax list indicates that they owned a two-story brick house and a frame weaving shop. Coverlets made by Andrew and Henry Seifert bear the inscription "Woven Superior Tight Work Manufactured On The Latest Fashion By H. & A. Seifert Mechanicsburg Cumberland County Pennsylvania AD . . ." (followed by the date). This same inscription is found on coverlets made by Henry alone from 1847 to 1849. Henry attended Pennsylvania College and Seminary at Gettysburg, Pennsylvania (Adams Co.), from approximately 1852 to 1856, and became a Lutheran minister, at which time he stopped weaving. (See also entry for Seifert & Co.) 2 (Henry alone), 1847 and 1849; 4 (with Andrew), 1843–1850.

SEIFERT & COMPANY. This organization appears in *Boyd's Business Directory, Adams–York*, as carpet weavers on Main Street in Mechanicsburg, Pennsylvania (Cumberland Co.). It is not known which or how many of the Seifert brothers were responsible for the three undated coverlets by the company that have been recorded.

SEIGRIST, Henry (1788–1860). Born in Lancaster County, Pennsylvania, Seigrist moved in 1826 to Wayne County, Ohio, and in 1830 to Richland County, Ohio, where he wove in Washington Township. *

SEIP, ———. See entry for Henry Probst.

SERFF, Abraham (1791–1876). Born in Pennsylvania, he was weaving in Codorus (later North Codorus) Township, Pennsylvania (York Co.), where he appears in 1823 tax records without an occupation, although he is described as a weaver in the 1850 U. S. census of North Codorus Township. His account and pattern books are in the Historical Society of York County, York, Pa. Serff's account book for 1844–1864 shows that he sold coverlets at prices that ranged from $1 to $1.75. He made overshot coverlets but is not known to have had a Jacquard-type attachment for his loom. Serff also wove linen, bagging, carpets, tow linen, and flannels. He is buried in the Lischy cemetery, North Codorus Township. *

SETZER, Jacob (1819–1892). A Pennsylvania native,

*Coverlet border design with castlelike buildings, a church, houses, large American flags, and palm trees; double weave in blue wool and white cotton. Attributed to the Hay Weaving Shop, Batavia, Ohio, ca. 1845. Clermont County Historical Society, Batavia, Ohio.*

[ 105 ]

he is included in the 1850 U. S. census for Jackson Township, Pennsylvania (Monroe Co.), as a weaver. 3, undated.

SHAFER, J. One coverlet woven in Martinsburg, Pennsylvania (Blair Co.), in 1847 has been recorded.

SHALK, Jacob ( –1864). He was weaving in Lebanon, Pennsylvania (Lebanon Co.), in 1833 and 1835. Shalk died intestate before October 1, 1864; letters of administration are filed in the Lebanon County Courthouse. It is not known if he was the Jacob Shalk who was a weaver in Ohio between 1840 and 1850. 7, 1833–1835.

SHALK, Jacob. He is listed by the O.H.S. as weaving in Licking County, Ohio, between 1840 and 1850. He may have been the Jacob Shalk who was weaving in Pennsylvania in the 1830s and died there in 1864. *

SHALK, John. One coverlet with this name and the date 1835 has been recorded; it is not known where the coverlet was made or whether Shalk was the weaver or the client.

SHALLENBERGER, Peter. Shallenberger was weaving in Juniata County, Pennsylvania, in 1836 because his name appears on a coverlet with that date and location. He probably is the weaver, working in Juniata County in 1838 and 1839, who signed his coverlets "P. S." 3, 1836–1839.

SHAMP, D. One coverlet with this name, 1847, and Perry, New York (Wyoming Co.), has been recorded; it is not known whether Shamp was the weaver or the client.

SHANK, H. One coverlet inscribed with this name and woven in Shelby County (state unknown) in 1847 has been recorded; it is not known whether Shank was the weaver or the client.

SHANK, M. One coverlet inscribed with this name and woven in Fairfield County, Ohio, in 1843 has been recorded; it is not known whether Shank was the weaver or the client.

SHANK, W. He was weaving in Montgomery County, Ohio, between 1831 and 1839, according to recorded coverlets. It is not known if he was related to H. or M. Shank (see entries). 5, 1831–1839.

SHAW, Robert. See entry for William Muir.

SHEAFFER, Franklin D. He is included by the C.C.G.A., Safford and Bishop, and Kovel and Kovel as weaving in 1849, location unknown. 1, 1849.

SHEAFFER, Isaac. Reinert locates Sheaffer in 1836 at Rabbit Hill, Warwick Township, Pennsylvania (Lancaster Co.), which he abbreviated in his inscriptions to "Isaac Sheaffer 1836 R.H.W.T.L.C." It is not known whether he is the same Isaac Sheaffer who was weaving in Stark County, Ohio, at a later date. In 1838 an Isaac Sheaffer was weaving in Plain Township, Ohio (Stark Co.); in 1842 he wove at least one coverlet there and at least one in Jackson Township (Stark Co.). He was weaving in New Berlin, now North Canton, Ohio (Stark Co.), in 1844 and 1845. 1 (Pennsylvania), 1836; 7 (Ohio), 1838–1845.

SHEARER, Henry (ca. 1805– ). He is listed in the 1850 U. S. census for Richland County, Ohio, as a German-born weaver in whose house was living another weaver, Sebastian Hipp (see entry). *

SHEARER, Michael. He appears in W. W. Reilly & Co. as a coverlet weaver in New Lebanon, Ohio (Montgomery Co.). *

SHERMAN, Jacob (ca. 1820– ). Born in Germany, he is included by the C.C.G.A., Safford and Bishop, and Kovel and Kovel as weaving in Attica, Ohio (Seneca Co.), in 1839. The 1850 U. S. census for Seneca County describes Sherman as a weaver. 6, 1838–1867.

SHERMAN, John. The C.C.G.A., Safford and Bishop, and Kovel and Kovel locate Sherman in Mount Morris, New York (Genesee Co.), in 1838. He was weaving in Kendall Mills, New York (Orleans Co.), by 1848. 5, 1837–1848.

SHIVE, M. This weaver is identified by Reinert as working in New Britain Township, Pennsylvania (Bucks Co.), in 1836. *

SHOTWELL, ———. He is listed by Safford and Bishop as weaving in Shotwell's Landing (now Rahway), New Jersey (Union Co.), in 1845. *

SHOUSE, Nicholas. Montgomery believes that Shouse may have been weaving in Vincennes, Indiana (Knox Co.), early in the nineteenth century, but no further information about him has been found in any Indiana records. *

SHREFFLER, Henry. He is located by Reinert and Kovel and Kovel in Salona, Pennsylvania (Clinton Co.), in 1851, but he does not appear in the 1850 U. S. census for Clinton County. *

SHREFFLER, Israel (ca. 1826– ). He is described as a Pennsylvania-born "coverlid weaver" in the 1850 U. S. census for Salona, Pennsylvania (Clinton Co.). *

SHREFFLER, Samuel (ca. 1804– ). Born in Pennsylvania, he is identified by Reinert and Kovel and Kovel as weaving in Salona, Pennsylvania (Clinton Co.), in 1851, and is listed in the 1850 U. S. census for Clinton County as a coverlet weaver. *

SIMPSON, George (1795– ). Born in Scotland, he is included by the C.C.G.A., Safford and Bishop, and Kovel and Kovel as weaving in Switzerland County, Indiana, in 1840. According to Montgomery, he worked first in Windsor, Vermont (Windsor Co.), and then for almost ten years in New Haven, Connecticut (New Haven Co.), before he moved to Caledonia, Indiana (Switzerland Co.). He is listed in the 1850 and 1860 U. S. census records for Switzerland County as a weaver. The 1860 U. S. census states that he was assisted by his son Joseph (see entry), a weaver and schoolmaster. One coverlet that is believed to be his work has been located, according to Montgomery.

SIMPSON, Joseph. In the 1860 U. S. census for Caledonia, Indiana (Switzerland Co.), he is reported as assisting his father, George (see entry), in the weaving trade. Joseph worked as a weaver and schoolmaster. *

SINGER, John. Safford and Bishop identify Singer as weaving in Osnaburg Township, Ohio (Stark Co.), in 1846. According to W. W. Reilly & Co., he worked as a coverlet weaver in Mapleton, Ohio (Stark Co.), in 1853. 5, 1844–1853.

SLAYBAUGH, Charles. He was probably born in Pennsylvania and is identified by the O.H.S. as weaving with his brother Josiah (see entry) on Sandusky Avenue in Bucyrus, Ohio (Crawford Co.), between 1845 and 1850. *

SLAYBAUGH, Josiah (ca. 1825–    ). Born in Pennsylvania, he was weaving with his brother Charles (see entry) in Bucyrus, Ohio (Crawford Co.), between 1845 and 1850, according to the O.H.S. Montgomery states that he worked there with Samuel Slaybaugh (see entry), who was apparently his brother, and Samuel's son William from about 1848 to 1855. Josiah moved to Van Buren Township, Indiana (Kosciusko Co.), by 1863, and later still to Washington Township, Indiana (Elkhart Co.), 1 (Josiah and Samuel), 1845; 11 (Josiah alone), 1848–1878.

SLAYBAUGH, Samuel (ca. 1819–    ). A native of Pennsylvania, he wove with his brother Josiah (see entry) in Bucyrus, Ohio (Crawford Co.), where he is included as a coverlet weaver by the 1850 U. S. census. Living in his household was Lewis Fogle (see entry), a German-born weaver. W. W. Reilly & Co. identifies Samuel Slaybaugh as a coverlet weaver in Bucyrus in 1853, while Montgomery states that his brother Josiah and his nephew William worked with him from about 1848 to 1855. 4, 1843–1850; 1 (Josiah and Samuel), 1845.

SLAYBAUGH, William. See entries for Josiah and Samuel Slaybaugh.

SLOTHOWER, P. He was weaving in 1837 and 1838, probably in Pennsylvania. 2, 1837–1838.

SLUSSER, Eli M. (ca. 1823–    ). Born in Pennsylvania, he was weaving in Canton, Ohio (Stark Co.), in 1842 and 1844, where he is described as a weaver in the 1850 U. S. census. 2, 1842 and 1844.

SLUSSER, Jacob M. He is identified by the O.H.S. as weaving at Bethlehem (now Navarre), Ohio (Stark Co.), in 1840. 1, 1842.

SMITH, Daniel S. Reinert locates Daniel S. Smith in Upper Hanover Township, Pennsylvania (Montgomery Co.), in 1841. 1, 1841.

SMITH, George (ca. 1844–    ). Born in Pennsylvania, he appears in the 1860 U. S. census as a coverlet weaver in the third ward of Allentown, Pennsylvania (Lehigh Co.). He was living in the home of George M. Smith (see entry), a "coverlid pedlar" born in Saxony, Germany, who probably was his father. *

SMITH, George M. (ca. 1821–    ). He is listed in the 1860 U. S. census for the third ward of Allentown, Pennsylvania (Lehigh Co.), as a "coverlid pedlar" who was born in Saxony, Germany. Probably his son, George Smith (see entry), described as a coverlet weaver, was also in the household. *

SMITH, John (ca. 1794–    ). Born in Pennsylvania, he appears in the 1850 U. S. census as a weaver in Schaefferstown, Heidelberg Township, Pennsylvania (Lebanon Co.). Tax lists for Heidelberg Township describe Smith as a weaver and dyer in 1843 and as a weaver in 1848. Charles H. Huber, *Schaefferstown, Pennsylvania 1763–1963* (Schaefferstown, Pa., 1963), states that he supposedly invented a process for weaving "tapestry blankets" for which he received a U. S. patent. There is an outer border of two rows of stars or snowflakes and the legend "J. S. Patent" on some of his coverlets. 14, 1833–1839.

SMITH, John. The O.H.S. locates him in Cincinnati, Ohio (Hamilton Co.), between 1840 and 1844. 5, 1851–1854, West Salem, Ohio (Ashland Co.).

SMITH, Joseph. Reinert lists him as weaving in Millerstown (now Annville), Pennsylvania (Lebanon Co.), in 1840; Millerstown tax records indicate that he was weaving there in 1842 and 1843. Two of his recorded coverlets, one dated 1837 and the other undated, are signed "Joseph Smith & Son"; his son's identity is unknown. 6, 1835–1842.

SMITH, William (ca. 1842–    ). Montgomery states that he was born in Kentucky and was weaving coverlets in Salem, Indiana (Washington Co.), date unknown. *

SNIDER, J. He appears in Montgomery as weaving in Pipe Crick, Harrison Township, Indiana (Miami Co.), in 1843. Snider used a design identical to that employed by William Deeds (see entry), to whom he may have sold his loom and patterns some years later. (See also entry for John Snyder.) 1, 1843.

SNIDER, Samuel (ca. 1820–    ). Born in Pennsylvania, he sometimes spelled his name "Snyder" on his coverlets. Montgomery states that he was weaving in New Paris, Indiana (Elkhart Co.), in 1843; he remained there until at least 1855. 6, 1843–1855.

SNYDER, Daniel. He is located by Reinert and Kovel and Kovel in Hanover Township, Pennsylvania (Montgomery Co.), in 1838, where he wove until 1844. 5, 1838–1844.

SNYDER, Isaac (ca. 1827–    ). Born in Pennsylvania, he is described in the 1850 U. S. census as a coverlet weaver in Bethel Township, Pennsylvania (Berks Co.) *

SNYDER, Jacob (ca. 1825–ca. 1872). A native of Pennsylvania, Snyder is identified by Safford and Bishop as weaving in Stark County, Ohio, in 1849. According to Montgomery, he moved from Ohio to Jackson Township, Indiana (De Kalb Co.), in 1852 and lived the rest of his life there. When Snyder was weaving in Indiana, an apprentice, Aaron C. Osbon (see entry), worked for him. 6 (Ohio), 1847–1850; 3 (Indiana), 1854–1857.

SNYDER, John. He is included by Safford and Bishop as weaving in Milton, Indiana (Wayne Co.), in 1843, where he worked for John Wissler (see entry), according to an account by Wissler's son that is cited by Montgomery. Montgomery could not locate Snyder in the census records for Indiana, and believes that he may have been the J. Snider (see entry) of Miami County, Indiana. *

SNYDER, Mary. According to Safford and Bishop, Mary Snyder was in Tappan, New York (Rockland Co.), in 1837 *

SPECK, Johan. He is listed by the C.C.G.A. and Kovel and Kovel as weaving in Pennsylvania in 1725, and by Safford and Bishop as weaving there in 1825, and it may be assumed he was not using a Jacquard mechanism on his loom. Reinert identifies him as Johan Ludwig Speck and says that he was weaving in 1723, place unknown. Speck's weaving pattern book, which contains more than 80 patterns, is owned by the Philadelphia Museum of Art. *

SPECK, John C. He may have been weaving in Martinsburg, Virginia (Berkeley Co.), now in West Virginia, prior to 1863, since his name is on an undated coverlet with that location.

SPENCER, William (ca. 1829–    ). The 1850 U. S. census for Wolcott, New York (Wayne Co.), includes Spencer as a New York-born weaver living in the household of Daniel Conger (see entry). *

SPERLING, Louis. He is identified by Reinert as weaving in Jacksonville, Pennsylvania (Lehigh Co.), in 1875. *

STABLER, G. One coverlet with this name has been recorded, but the location and date of manufacture are not indicated. It is not known if Stabler was the weaver or the client.

STAGER, Henry F. (ca. 1820–1888). Born in Pennsylvania, he was weaving in Mount Joy, Pennsylvania (Lancaster Co.), by at least 1843. He is identified as a weaver in Mount Joy borough tax lists for 1857, 1858, and 1864, and in the U. S. census for 1850, 1860, and 1870. Stager used a variety of inscriptions, including "M. By H. Stager, Mount Joy, Lancaster Co., Pa., Warranted Fast Coller [color]"; "Made By H. F. Stager, Mount Joy, Lancaster Co., Pa., Fast Color No. 1"; and "Manuf. By H. F. Stager & Son, Fast Colors, Mount Joy, Lancaster County, Penn." Stager's son is not mentioned in census records, and no information about him has yet been discovered. 40, one dated 1843 and one dated 1844. 6 (Stager & Son), undated.

STALEY, Andrew. He appears in the O.H.S. as weaving in Mechanicsburg, Ohio (Champaign Co.), in 1870. *

STARR, F. One coverlet with this name, but with location and date of manufacture unverified, has been recorded. It is not known whether Starr was the weaver or the client.

STAUCH, David, Jr. (1807–1879). He first appears as a

*A row of half-timbered buildings with pennants, cupolas, and chimneys is featured in this coverlet border design; Beiderwand weave in red, blue, and green wool and natural cotton. Woven by Henry K. Frederick, Cumberland Co., Pa., 1846. Courtesy of E. T. Wilson. See color plate facing page 102.*

[ 108 ]

weaver in the tax lists of Weigelstown, Dover Township, Pennsylvania (York Co.), in 1833. He was there in 1836, but his whereabouts from 1837 to 1849 are not known. Stauch's coverlets often include the word "Patent" below his inscriptions along the border. He is buried in St. Paul's cemetery, North Codorus Township, Pennsylvania (York Co.). 12, 1836–1849.

STAUCH, David, Sr. ( –1839). Reinert locates him in York County, Pennsylvania, dates unknown, and tax lists for Dover borough, Dover Township, Pennsylvania (York Co.), show that he was a weaver there from 1820/21 to 1839. An inventory taken soon after his death includes 10 coverlets and quilts valued at $30, 1 reel at 25¢, 2 looms at $8, flax at $10, and a "weavers apparatus" valued at $5. *

STAUDT, Simon. He is listed by the O.H.S. as weaving in Troy, Ohio (Miami Co.), in 1844. According to recorded coverlets, Staudt was weaving in Miami County from at least 1842 to 1848. 4, 1842–1848.

STAUFFER, R. One coverlet has been recorded with this name and 1855, but with no location of manufacture indicated. It is not known whether Stauffer was the weaver or the client.

STEIER, W. He appears in Reinert as weaving in Upper Hanover Township, Pennsylvania (Montgomery Co.), in 1842; Safford and Bishop and Kovel and Kovel locate him there in 1848. Steier's coverlets bear either the inscription "W. Steier, Ober Hanover in Montgomery," or "Made by W. Steier in Ober Hanover T. Montgomery C." 3, 1844–1848.

STEINER, David. Steiner was weaving in Brecknock Township, Pennsylvania (Lancaster Co.), dates unknown. The inscriptions on his recorded coverlets include the word "Patent." 3, undated.

STEINHILBER, Martin (1833–1920). He was weaving in Ross County, Ohio, from 1840 to 1845, and, according to the O.H.S., in Covington, Ohio (Miami Co.), dates unknown. A great-grandchild of the weaver says that Steinhilber wove in a shop on South High Street, assisted by his son and five daughters. He often included the term "Fancy Coverlet" in his inscriptions. 5, 1843–1852.

STEINHILL Brothers. One coverlet has been recorded, woven by them in 1840 in Ross County (probably Ohio).

STEPHEN, Jacob. He is included in the O.H.S. as weaving in Springville, Ohio (Seneca Co.), in 1853. *

STEPHENSON, Daniel (1823–1892). He was born in Yorkshire, England, and, according to the Art Institute of Chicago, came to America in 1840. His father was a weaver in a factory in Geneva, New York (Seneca Co.). "It is known that Daniel was in Canada in 1850 as an employee for Messrs. Clark and Roblett, as head weaver. Thereafter, he went to Springfield, Ohio (Clark Co.), as an apprentice to a weaver named Robert Crossley for two years. Some records say he came to Iowa in 1845, but did not stay. He returned from Ohio to Fairfield, Iowa (Jefferson Co.), in 1852 and set up his shop. He is said to have brought his loom from Ohio, and the flying shuttles he used were shipped from England by an uncle. His designs were his own. His customers made their selections. The cost of weaving was between

*Border design of repeating patterns of a house, church, monument, and Centennial buildings; double weave in red and blue wool. Woven by J. A. Van Vleck, Gallipolis, Ohio, ca. 1845. Western Reserve Historical Society, Cleveland, Ohio, gift of Mrs. Frank L. Wiley.*

$3.50 and $5.00 per coverlet. To weave the name of the customer and date in the corner was 25 cents extra." Art Institute of Chicago. The C.C.G.A., Safford and Bishop, and Kovel and Kovel believe that Stephenson was weaving in Fairfield, Iowa (Jefferson Co.), in 1849. 6, 1855–1870.

STERNBERG, William. He is located by the C.C.G.A., Safford and Bishop, and Kovel and Kovel in New York state in 1838. One coverlet with the inscription "E. B. Wm. Sternberg, Cambria, Niagara County, N.Y. 1834" has been recorded, although there is some question concerning the date because the inscription is worn in this area. 1, 1834.

STEURNAGLE, Andrew. He appears in W. W. Reilly & Co. as a coverlet weaver in Inland, Ohio (Summit Co.), in 1853. *

STICH, G. Safford and Bishop and Kovel and Kovel identify Stich as weaving in Newark, Ohio (Licking Co.), in 1839. According to a February 27, 1836, issue of the *Advocate* (Newark, Ohio), Stich had started weaving single and double coverlets and had bought Robert Moore's (see entry) establishment. 14, 1838–1848.

STIERWALT, Moses. He is included in the O.H.S. as weaving in Washington Township, Ohio (Sandusky Co.), between 1840 and 1850. *

STIFF, J. Stiff was weaving in Stillwater, New Jersey (Sussex Co.), in 1836 and 1837. He worked in Montague, New Jersey (Sussex Co.) in 1838 and 1839 and was in Milford, Pennsylvania (Pike Co.), between 1841 and 1844. The borders of Stiff's coverlets often feature American eagles beneath the word "Liberty," alternating with single trees. 9, 1836–1844.

STIMMEL, S. He was weaving in 1851 and 1853, but the locations of manufacture are not indicated on his coverlets. 2, 1851 and 1853.

STINGER, Samuel (ca. 1801–1879). Montgomery believes that Stinger was born in Pennsylvania and moved to Montgomery County, Ohio, in 1832. In Germantown he purchased a loom for $100 that apparently had a Jacquard-type attachment. In 1838 he moved to Carthage, Indiana (Rush Co.), and is described in the 1850 U. S. census for Rush County as a "farmer and weaver," being assisted by Nicholas Reiter (see entry), a German-born weaver. Stinger used a large 8-pointed star surrounded by a group of smaller stars as a trademark. 9, 1848–1857.

STOHL, F. He was weaving in Lampeter Township, Pennsylvania (Lancaster Co.), by at least 1834. 3, 1833–1834.

STONER, Henry. One coverlet with this name and the date 1841 has been recorded; the location of manufacture is unknown. It is not known whether Stoner was the weaver or the client.

STRACKE, Barnhardt. He is listed by the C.C.G.A., Safford and Bishop, and Kovel and Kovel as weaving in Hocking County, Ohio, in 1856. *

STRAUSER, Elias (ca. 1826–    ). Born in Pennsylvania, he is identified in the 1850 U. S. census as a weaver in Plain Township, Ohio (Wayne Co.). 1, 1850.

STRIEBIG, John K. (1809–1868). Beginning in 1840, tax records for York Township, Pennsylvania (York Co.), include Striebig as a weaver, although Reinert locates him in Maryland in 1842. The C.C.G.A., Safford and Bishop, and Kovel and Kovel indicate that he was weaving in Wayne County, Indiana, between 1834 and 1840. Montgomery states on p. 109: "Over the years the name of John Striebig has appeared on several lists as a weaver in Wayne County, Indiana, despite positive proof that he was working in Pennsylvania at the same time he was credited with weaving in Indiana. Through the research of Mrs. Janet Gray Crosson, Lancaster, Pennsylvania, in the files of the Historical Society of York County, York County, Pennsylvania, the author is in possession of records which offer indisputable proof that he could not have been an Indiana weaver." Striebig is known to have died in York County, Pennsylvania. 13 (location not indicated), 1834–1847.

STROBEL, Lorenz (ca. 1812–1900). Born in Germany, he came to America about 1840 and settled in Summit County, Ohio. William B. Doyle, ed., *Centennial History of Summit, Ohio* (Chicago, 1908). A few years later, he moved to Coventry Township, Summit Co., where he was weaving between 1846 and 1850. The 1850 U. S. census identifies him as a farmer in Coventry Township. 2, 1846 and 1850.

STROUD, William. He appears in Kovel and Kovel as weaving in Cadiz, Ohio (Harrison Co.), about 1830. 2, 1836 and 1838.

STRUNK'S MILLS. See entry for Joseph F. Schnee.

SULSER, Henry. W. W. Reilly & Co. describes Sulser as a coverlet weaver in Greenfield, Ohio (Highland Co.), in 1853. *

SUTHERLAND, J. (ca. 1808–    ). Born in Pennsylvania, he appears in the 1850 U. S. census of Brighton Township, Pennsylvania (Beaver Co.), as a farmer. One coverlet with this name, which was woven in Beaver, Pennsylvania, in 1840, has been recorded; it is not known whether Sutherland was the weaver or the client.

SWAN, Cyrus (ca. 1824–    ). The 1850 U. S. census lists him as a Pennsylvania-born weaver living in Salt Creek Township, Ohio (Holmes Co.). 1, 1848.

SWANK, J. He is identified by the O.H.S. as weaving in Knox County, Ohio, in 1846. 1 (attributed), 1846.

SWEENY, T. W. W. Reilly & Co. locates Sweeny as a coverlet weaver at Armstrong's Mills, Ohio (Belmont Co.), in 1853. *

SWEITZER, ———. See entry for Kepner's Woolen Mill.

[110]

# T

TATHAM, Thomas. He appears in French as a "carpet coverlet weaver" in Middletown, New York (Orange Co.). *

TEST WOOLEN MILLS. This mill was in operation in Hagerstown, Indiana (Wayne Co.), during the 1850s. See entries for Elias Favorite, John Hoover, and Thomas Jordan. *

THOMPSON, George. He is identified by Montgomery as a weaver who advertised in the January 5, 1838, issue of the Corydon, Indiana, *Investigator* that he was ready to weave coverlets in Harrison County, Indiana. *

THOMPSON, Ritchie. The C.C.G.A., Safford and Bishop, and Kovel and Kovel locate Thompson in Brownsville, Indiana (Union Co.), in 1834. Montgomery writes that no record of this weaver was found in Indiana. *

TOBIN, John (ca. 1827– ). Born in Ireland, W. W. Reilly & Co. says that Tobin was a coverlet weaver in Newark, Ohio (Licking Co.), in 1853, where he also appears in the 1850 U. S. census. *

TRAPPE, Samuel J. He is listed by the C.C.G.A., Safford and Bishop, and Kovel and Kovel as weaving in 1856, location unknown. *

TURNBAUGH, Joseph (ca. 1829– ). Born in Pennsylvania, he was weaving at Sugarloaf, Pennsylvania (Luzerne Co.). The 1850 U. S. census for Black Creek Township (Luzerne Co.) lists him as a "coverlid" weaver living in the home of Samuel Turnbaugh, a farmer. Samuel Turnbaugh, who was also a weaver, was probably his father. Coverlets woven by Joseph and Samuel together have been recorded. 5 (Joseph alone), 1851–1852; 3 (Joseph and Samuel), 1849–1851.

TURNBAUGH, Samuel. See entry for Samuel Dornbach.

TURNER, William (ca. 1802– ). Born in England, he is described in the 1850 U. S. census as a dyer and weaver in the fourth ward of Dayton, Ohio (Montgomery Co.). W. W. Reilly & Co. also describes Turner as a coverlet weaver in Dayton. *

TYLER, Elman ( –1906). Born in Oswego County, New York, the son of Harry Tyler (see entry), Elman was his father's first assistant. According to his daughter, Etta Tyler Chapman, he was a fast, efficient weaver who could produce two strips of a coverlet in two and one-half days. Believing that the lion used by his father as a trademark was too British, he designed the eagle trademark that the Tylers used from 1845 onward. Elman was a penmanship teacher and conducted classes in the evenings. *

TYLER, Harry (1801–ca. 1858). Born in Connecticut, he settled in Boston, New York (Erie Co.), in 1832 and began farming. According to Tyler's granddaughter, Etta Tyler Chapman, Tyler disliked farming, and after one year relocated in Butterville, New York (Jefferson Co.), where he began weaving coverlets and carpets. "The Tyler Coverlets," *Antiques*, XIII (March 1928), pp. 215–218. Tyler built both his looms (one for coverlets and one for ingrain carpets) and drew his own designs, except for the bowl of fruit motif and the eagle trademark that were developed by his son Elman (see entry). Tyler first used a regal lion as a trademark. In 1845 he began using an American eagle with the motto "E Pluribus Unum." Tyler, with assistance from his family, would also dye the yarn for a coverlet. He purchased

On this border design a three-story house is flanked by trees and towering rose bushes; Beiderwand weave in red and blue wool and natural cotton. Woven by Martin Hoke, York, Pa., 1843. Courtesy of Dr. and Mrs. Willard J. Davies.

dyes from Elisha Camp, in Jefferson County, using indigo for blue and cochineal for red. The dyeing was done in a small building behind the home. Tyler trademarked coverlets dating after 1858 were apparently woven by Elman Tyler or other members of the Tyler family. (See n. 21, p. 14, and n. 24, p. 15.) 94, 1834–1860.

## U

UHL, Peter. Three coverlets woven by Uhl have been recorded. At least one of them, signed and dated 1838, is in an overshot weave. Another, woven with the aid of a Jacquard-type attachment, is dated 1841; presumably Uhl did not have the Jacquard mechanism until after 1838. The coverlets were woven in Trumbull County, Ohio.

UMBARGER, Michael, Jr. (ca. 1811– ). Born in Pennsylvania, he is listed by the C.C.G.A., Safford and Bishop, and Reinert as weaving in Middle Paxton Township, Pennsylvania (Dauphin Co.). The 1850 U. S. census includes Umbarger as a weaver in West Hanover Township (Dauphin Co.), in whose household was Michael Umbarger, Sr., aged 72 years, also a weaver. By 1850 the younger Umbarger had purchased land in Dauphin County from Philip Michael, probably the same Philip Michael (see entry), also a coverlet weaver, who moved to Indiana in 1849. 12, 1839–1851.

UNGER, I. He was weaving in Lancaster County, Pennsylvania, in 1844, according to recorded coverlets. He does not appear in tax, census, deed, or estate records of Lancaster County; perhaps he only worked there briefly. 2, 1 dated 1844.

## V

VAN BUSKIRK, Jacob (ca. 1803– ). Born in Pennsylvania, he appears in the 1850 U. S. census for Woodview, Ohio (Morrow Co.). W. W. Reilly & Co. identifies van Buskirk as a coverlet weaver at Woodview in 1853. *

VAN DOREN, Abram William (1808–1884). Born in Millstone, New Jersey (Somerset Co.), he was one of a family of weavers. Van Doren went to Oakland County, Michigan, in 1838, where he worked as a weaver until he began farming in 1864. Later he moved to Supply Creek, Nebraska, where he died. He purchased his looms and other equipment from a J. J. Davidson of New York. Mildred Davison, "Hand-Woven Coverlets in the Art Institute of Chicago," *Antiques*, XCVII (May 1970), p. 739. A "J. J. Davidson" has not been recorded in this survey, although he may be the J. Davidson or J. M. Davidson mentioned previously (see entries). 8, 1845–1849.

VAN DOREN, Garret William (ca. 1811– ). A native of New Jersey and a brother of Abram, Isaac, and Peter van Doren (see entries), Garret van Doren signed his coverlets with the initials "G. W. V. D." rather than his full name. 1 (Farmerville, state unknown), 1833; 4 (Millstone, New Jersey [Somerset Co.]), 1835–1841.

VAN DOREN, Isaac William (1798–1869). He was born at Millstone, New Jersey (Somerset Co.), a brother of Abram, Garret, and Peter van Doren (see entries); he wove at Millstone and signed his coverlets with his initials "I. W. V. D." The account book (1835–1851) of the business of Issac van Doren is privately owned. 3, 1849 and 1853.

*Large public buildings alternate with smaller houses that are tucked behind trees; double weave in red and blue wool and white cotton. Weaver unidentified, possibly Ohio, ca. 1840–1850. Courtesy of Mrs. Henry B. Wilson. See color plate facing page 102.*

VAN DOREN, Peter Sutphen (1806–1899). Like his brothers, Peter van Doren was born in Millstone, New Jersey (Somerset Co.), where he made double woven coverlets that he signed "P. S. V. D." 6, 1838–1846.

VAN FLECK, Peter. One undated coverlet bearing his name and woven in Gallipolis, Ohio (Gallia Co.), has been recorded. A possible relationship to the weaver Jay A. van Vleck (see entry) has not been verified.

VAN GORDON, William H. (ca. 1824– ). Born in Pennsylvania, Safford and Bishop locate van Gordon in Covington, Ohio (Miami Co.), in 1852; he is described as a weaver in the 1850 U. S. census for Miami County. 15, 1849–1853.

VAN METER, Joel. In an 1826 issue of the *Bridgeton Observer* (Cumberland County, New Jersey), van Meter informed the public that he was "prepared to weave double coverlets at his house about 1½ miles on the road from Bridgeton to Centerville." *

VAN NESS, James (ca. 1816– ). Van Ness appears in Safford and Bishop and Kovel and Kovel as weaving in Palmyra, New York (Wayne Co.), in 1848 and 1850; the C.C.G.A. also places him in New York in 1850. The 1850 U. S. census describes him as a New York-born coverlet weaver living in Palmyra next door to Ira Hadsell (see entry), also a coverlet weaver. Van Ness often used an American eagle under the motto "E Pluribus Unum" in the corners of his coverlets. 14, 1849–1852.

VAN NORTWICK (or NORTWIC), C. The C.C.G.A., Safford and Bishop, and Kovel and Kovel say that he was a weaver in Asbury, New Jersey (Warren Co.), in 1840. Van Nortwick's inscriptions include the term "Fancy Weaver," and many of his coverlets have the word "Liberty" above eagles in the border design. 16, 1837–1849.

VAN SICKLE, Sarah (1822–1914). Sarah van Sickle is described by Hall as a weaver in Indiana; the dates are unknown. She is actually Sarah LaTourette (see entry), who Montgomery states married John van Sickle in 1870 in Indiana and moved with him to Kentucky. No coverlets woven after her marriage are known.

VAN VLECK, Jay A. (ca. 1827– ). Born in New York, the C.C.G.A., Safford and Bishop, and Kovel and Kovel locate him in Ohio, and he is described as a weaver in the 1850 U. S. census for Gallipolis, Ohio (Gallia Co.). Van Vleck used the inscription "Manufacd by Jay A. van Vleck, Gallipolis, O" on his coverlets, but he did not date them. 8, undated.

VAN VLEET, Abraham. According to Montgomery, van Vleet advertised in the April 20, 1830, issue of the *Political Clarion* of Connersville, Indiana (Fayette Co.), that he was ready to weave coverlets and ingrain carpets. He had moved from Warren County, Ohio, to Fayette County, Indiana, in the 1820s. In 1831 van Vleet sold his weaving business to Hiram Bundy (see entry) and nothing further has been learned about him, according to Montgomery. *

VARICK, ———. The C.C.G.A., Safford and Bishop, and Kovel and Kovel include him as weaving in 1835; the location is unknown. 2, 1835 and 1838.

VERPLANK, Samuel. He is listed by Safford and Bishop as weaving in Fishkill, New York (Dutchess Co.), in 1843. *

VOGEL, August (1801– ). According to Montgomery, Vogel, who was born in Germany, came to Baltimore in 1834. In April 1836 the Brookville *Indiana American* announced that three weavers, Vogel,

*Coverlet border design composed of classical style houses with picket fences and large trees; double weave in red wool and white cotton. Woven by D. Shamp, Wyoming Co., N. Y., 1847. Margaret Woodbury Strong Museum, Rochester, N. Y. See color plate facing page 102.*

[113]

The interior design features churches juxtaposed with taverns, pagodas, and palm trees, and is an elaboration of the more common "Boston Town Border." This example has a grapevine border; double weave in blue wool and white cotton. Weaver unidentified, probably Ohio, ca. 1845. Iroquois County Historical Society Museum, Wateska, Ill.

Jacob Walter, and Gottlieb Eckert, had leased the G. W. Kimble Woolen Factory (see entries) and were ready to weave blankets and coverlets, as well as dyeing, fulling, dressing, and carding wool. The three men are not listed in the 1840 U. S. census for Franklin County, so the business does not appear to have lasted long. The C.C.G.A., Safford and Bishop, and Kovel and Kovel locate Vogel in Crawfordsville, Indiana (Montgomery Co.), in 1846. He bought a lot there in 1848 and set up his loom in a two-story building on South Washington Street. Vogel cannot be traced after 1854, when he married and sold his property. 2, 1851 and 1853.

VOGLER, Milton (1825– ). He is said to have been weaving in Ohio—possibly Adams County—in 1855 and 1856. 1 (attributed), 1855.

## W

WAGNER, John. Reinert says that Wagner was weaving in 1846, probably in Lebanon County, Pennsylvania. 1, 1844.

WALHAUS, Henry. He is identified by Madden as weaving in Belleville (St. Clair Co.) and Quincy (Adams Co.), Illinois, dates unknown. *

WALK, Jacob M. He appears in W. W. Reilly & Co. as a coverlet weaver in Stark County, Ohio. 1, undated.

WALTER, Jacob (1800– ). Montgomery states that Walter was born in Hesse-Darmstadt, Germany, and came to America in 1832. He advertised in the Brookville *Indiana American* that he was beginning to weave coverlets and other materials in Franklin County, working with August Vogel and Gottlieb Eckert (see entries). Nothing further is known about him. *

WANTZ, ———. See entry for John Keener. *

WARWICK, J. He is listed by the C.C.G.A., Safford and Bishop, and Kovel and Kovel as weaving in 1849, location unknown, and may be the same man identified by the C.C.G.A. as "Varick" (see entry). *

WARNER, P. Reinert locates Warner at Lineboro, Maryland (Carroll Co.), in 1845. Warner sometimes used the terms "Fancy Patent" and "Beauty Patent" in his coverlet inscriptions. 5, 1846–1857.

WATSON WOOLEN MILL. According to the Shelburne Museum, the mill was operating about 1815 in Chelsea Upper Village, Vermont (Orange Co.). It apparently made coverlets, since one is attributed to the Watson Woolen Mill.

WEAND, William (ca. 1826– ). He appears in *Boyd's Business Directory, Berks-Schuylkill*, as weaving "coverlids" on North Eighth Street near Linden in Allentown, Pennsylvania (Lehigh Co.). The 1860 U. S. census includes him as a Pennsylvania-born weaver. *

WEAND. See entries under Wiand.

WEAREHS, ———. He was a weaver in Loudonville, Ohio (Ashland Co.), in 1852 and 1853, according to recorded coverlets, and may be the F. Yearous (see entry) who was weaving there from 1853 to 1858. 2, 1852 and 1853.

WEAVER, Frederick ( –1885). Reinert locates him near Aaronsburg, Pennsylvania (Centre Co.), in 1851. Weaver's will indicates that he was a weaver in Haines Township, Pennsylvania (Centre Co.). Centre County Courthouse. He is buried at Aaronsburg. 4, 1848–1868.

WEAVER, J. G. He was weaving at least between 1836 and 1838, location unknown. 7, 1836–1838.

WEAVER, John (ca. 1824– ). Born in Pennsylvania, Weaver is included in the 1850 U. S. census as a coverlet weaver in Rowsburg, Ohio (Ashland Co.). In his household was Samuel Weaver (see entry), a Pennsylvania-born coverlet weaver who was probably his brother. John Weaver is also listed by W. W. Reilly & Co. as weaving in Rowsburg. 5, 1850–1857.

WEAVER, Samuel (ca. 1830– ). Born in Pennsylvania, the 1850 U. S. census indicates that he was living with John Weaver (see entry), a coverlet weaver, in Rowsburg, Ohio (Ashland Co.). 2, 1 undated, 1 dated 1862.

WEAVER, Thomas ( –1843). An inventory taken shortly after Weaver's death includes a weaving reel valued at $2, a "pattent coverlit weaving loom" valued at $50, a "common weaving loom" valued at $10, 47 coverlets valued at $140, a coverlet on the loom valued at $3, and cotton yarn on the loom valued at $2.70. Inventory, May 8, 1843, Lehigh County Courthouse. When he died, he was living in Upper Milford Township, Pennsylvania (Lehigh Co.). 7, 1837–1843.

WEBER, R. Kovel and Kovel locate Weber in Emmaus, Pennsylvania (Lehigh Co.), dates unknown. *

WEBER, T. Reinert states that Weber was working in Emmaus, Pennsylvania (Lehigh Co.), in 1838. All coverlets recorded in this survey are inscribed with an Emmaus location. 6, 1837–1843.

WEDDEL, Liza Jane. According to Kovel and Kovel, she was weaving in Floyd, Virginia (Scott Co.), in 1819. *

WEIDEL, George (ca. 1815– ). He was born in Pennsylvania. Weidel's name is sometimes spelled "Widle" in the tax records of Bedford Township, Pennsylvania (Bedford Co.), from 1848 to 1855. The 1850 U. S. census describes him as a coverlet weaver in Bedford borough. *

WEIL, George P. He appears in *Boyd's Business Directory, Berks-Schuylkill*, as a coverlet manufacturer with Henry Gabriel at the foot of South Seventh Street, Allentown, Pennsylvania (Lehigh Co.). The

The interior pattern is composed of six large foliate wreaths, the wide side border features churches and symmetrically placed houses or taverns with two-story porches, the bottom border is a stylized vine, and the corner blocks contain a large peacock perched on a flowering branch; Beiderwand weave in red wool and natural cotton. Weaver unidentified, probably Pennsylvania or Ohio, ca. 1845. Abby Aldrich Rockefeller Folk Art Center. See frontispiece.

1860 Allentown city directory shows him weaving coverlets there on Union Street at Eighth Street. *

WELK, George (ca. 1795– ). Born in Pennsylvania, he is described as a weaver in the 1850 U. S. census in Springfield Township, Ohio (Mahoning Co.). W. W. Reilly & Co. also locates him as a coverlet weaver in Mahoning County. *

WELTY, John B. Reinert shows Welty as weaving in Boonsboro, Maryland (Washington Co.), in 1839, while the C.C.G.A. and Safford and Bishop place him in the same location in 1848. 17, 1833–1851.

WENSEL, Charles (ca. 1828– ). Born in Saxony, Germany, Wensel appears as a coverlet weaver in the 1860 U. S. census for the third ward of Allentown, Pennsylvania (Lehigh Co.). *

WEST, James. He is listed by the O.H.S. as an English-born weaver who came to America with his father. They settled in Ohio and began weaving in 1837. 2, 1843 and 1848.

WEST, William. In an 1826 issue of the *New Jersey Mirror and Burlington County Advertiser*, West advertised that he was weaving double and figure work coverlets, bedspreads, and so forth in a shop four doors above General Read's on Garden Street, Mount Holly, New Jersey (Burlington Co.). *

WEVER, H. S. One coverlet with this name and 1844 has been recorded; the location is unknown.

WHISLER, John. See entry for John Wissler.

WHITE, ———. One coverlet with the following inscription has been recorded: "Wove/by/White/near/Hunting/ton." No further information has been recorded to date.

WHITE, Abel. According to Weiss and Ziegler, White advertised in an 1820 issue of the *New Jersey Mirror and Burlington County Advertiser* that he had taken the shop formerly occupied by James Holland in Lumberton, New Jersey (Burlington Co.), where he would weave "Double and Figure Work, Coverlids, Diaper and other Country weaving in its various branches." White was in business until 1826. *

WIAND (or WEAND), Charles (ca. 1818– ). Born in Pennsylvania, Reinert says that Wiand was weaving in Trexlertown, Pennsylvania (Lehigh Co.), in 1839 and in Allentown, Pennsylvania (Lehigh Co.), in 1840. The 1850 U. S. census includes him as a weaver in Allentown in whose household was John Kramlich (see entry for John Gramlyg), a German-born weaver. Wiand was located by Safford and Bishop and Kovel and Kovel in Allentown, Pennsylvania (Lehigh Co.), in 1854. 24, 1840–1859.

WIAND (or WEAND), David. Wiand is listed by Safford and Bishop as weaving in Zieglersville, Pennsylvania (Montgomery Co.), in 1837, and in 1841 he was weaving in Lower Salford Township, Pennsylvania (Montgomery Co.). 4, 1837–1841.

WIAND, Joel (ca. 1820– ). Born in Pennsylvania, Wiand is listed in the 1850 U. S. census of the third ward, Allentown, Pennsylvania (Lehigh Co.), as a weaver, and as a carpet weaver in the 1860 U. S. census. *

WIAND, John (ca. 1844– ). A native of Pennsylvania, Wiand is listed in the 1860 U. S. census of the third ward, Allentown, Pennsylvania (Lehigh Co.), as a coverlet weaver. He was living in the household of Joel Wiand (see entry), a carpet weaver who probably was his father. *

WIAND (or WIEAND or WIEND), Jonathan D. (ca. 1828–1884). Born in Pennsylvania, he probably can be identified as the J. D. Wieand located by Reinert and Kovel and Kovel in Allentown, Pennsylvania (Lehigh Co.), in 1868. The 1850 U. S. census places him as a weaver in Allentown in the house of Daniel Wiand, who may have been his father. An inventory of Jonathan's estate, dated 1884, includes 6 carpet looms and fixtures valued at $15 each. Lehigh County Courthouse. 1, 1868.

WIEND (or WEAND), Michael. According to Reinert, Wiend was weaving in Pottstown, Pennsylvania (Montgomery Co.), in 1838. 1, 1838.

WILDIN, John (ca. 1803– ). Born in Germany, he is identified as a weaver in the tax records for York Township, Pennsylvania (York Co.), from 1840 to 1850, although the 1850 U. S. census includes him as a mason. He does not appear in the 1860 U. S. census, and no deed or estate settlement for Wildin can be found in York County. 7, 1839–1846.

WILKISON, Emily. She is listed by Safford and Bishop as weaving in Bethany, New York (Genesee Co.), in 1836. *

WILL, William (ca. 1798– ). Born in Germany, he was weaving in Knox Township, Ohio (Columbiana Co.), according to the 1850 U. S. census. He is included by W. W. Reilly & Co. as a coverlet weaver in Columbiana County. *

WILLIAMS, H. R. (ca. 1809– ). Williams, Pennsylvania-born, is located by Kovel and Kovel and Reinert as weaving at Mill Hall (Clinton Co.) in 1850, where the 1850 U. S. census identified him as a clothier with a woolen factory. 1, 1848.

WILLIAMS, Henry T. One undated coverlet with this name, woven in Dover Township, Pennsylvania (York Co.), has been recorded; it is not known whether Williams was the weaver or the client.

WILLIAMS, John T. Williams was weaving in Mechanicsburg, Pennsylvania (Cumberland Co.), between 1834 and 1836. He first appears in the tax rolls as a weaver and dyer in 1835, and may be the T. J. Williams listed therein in 1838 and 1840. A deed of April 1844 shows that Charles Young, a Mechanicsburg coverlet weaver, sold property to Henry and Andrew Seifert, also coverlet weavers (see entries). This same property, which was situated on the south side of Main Street, was bought by Young from Williams in 1840. Cumberland County Courthouse, Mechanicsburg. 3, 1834–1836.

WILLIAMS, May. Kovel and Kovel identify her as weaving in Falmouth, Kentucky (Pendleton Co.), in 1817. *

WILLIAMS, William T. (ca. 1816– ). He was born in Pennsylvania and was weaving in Paradise Township, Pennsylvania (York Co.), in 1844. Tax records for Dover Township, York County, include Williams as a weaver in 1846 and 1847; the 1850 U. S. census identifies him as a butcher there. 2, 1844 and 1847.

WILSON, Henry. According to the C.C.G.A., Kovel and Kovel, and Safford and Bishop, he was weaving in Hendricks County, Indiana, in 1850. See also entry for Hugh Wilson. *

WILSON, Hugh (1803–1884). According to Montgomery, Wilson was born in Paisley, Scotland, where he was apprenticed to a weaver at about age fifteen. After two years, he fled to America and worked in several locations until he settled in Shelbyville, Kentucky (Shelby Co.), where he started his own weaving business in 1824. With his wife and eleven children, Wilson moved on to Hendricks County, Indiana, in 1849. In 1850 he was included in the manufacturers' census as having two employees and producing woven goods valued at $1,000 annually. He moved to Coatesville (Hendricks Co.), in 1860, dying there in 1884. 17, 1848–1874.

WILSON, John. In 1806 Wilson was weaving for James Alexander near Newburgh, New York (Orange Co.) Alexander's account book indicates that Wilson wove coverlets at 16 shillings each, plus diaper, wide cloth, cotton, and flannel. New York State Historical Association, Cooperstown. No coverlets bearing Wilson's name are known, but none of Alexander's coverlets shows a maker's name. *

WILSON, Jonathan. See entry for William Muir.

WILSON, Robert B. (ca. 1792– ). Born in Scotland, he is identified as a carpet weaver in New Philadelphia, Ohio (Tuscarawas Co.), in the 1850 U. S. census. The O.H.S. locates him there in 1842, as does W. W. Reilly & Co. *

WILSON, William. Wilson came to America from Scotland in 1818, settling in Madison County, New York. One coverlet, dated 1836 and marked "A. Wilson," is attributed to him, as is another made for a member of his family. Wilson's account book that lists items received in trade for his coverlets is privately owned. Two coverlets are attributed to him; one is an overshot weave.

WINGERT, George S. According to the C.C.G.A. and Safford and Bishop, Wingert was weaving in Landisburg, Pennsylvania (Perry Co.), in 1838. Any relationship to Henry Wingert (see entry) has not been determined. 7, 1832–1838.

WINGERT, Henry (ca. 1826– ). Born in Pennsylvania, he is located by the C.C.G.A. and Safford and Bishop in Landisburg, Pennsylvania (Perry Co.), in 1846. Kovel and Kovel say that he was weaving there in 1838. The 1850 U. S. census for Perry County identifies him as Henry, Jr., a weaver living with his father, who was a farmer. A relationship to George S. Wingert (see entry) has not been determined. 4, 1841–1848.

WIRICK, John (ca. 1808– ). A native of Pennsylvania, he is included by Safford and Bishop as weaving in Midway, Ohio (Clark Co.), in 1849. The 1850 U. S. census for Johnson Township, Champaign Co., identifies Wirick as a weaver. Living in his household was William Wirick, a young Pennsylvania-born weaver, probably his son. 11, 1848–1861.

WIRICK, William. See entry for John Wirick.

WISE, E. He was probably weaving in Derry Township, Pennsylvania (Mifflin Co.), in 1842. Two coverlets bearing this name and date have been recorded, but no weaver named Wise has been found in the 1840 U. S. census for Mifflin County. 2, 1842.

The "Hemfield Railroad" pattern features a locomotive and engineer; double weave in red and blue wool and natural cotton. Weavers believed to have produced coverlets in this pattern include Daniel Campbell, William Harper, Martin Burns, George Coulter, and Harvey Cook. Weaver unidentified, possibly West Virginia or Pennsylvania, ca. 1840–1850. Collection of Mr. and Mrs. Foster McCarl, Jr.

The floral, carpetlike interior of the coverlet is surrounded by rows of locomotives on the borders; double weave in red and blue wool and natural cotton. The bust in the corner is said to be the president of the Hemfield Railroad, the opening of which this coverlet pattern is thought to commemorate. Weavers believed to have produced coverlets in this pattern include Daniel Campbell, William Harper, Martin Burns, George Coulter, and Harvey Cook. Weaver unidentified, possibly West Virginia or Pennsylvania, ca. 1840–1850. Collection of Mr. and Mrs. Foster McCarl, Jr. See color plate facing page 103.

WISE, H. He was weaving in Leacock Township, Pennsylvania (Lancaster Co.), in 1838 and 1839. 2, 1838 and 1839.

WISSLER, John (1816–1896). Born in Lancaster County, Pennsylvania, he appears in the C.C.G.A., Safford and Bishop, and Kovel and Kovel as weaving in Milton, Indiana (Wayne Co.), in 1826. Montgomery states that the Wissler family moved to Wayne County, Indiana, in 1828. After his marriage in 1833, Wissler moved south of Milton and opened a weaving shop. During the next eleven years many weavers worked with him, including John Marr, John Snyder, Henry Adolf, and possibly Peter Lorenz (see entries). The Wisslers moved to Milton in 1844, where he is identified in the 1850 U. S. census as a coverlet weaver, in the 1860 census as a carpenter, and in the 1870 census as a coverlet weaver. By the 1870s he was mostly weaving grain sacks and carpeting. The family came from Holland and originally spelled their name Whisler; several coverlets have this spelling. In order to conform to the usage preferred by other Indiana relatives, John changed his name to Wissler in 1841, states Montgomery. 9, 1838–1846.

WITMER, Jacob (ca. 1814–ca. 1887). Born in Pennsylvania, he is located by Reinert and Kovel and Kovel in Lancaster County, Pennsylvania, in 1838. The C.C.G.A. and Safford and Bishop place Witmer there in 1841. The 1850 U. S. census for Manor Township, Lancaster Co., includes him as a coverlet weaver. He is probably the Jacob H. Witmer who died in Lancaster City in early 1887, an inventory of whose estate valued tools for making carpets at $3. Lancaster County Courthouse. 27, 1837–1851.

WITT, ———. According to the C.C.G.A., Kovel and Kovel, and Safford and Bishop, Witt was weaving in New York in 1847. The New York State Historical Association, Cooperstown, also gives a date of 1848. *

WOHE, W. He is included by Safford and Bishop as weaving in Pittsford, Michigan (Hillsdale Co.), in 1860. See entry for W. Wolfe. *

WOLF, Adam (ca. 1816– ). Born in Pennsylvania, he appears in the C.C.G.A., Kovel and Kovel, and Safford and Bishop as weaving in Ohio in 1849. The 1850 U. S. census identifies Wolf as a coverlet weaver in Blooming Grove, Ohio (Richland Co.). 1 (Pennsylvania), 1835; 20 (Ohio), 1843–1852.

WOLF, H. He was weaving in Ohio. 3, 1852–1858.

WOLF, William. The O.H.S. locates Wolf in Hanover, Ohio (Licking Co.), in 1836. 2 (one attributed), 1836.

WOLFE, W. He is listed by Safford and Bishop as weaving in Pittsford, Michigan (Hillsdale Co.), in 1860. This is the same weaver they identify as "W. Wohe," who was weaving there in 1860. *

WOOD, J. C. ( –1860). According to the O.H.S., Wood was weaving in East Village, Ohio (Ashtabula Co.), in 1836. He is probably the John C. Wood who died on March 26, 1860, in East Ashtabula, Ohio (Ashtabula Co.). *

WOODCOCKE, ———. Woodcocke operated a coverlet weaving business with a man named Frederick in Middle Woodberry Township, Pennsylvania (Bedford Co.), in 1850. According to the 1850 U. S. census of manufacturers, the establishment used water power, had three looms, and employed three men. Woodcocke's firm produced 1,000 coverlets valued at $500 annually, as well as other woven goods. *

WOODRING, ———. Woodring was weaving in Allentown, Pennsylvania (Lehigh Co.), with a weaver named John Seidenspinner (see entry). They signed

*The steamboats on the interior of this coverlet are said to commemorate a race between The Fox and The Lark on the Monongahela River in Pennsylvania on July 4, year unknown; double weave in blue wool and white cotton. Weaver unidentified, possibly Ohio, ca. 1835–1845. Collection of the Colonial Coverlet Guild of America.*

The floral interior is bordered by eagles and stars, while Washington on horseback and the motto "United We Stand, Divided We Fall" appears in each corner block; double weave in blue wool and white cotton. Woven by James Cunningham, Oneida Co., N. Y., 1845. Collection of Mr. and Mrs. Foster McCarl, Jr.

their work "Manufactured by Woodring and Seidenspinner in Allentown." He is probably the David Woodring included in the 1860 Allentown city directory as a weaver boarding on Union Street near Seventh Street. A 45-year-old Pennsylvania-born carpet weaver, William David Woodring, appears in the 1870 U. S. census of Emmaus, Pennsylvania (Lehigh Co.). One undated coverlet made by Woodring and Seidenspinner is known.

WOOLRICH WOOLEN MILLS. See entry for John Rich.

WORLEY, W. C. Madden locates Worley in Lewistown, Illinois (Fulton Co.); the dates are unknown. *

WUNTERLICH, John. Coverlet inscriptions indicate he was weaving in Norton Township, Ohio (Summit Co.), in 1857 and 1858. 2, 1857 and 1858.

## Y

YARDY, C. See entry for Christian Yordy.

YEAROUS, Adam (ca. 1827–    ). Born in Germany, he is included as a weaver in the 1850 U. S. census for Jackson Township, Ohio (Knox Co.). 4, 1847–1867.

YEAROUS, F. He is identified by the C.C.G.A., Kovel and Kovel, and Safford and Bishop as weaving in Ashland County, Ohio, in 1853. Recorded coverlets reveal that he was in Loudonville, Ashland County, from at least 1840 to 1858. 18, 1840–1858.

Interior design featuring soldiers with drawn swords on horseback; double weave in blue wool and white cotton. Weaver unidentified, possibly New York, 1838. Collection of Mr. and Mrs. Foster McCarl, Jr.

YERGIN, William K. (ca. 1813–    ). Born in Pennsylvania, he is described as a joiner in the 1850 U. S. census for Sugar Creek Township, Ohio (Wayne Co.). 4, 1850–1852.

YINGST, David (ca. 1818–1889). A native of Pennsylvania, Yingst appears in the 1842 tax roll for Lebanon borough, Pennsylvania (Lebanon Co.), as a weaver living in the household of Emanuel Meily, Jr. (see entry), also a weaver. The 1848 tax list and the 1850 U. S. census for Lebanon County both identify Yingst as a weaver, while the 1860 Lebanon city directory indicates that he was weaving on Hill Street at the corner of Market Street. An inventory of his belongings taken in 1889 includes looms, spinning wheels, and other textile equipment. Lebanon County Courthouse. 3, 1854.

YORDY, Benjamin (ca. 1820–    ). Yordy was in Pennsylvania and appears as a weaver in the 1850 U. S. census for Conestoga Township, Pennsylvania (Lancaster Co.). In his household was Thomas Patterson (see entry), a 69-year-old Pennsylvania-born weaver. 3, 1853–1858.

YORDY, Christian (ca. 1811–    ). Born in Pennsylvania, he is identified by Reinert as weaving in West Lampeter Township, Pennsylvania (Lancaster Co.), in 1840. From recorded coverlets, it has been learned that Yordy was weaving in Conestoga Township (Lancaster Co.) in 1835 and 1836, in Lampeter Square (Lancaster Co.) between 1837 and 1839, and in the borough of Willow Street (Lancaster Co.) from at least 1841 to 1852. The 1850 U. S. Lancaster County census includes Yordy as a coverlet weaver. The C.C.G.A., Kovel and Kovel, and Safford and Bishop list a "C. Yardy" as weaving in Lampeter Square in 1853; this is probably Christian Yordy. 32, 1835–1852.

YOUNG, ———. According to the O.H.S., Young was weaving in Cincinnati, Ohio (Hamilton Co.), in the 1840s. *

YOUNG, Abraham. One coverlet by Abraham Young, woven in Walkersville, Maryland (Frederick Co.), has been recorded. 1, 1840.

YOUNG, Charles. He is identified in the 1835 tax list for Mechanicsburg, Pennsylvania (Cumberland Co.), as a mason; in 1838 as weaving and coloring; and from 1841 to 1844 as a weaver owning a two-story brick house and a frame weaving shop. He bought real estate on the south side of Main Street in Mechanicsburg from John T. Williams (see entry), a coverlet weaver, in 1840, and sold it in 1844 to Henry and Andrew Seifert (see entries) coverlet weavers from York County, Pennsylvania. 12, 1836–1843.

YOUNG, John. He is described by W. W. Reilly & Co. as a coverlet weaver at Fort Jefferson, Ohio (Darke Co.), in 1853. *

Young, John (ca. 1804– ). He is identified as a weaver in the 1850 U. S. census for Center Township, Indiana (Lake Co.). Montgomery says that Young was born in New York, relocated in Pennsylvania, but moved back to New York and then to Indiana around 1843. *

Young, Matthew (1813–1890). Born in Kilmarnock, Ayrshire, Scotland, Young and his wife immigrated to America in 1852. They joined James Craig (see entry), Young's brother-in-law, in Canton, Indiana (Washington Co.), and the two men wove together for the next thirteen years, according to Montgomery. Craig left in 1864, but Young remained until 1881, when he moved to Greensburg, Indiana (Decatur Co.). Since they wove together, it is impossible to determine which coverlets were woven by Craig and which by Young. 6, undated and attributed to Craig and Young.

Young, N. One coverlet by this weaver dated 1839 has been recorded; the location of manufacture is unknown. N. Young may be the Nathaniel Young who, according to White, traveled around Bergen and Hudson counties in New Jersey. Two additional coverlets, dated 1837 and made for John and Ellen Winner, have been ascribed to Nathaniel Young by Winner family descendants.

Young, Peter (ca. 1826– ). Born in Bavaria, Germany, he is listed as a coverlet weaver in the third ward of Allentown, Pennsylvania (Lehigh Co.), in the 1860 U. S. census. *

## Z

Zarn, George. According to Reinert, Zarn was weaving in Schaefferstown, Pennsylvania (Lebanon Co.), in 1843. Tax records of Heidelberg Township (Lebanon Co.), for 1848 identify him as a laborer. Pennsylvania State Archives, Harrisburg. 1, 1843.

Zelner, Aaron (1812–1893). Zelner was born in Pennsylvania, where he learned to weave in Bucks County. He was weaving in Plumstead Township (Bucks Co.), in 1840. By 1845 he had moved to Canada and wove there until his death, according to Burnham and Burnham. 1, 1840.

Zinck, John L. (ca. 1827–1880). Born in Gunzenhausen, Bavaria, Germany, he came to the United States with his parents at the age of 9. In 1851 he advertised in York, Pennsylvania (York Co.), papers that he was starting a coverlet weaving business. He appears in the 1850 U. S. census for York as a carpet weaver using two hand-powered looms; he employed one man at that time. He is also identified in the York tax records as a butcher, and by 1863, as a beer dispenser; in 1868 and 1869 he had a saloon in York. Identifying him as a well-known citizen, Zinck's obituary does not mention his weaving. *Hanover Spectator*, January 14, 1880. *

Zoar. See entry for Gottfried Kappel.

Zufall, Moses (ca. 1830– ). Zufall is included in the 1850 U. S. census for Somerset Township, Pennsylvania (Somerset Co.), as a Pennsylvania-born weaver living in the household of Aaron Casebeer (see entry). *

One-quarter section of a coverlet pattern depicting many Masonic symbols, among which are a beehive, representing industry, a key (Masonic secrets), and a square, level, and compass (the Masonic code of conduct); double weave in blue wool and white cotton. Weaver unidentified, possibly New York, ca. 1835–1840. Scottish Rite Museum of Our National Heritage, Lexington, Mass., gift of Mr. and Mrs. Foster McCarl, Jr.

# Supplementary List

## WEAVERS DISCOVERED SINCE THE CHECKLIST WAS FIRST PUBLISHED

Brailer, Augustin. The single coverlet recorded for this weaver indicates that he was active in 1847, location unknown. 1, 1847.

Davis, E. One coverlet with this name and the date 1832 has been recorded. It is not known whether Davis was the weaver or the client.

Davis, J. The single coverlet recorded for this weaver indicates that he was active in 1850, location unknown. 1, 1850.

Ely, Edwin. One coverlet with this name but no date or location has been recorded; it is not known whether Ely was the weaver or the client.

Heffner, ———. One coverlet bearing this weaver's name, an 1856 date, and a Muncie, Indiana (Delware Co.), location has been recovered. 1, 1856.

Henning, A. A single coverlet with this name, an 1847 date, and a Sucer Creek, Ohio (Stark Co.), location has been recorded. It is not known whether Henning was the weaver or the client.

Hesse, F. A single coverlet with the date 1849 and this name has been recorded; it is not known if Hesse was the weaver or the client.

Landis, M. A. A single coverlet bearing this name, an 1849 date, and Leacock Township, Pennsylvania (Lancaster Co.), has been recorded. Whether Landis was the weaver or the client is unknown.

Lehr, George. (1795–1871). Born in Mountainville, Pennsylvania (Lehigh Co.), he moved to Weathersfield (later Oldtown), Ohio (Mahoning Co.), by 1838. In 1840 he moved to New Baltimore, Ohio (Stark Co.), and in 1843 to Wayne County, Ohio where he is said to have established a weaving business.*

Morgan, William S. Two coverlets with this weaver's name, "Somerset Co., and the date 1871 have been recorded.

Nusser, Christian. Two coverlets woven by Nusser in Findlay, Ohio (Hancock Co.), have been recorded. 2; 1 dated 1844.

Oberholser, Jacob. One coverlet with this name and the date 1851 has been recorded; it is not known whether Oberholser was the weaver or the client.

Satler, J. M. Woven in Farmington, Illinois (Fulton Co.), in 1846, one coverlet with this name has been recorded. It is not known if Satler was the weaver or the client.

Sutherland, H. A coverlet with this name has been recorded, but it is not known whether Sutherland was the weaver or the client.

Wiggins, C. One coverlet made by this weaver, located at "DeKalb" in 1840, has been recorded. 1, 1840.

# Trademarks

*Gilmour Brothers*

A WEAVER sometimes identified himself as the maker of a particular coverlet with a trademark rather than by using his name or initials. This section illustrates nineteen trademarks and identifies the weavers who employed them.

Coverlet signature blocks of weavers who routinely combined their names with a trademark are not pictured because the identification is obvious. In other cases, it is difficult to distinguish whether a particular pictorial motif is a trademark or simply an element of the overall coverlet design. A specific motif may appear to be a weaver's trademark, but when only one or two related coverlets have been recorded, the evidence is so limited that we are unable to arrive at a definitive conclusion.

Only those trademarks that can be fully documented and supported by our index are included here. Many more trademarks undoubtedly exist, and continued research should uncover new ones and substantiate those now held in question.

Charles Adolf

Craig Family

I. Christie

Thomas Cranston

Cockfair Mills

Gilmour Brothers

Samuel Graham
(after 1850)

Klein Family

Samuel Graham
(before 1850, for the most part)

John LaTourette

David Haring

Sarah and Henry LaTourette

[ 127 ]

John Henry Meily

John Rogers

Muir Family

Samuel Stinger

Matthew Rattray

Harry Tyler (lion)

[ 128 ]

*Harry Tyler (eagle)*

# Where To See Coverlets

THE range of colors, textures, and patterns so vital to coverlet design are best appreciated when viewed firsthand, and fortunately, excellent and exciting Jacquard-type coverlets are to be seen nationwide. Some form a part of fine private collections, while many others are housed in museums, historical societies, and university collections.

Although by no means inclusive, the following list provides a starting point for those interested. Due to space limitations and the fragile nature of textiles, many of these museums cannot have coverlets on constant display. Prior appointments are often advisable and always appreciated.

**California**
  Charles W. Bowers Memorial Museum, 2002 N. Main Street, Santa Ana.
**Colorado**
  The Denver Art Museum, 100 W. 14th Avenue Parkway, Denver.
**Connecticut**
  Litchfield Historical Society, On-the-Green, Litchfield.
  Stamford Historical Society, Inc., 713 Bedford Street, Stamford.
**Delaware**
  The Henry Francis du Pont Winterthur Museum, Winterthur.
**District of Columbia**
  Daughters of the American Revolution Museum, 1776 D Street, N.W.
  The National Museum of History and Technology (Smithsonian Institution) 14th Street and Constitution Avenue, N.W.
**Illinois**
  Art Institute of Chicago, Michigan Avenue & Adams Street, Chicago.
  Chicago Historical Society, North Avenue & Clark Street, Chicago.
  Illinois State Museum, Spring & Edward streets, Springfield.

World Heritage Museum, University of Illinois at Urbana-Champaign, 484 Lincoln Hall, Urbana.

**Indiana**
Children's Museum of Indianapolis, Inc., 3010 N. Meridian Street, Indianapolis.
Conner Prairie Pioneer Settlement, 30 Conner Lane, Noblesville.
Indiana State Museum, 202 N. Alabama Street, Indianapolis.
Indianapolis Museum of Art, 1200 W. 38th Street, Indianapolis.
The Northern Indiana Historical Society, 112 S. Lafayette Boulevard, South Bend.
Tippecanoe County Historical Museum, 909 South Street, Lafayette.

**Maryland**
The Baltimore Museum of Art, Art Museum Drive, Baltimore.

**Massachusetts**
Historic Deerfield, The Street, Deerfield.
Merrimack Valley Textile Museum, 800 Massachusetts Avenue, North Andover.
Old Sturbridge Village, Sturbridge.

**Michigan**
Greenfield Village and Henry Ford Museum, Oakwood Boulevard, Dearborn.
Kimball House Museum, 196 Capital Avenue, N.E., Battle Creek.

**New Jersey**
Monmouth County Historical Association, 70 Court Street, Freehold.
The Newark Museum, 49 Washington Street, Newark.
Pascack Historical Society, 19 Ridge Avenue, Park Ridge.

**New Mexico**
Museum of International Folk Art, Camino Lejo, Santa Fe.

**New York**
Adirondack Center Museum, Court Street, Elizabethtown.
Albany Institute of History & Art, 125 Washington Avenue, Albany.
American Life Foundation and Study Institute, Old Irelandville, Watkins Glen.
Huntington Historical Society, 2 High Street, Huntington.
Jefferson County Historical Society, 228 Washington Street, Watertown.
The Landmark Society of Western New York, 130 Spring Street, Rochester.
Metropolitan Museum of Art, Fifth Avenue at 82nd Street, New York City.
New York Historical Society, 170 Central Park West, New York City.
New York State Historical Association, Lake Road, Cooperstown.

**Ohio**
Campus Martius Museum, 601 2nd Street, Marietta.
Cincinnati Art Museum, Eden Park, Cincinnati.
Clark County Historical Society, 300 W. Main Street, Springfield.
Columbus Gallery of Fine Arts, 480 E. Broad Street, Columbus.
Dunham Tavern Museum, 6709 Euclid Avenue, Cleveland.
The Massillon Museum, 212 Lincoln Way, East, Massillon.
Milan Historical Museum, 10 Edison Drive, Milan.
Ohio Historical Center, I-71 and 17th Avenue, Columbus.
Wayne County Historical Museum, 546 E. Bowman Street, Wooster.

**Pennsylvania**
    Allentown Art Museum, Fifth and Court streets, Allentown.
    Historical Society of Berks County, 940 Centre Avenue, Reading.
    The Historical Society of York County, 250 E. Market Street, York.
    Lehigh County Historical Society, 414 Walnut Street, Allentown.
    Old Economy Village, 14th and Church streets, Ambridge.
    Packwood House Museum, 10 Market Street, Lewisburg.
    Pennsylvania Farm Museum of Landis Valley, 2451 Kissel Hill Road, Lancaster.
    Philadelphia Museum of Art, 26th Street & Benjamin Franklin Parkway, Philadelphia.
    William Penn Memorial Museum, Third and North streets, Harrisburg.

**Rhode Island**
    Museum of Art, Rhode Island School of Design, 224 Benefit Street, Providence.

**Tennessee**
    Houston Antiques Museum, 201 N. High Street, Chattanooga.

**Texas**
    The Bayou Bend Collection, #1 Westcott, Houston.
    University of Texas at Austin, Winedale Museum, Round Top.

**Vermont**
    Shelburne Museum, U. S. Route 7, Shelburne.

**Virginia**
    Abby Aldrich Rockefeller Folk Art Center, Williamsburg.
    Valentine Museum, 1015 E. Clay Street, Richmond.

**Wisconsin**
    Elvehjem Art Center, University of Wisconsin at Madison, 800 University Avenue, Madison.

**Canada**
    Ontario Science Centre, 770 Don Mills Road, Toronto, Ontario.

**England**
    American Museum, Claverton Manor, Bath.
    John Judkyn Memorial, Freshford Manor, Bath.

# Glossary

**Beiderwand**   German term for a compound weave consisting of a warp-faced plain weave combined with a weft-faced plain weave. It is characterized by the vertical alignment of the pattern and is color reversible.

***Binding System**   System in accordance with which warp ends and weft picks are bound.

***Bobbin**   Tube of wood, paper, or other material on which the weft is wound for insertion in the shuttle.

**Cochineal**   Dyestuff made from the dried crushed bodies of an insect (*Dactylopius coccus*) native to South America. Colors produced vary from pinkish purple shades to scarlet, depending on the mordant.

***Compound Weave**   Weave in which the weft or the warp is divided into two or more series, one of which appears on the face and the other on the reverse.

***Construction**   The weave or combination of weaves of which a textile is composed.

**Coverlet, Coverlid**   Both words may be traced back to the fourteenth century and refer to a bedcover, usually of wool and cotton, but occasionally of wool and linen, that is woven on a loom. "Couvrir" is from the French and means "to cover;" "lit" means "bed."

***Damask**   Figured textile with one warp and one weft in which the pattern is formed by a contrast of binding systems. In its classic form, it is reversible, the contrast being produced by the use of warp and weft faces of the same weave. By extension, two distinct binding systems may also be employed.

**Diaper**   A fabric having a small, allover repeating pattern; a diamond or birdseye. (Not necessarily a damask.)

**Double Cloth Weave**   Two cloths, woven simultaneously, one above the other, being interwoven at specified intervals to form an allover patterned cloth in which the colors are reversible from front to back.

***Draft**   A diagram for setting up the loom; a complete draft shows the order of entering the warp ends in the heddles, the arrangement for connecting the shafts and the treadles, and the shedding order.

**Drawboy**  The workman who pulls the lashes on a drawloom.

**Drawloom**  A hand loom for weaving figured textiles, which is equipped with a special type of figure harness that controls some or all of the warp ends. This drawloom figure harness consists of the leashes. In the most developed type of drawloom, the leashes are connected with necking cords which, after passing through the comber board, are attached to pulley cords. After passing through the pulley box, they become the tail cords to which the cords of the simple are attached. The cords controlling the drawloom figure harness permit the automatic repeat of a pattern in the width of the textile by joining the necking cords that correspond to the different comber units to each pulley cord. The automatic repeat of the pattern in the length of the textile is repeated by means of lashes attached to the tail cords or to the simple.

**Dyestuff**  Coloring substance used in dyeing.

**Face**  The right side of a textile or weave. By extension, in the terms warp-face and weft-face, it is used for the side on which the warp or the weft predominates.

**Float**  The segment of end or pick that crosses at least two yarns between the points of binding.

**Fly Shuttle**  An attachment invented by John Kay in England in 1733. A means of propelling the shuttle by battens or picker sticks mounted on either side of the loom, connected by a cord manipulated by the weaver as he simultaneously operated the treadles to open the shed. This attachment allowed a single person to weave wide (broad) cloths where previously at least two operators were necessary.

**Ground**  The field or background of the pattern.

**Ground Fabric**  Any construction that serves as a foundation for pattern, texture, or pile.

**Ground Harness**  The harness that operates the ends forming the ground weave when additional harnesses are also in operation.

**Hand Loom**  All looms, including the Jacquard, which are not operated by power and require a human operator to perform certain of the weaving operations. The term is often used, wrongly, instead of shaft loom to distinguish a loom with shafts from a drawloom.

**Hank**  Skein of thread or yarn that contains a standard number of yards, usually 840 for cotton and 560 for wool.

**Harness**  A group of shafts or leashes that perform one function in the weaving of a textile. The term is also applied to all the shafts in a loom.

**Heddle**  The loop of thread, or other material, through which an end is passed so that it may be raised or lowered to open the shed, permitting the passage of the pick. In a shaft loom, the heddles are suspended between upper and lower bars.

**Heddle Bars**  The wooden or metal bars between which the heddles are suspended to form the shaft.

**Indigo** (*Indigofera tinctora*)  The fermented leaves of this shrub are used for a dyestuff to produce a strong, fast blue.

**Ingrain Carpet**  Double cloth carpeting, also known as Scotch, Kidderminster, and Kilmarnock. The name ingrain possibly comes from the fact that the materials used in the production of the carpet were dyed "in the grain," i.e., in the fiber.

***Jacquard-Equipped Loom***   A loom developed from the drawloom in which the simple, lashes, and drawboy are replaced by a mechanism employing punched cards for the automatic selection and pulling of the cords.

**Jeans**   A twill-woven heavy cotton fabric.

*__Lashes__   The loops of cord attached to the simple or to the tail cords of a drawloom that enable the drawboy to select and pull the cords controlling the warp ends that must be raised. The successive groups of warp ends are selected by means of the lashes; they are arranged in the simple or the tail cords before weaving, according to the required pattern.

*__Loom__   Any device on which a warp may be arranged and sheds formed by a shedding mechanism for the passage of picks. In its simplest form, a loom may be a single bar from which ends are stretched. More developed looms are the drawloom, the Jacquard-equipped loom, the power loom, and the shaft loom.

**Madder** (*Rubia tinctorum*)   A plant native to Asia Minor; red dyestuff is obtained from the root of the plant.

*__Main Warp__   The principal, or only, warp in a textile.

*__Main Weft__   The principal, or only, weft in a textile.

**Mordant**   Substance used to fix dyestuffs, such as tannic acid or salts.

*__Overshot Weave__   A supplementary weft thread which, with long skips or passes, "overshoots" the foundation warp threads to form a geometric pattern.

*__Pattern__   Design for the cloth.

*__Pattern Weft__   Weft, auxiliary to the main weft, passed from selvage to selvage to enrich the ground or to form a pattern.

*__Pick__   A single passage of the shuttle through the shed, carrying one or more weft threads. By extension, it is the weft threads so carried.

**Point of Binding**   Point at which an end is bound by a pick, or a pick by an end.

*__Power Loom__   A loom that does not require a human operator to perform any of the weaving operations, but which, once set up, operates independently by mechanical means.

**Quilt**   A bedcovering that has been wrought with a needle as distinct from an item woven on a loom.

*__Reed__   The instrument used to keep the warp ends evenly spaced and aligned. It is fastened in the batten, and serves to beat in the weft. It is generally of metal leaves fastened between two bars of wood or metal.

*__Reversible__   Having either side usable as the face.

*__Selvage__   The longitudinal edge of a textile, often distinguished by warp ends differing from those in the body of the textile, and sometimes by a change in the binding from the rest of the fabric.

*__Shaft__   A group of heddles fixed side by side so that they may be moved together at the same time. Most commonly the shaft consists of a series of heddles between two horizontal bars.

*__Shaft Loom__   A loom with shafts to raise and lower the warp. Frequently misnamed hand loom.

*Shed   The opening in the warp that permits the passage of the shuttle and thereby the pick.

*Shoot   See Pick.

*Shuttle   Tool by which the pick is passed through the shed in the warp. It holds the bobbin with the weft threads.

*Summer and Winter   A modern American term that refers to a weave which consists of a cotton or linen warp woven with a pattern of wool closely interwoven with the warp threads. Color and pattern reverse themselves causing the pattern to appear dark on light on one side and light on dark on the other.

*Tabby   Binding system or weave based on a unit of two ends and two picks, in which each end passes over one and under one pick, the points of binding being set over one end on successive picks.

*Treadle   A foot pedal of a loom, operated by the weaver to raise or lower a shaft.

*Treadling   The action of raising and lowering the shafts by means of the treadles in order to produce sheds for the passage of the weft.

*Twill   Binding system or weave requiring three or more ends and three or more picks in which, if the shift is always to the right or always to the left, continuous diagonals will be formed on both faces of the fabric.

*Warp (noun)   The longitudinal threads of a textile; those that are arranged on the loom. A single thread of warp is called an end. Alone, the term warp denotes all the warp ends in a textile. Suitably qualified, it denotes all the warp ends engaged in a specific function.

*Warp (verb)   To prepare the warp for the loom.

*Warp-Face   Term used to describe a weave or textile in which the warp predominates on one or both sides.

*Weave (noun)   System of interlacing ends and picks on a loom according to a predetermined pattern.

*Weave (verb)   To make a textile on a loom by interlacing warp and weft in a specific order.

*Weft   The transverse threads of a textile; those which are passed through the sheds. Also woof. Alone, the term weft denotes all the picks in a textile.

*Weft-Faced   Term used to describe a weave or textile in which the weft predominates on one or both sides.

The asterisked terms in this glossary have been taken from the Centre International d'Etude des Textiles Anciens, Lyons, France, which published its vocabulary in 1964.

# Bibliography

ANDERSON, IRMA PILLING. "Ohio Coverlets." *Antiques*, XLIX (January 1946), pp. 56–57.
BALTIMORE MUSEUM OF ART. *The Great American Cover-Up: Counterpanes of the Eighteenth and Nineteenth Centuries.* Baltimore: Baltimore Museum of Art, 1971.
BIRRELL, VERLA. *The Textile Arts, A Handbook of Fabric Structure and Design Processes: Ancient and Modern Weaving, Braiding, Printing, and Other Textile Techniques.* New York: Harper & Brothers, 1959.
BOYD, WILLIAM H. *Business Directory of the Counties of Adams, Bucks, Chester, Cumberland, Dauphin, Delaware, Franklin, Lancaster, Montgomery, and York.* Philadelphia: William H. Boyd, 1860.
———. *Business Directory of the Counties of Berks, Lebanon, Lehigh, Northampton, and Schuylkill.* Philadelphia: William H. Boyd, 1860.
———. *Lancaster County Directory.* Lancaster: Sprenger & Westhaffer, 1859.
BRADSBY, H. C. *History of Bradford County, Pennsylvania, with Biographical Selections . . .* Chicago: S. B. Nelson & Co., 1891.
BRIDGENS, H. F. *Bridgens' Atlas of Lancaster County, Pennsylvania.* Lancaster: D. S. Bare, 1864.
BURNETT, LYNN HASTINGS. "The Coverlets of Daniel Stephenson, Weaver." *Antiques Journal*, XXIX (July 1974), pp. 18–21, 46–47.
BURNHAM, HAROLD B., AND BURNHAM, DOROTHY K. *"Keep Me Warm One Night": Early Handweaving in Eastern Canada.* Toronto: University of Toronto Press, 1972.
CHAPMAN, ETTA TYLER. "The Tyler Coverlets." *Antiques*, XIII (March 1928), pp. 215–218.
*Commemorative Biographical Record of Prominent & Representative Men of Indianapolis & Vicinity.* Chicago: J. H. Beers & Co., 1908.
CRAFT AND FOLK ART MUSEUM. *Nineteenth Century American Coverlets.* Los Angeles: Craft and Folk Art Museum, 1976.

Davison, Mildred. "Five related coverlets." *Antiques*, CII (October 1972), pp. 650–652.

Davison, Mildred, and Mayer-Thurman, Christa C. *Coverlets: A Handbook on the Collection of Woven Coverlets in The Art Institute of Chicago.* Chicago: Art Institute of Chicago, 1973.

Denver Art Museum. *Quilts and Coverlets.* Denver: Denver Art Museum, 1974.

Doyle, William B., ed. and comp. *Centennial History of Summit County, Ohio, and Representative Citizens.* Chicago: Biographical Publishing Co., 1908.

Elvehjem Art Center. *American Coverlets of the Nineteenth Century from the Helen Louise Allen Textile Collection.* Madison: University of Wisconsin Press, 1974.

Fairbanks, Jonathan. "The Harry Tyler Coverlets." *House Beautiful*, LXII (November 1927), p. 537.

French, S., et al., comps. *New York State Mercantile Union Business Directory Carefully Collected & Arranged for 1850–1851.* New York: S. French, L. C. & H. L. Pratt, 1850.

Galley, Henrietta, and Arnold, J. O. *History of the Galley Family with Local and Old-Time Sketches in the Yough Region.* Rev. ed. Greensburg: C. Henry Printing Co., 1968.

Hall, Eliza Calvert [pseud.] *A Book of Hand-woven Coverlets.* Boston: Little, Brown & Co., 1912.

Hawes, George W., comp. *George W. Hawes' Ohio State Gazetteer and Business Directory, for 1859 and 1860.* Cincinnati: George W. Hawes, 1859.

Heald, Edward Thornton. *The Stark County Story.* I: 1805–1874, II: 1875–1901. Canton: Stark County Historical Society, 1949.

*History of Bedford, Somerset and Fulton Counties, Pennsylvania.* Chicago: Waterman, Watkins & Co., 1884.

*History of Cumberland and Adams Counties, Pennsylvania . . .* Chicago: Warner, Beers & Co., 1886.

*History of Miami County, Ohio . . .* Chicago: W. H. Beers & Co., 1880.

*History of Tuscarawas County, Ohio . . .* Chicago: Warner, Beers & Co., 1884.

Horstmann, Wm. H. Co. *One Hundred Years, 1816–1916; The Chronicles of an Old Business House in the City of Philadelphia.* Philadelphia: Wm. H. Horstmann Co., 1916.

Huber, Charles H., comp. *Schaefferstown, Pennsylvania, 1763–1963.* Schaefferstown: Schaefferstown Bicentennial Committee, 1963.

Kovel, Ralph, and Kovel, Terry. *Know Your Antiques: How To Recognize and Evaluate any Antique—Large or Small—Like an Expert.* New York: Crown Publishers, 1973.

Linn, John Blair. *History of Centre and Clinton Counties, Pennsylvania.* Philadelphia: L. H. Everts, 1883.

Lord, Priscilla S., and Foley, Daniel J. *The Folk Arts and Crafts of New England.* Philadelphia: Clinton Books, 1965.

Madden, Betty I. *Arts, Crafts, and Architecture in Early Illinois.* Urbana: University of Illinois Press, 1974.

*Manufactories and Manufacturers of the Pennsylvania of the Nineteenth Century.* Philadelphia: Galaxy Publishing Co., 1875.

MONTGOMERY, MORTON L., comp. *Historical and Biographical Annals of Berks County, Pennsylvania.* Chicago: J. H. Beers Co., 1909.

MONTGOMERY, PAULINE. *Indiana Coverlet Weavers and Their Coverlets.* Indianapolis: Hoosier Heritage Press, 1974.

PARSLOW, VIRGINIA D. "James Alexander, weaver." *Antiques,* LXIX (April 1956), pp. 346–349.

PECK, JESSIE FARRALL. "Weavers of New York's Historical Coverlets." *Antiques,* XVIII (July 1930), pp. 22–25.

PERRIN, WILLIAM HENRY, ed. *History of Stark County, with an Outline Sketch of Ohio.* Chicago: Baskin & Battey, 1881.

RABB, KATE MILNER. "Indiana Coverlets and Coverlet Weavers." Indiana Historical Society, *Publications,* VIII (1928).

RAMSAY, JOHN. "Zoar and Its Industries." *Antiques,* XLVI (December 1944), pp. 333–335.

REILLY, W. W. & Co. *Ohio State Business Directory for 1853–1854.* Cincinnati: Morgan & Overend, 1853.

REINERT, GUY F. *Coverlets of the Pennsylvania Germans.* Pennsylvania German Folklore Society Yearbook, 1948. Allentown: Pennsylvania German Folklore Society, 1949.

RICH, MICHAEL BOND. *History of the First 100 Years in Woolrich.* Williamsport: Grit Publishing Co., 1930.

ROBACKER, EARL F. *Old Stuff in Up-Country Pennsylvania.* South Brunswick: A. S. Barnes, 1973.

ROBERTS, CHARLES RHOADS, et al., comps. *History of Lehigh County, Pennsylvania, and a Genealogical and Biographical Record of Its Families.* Allentown: Lehigh Valley Publishing Co., 1914.

ROGERS, GRACE L. "Peter Stauffer, Early Nineteenth Century Weaver." *Handweaver & Craftsman,* VII (winter 1955–1956), pp. 12–14, 55.

SAFFORD, CARLTON L., AND BISHOP, ROBERT. *America's Quilts and Coverlets.* New York: E. P. Dutton & Co., 1972.

SELKREG, JOHN H. *Landmarks of Tompkins County, New York.* Syracuse: D. Mason & Co., 1894.

STILL, JOHN S. "Ohio Coverlets." *Museum Echoes,* XXXI (April 1958), pp. 27–30.

SWYGERT, MRS. LUTHER M., ed. *Heirlooms From Old Looms.* Chicago: Colonial Coverlet Guild of America, 1955.

WAGER, DANIEL E., ed. *Our County and Its People: A Descriptive Work on Oneida County, New York.* Boston: Boston History Co., 1896.

WEISS, HARRY B., AND ZIEGLER, GRACE M. *The Early Woolen Industry of New Jersey.* Trenton: New Jersey Agricultural Society, 1958.

WHITE, MARGARET E. *American Hand-Woven Coverlets in the Newark Museum.* Newark: Newark Museum, 1947.

———. "The Pattern Books of Weavers." *Antiques,* LIII (February 1948), pp. 134–135.

———. "Weavers of New Jersey." New Jersey Historical Society, *Proceedings,* LXXXII (October 1964), pp. 283–288.

WILLIAMS BROTHERS. *History of Franklin and Pickaway Counties, Ohio, with Illustrations and Biographical Sketches of Some of the Prominent Men and Pioneers.* Cleveland, 1880.

# Geographical Index

Colorado, 78

Connecticut, 63
  Hartford County
    Thompsonville, 31
  New Haven County
    New Haven, 89, 106
  New London County
    Clark's Falls, 45

Illinois
  Adams County
    Quincy, 37, 100, 115
  Carroll County
    Lanark, 66
  Champaign County, 70
  Clark County, 56, 58
    Casey, 61
    Martinsville, 58
  Clinton County, 100
  Cook County
    New City [now part of Chicago], 35
    Wheeling, 34
  Du Page County
    Naperville, 92
  Edwards County
    Albion, 88
  Effingham County
    Effingham, 68
  Fulton County
    Farmington, 124
    Lewistown, 122
  Hancock County
    Nauvoo, 45
  Iroquois County
    Bluff Springs, 37
    Watseka. *See* Bluff Springs
  Kane County
    Aurora, 82
  Knox County, 100
  La Salle County
    Mendota City, 58
  Lee County
    Dixon, 77
  Menard County, 39
  Peoria County
    Peoria, 93
  Perry County
    Tamaroa, 96
  Saint Clair County
    Belleville, 63, 115
    O'Fallon, 104
    Ridge Prairie, 104
  Shelby County
    Shelbyville, 68
  Stephenson County, 66
  Vermilion County, 78
  Wayne County
    Fairfield, 73
  Woodford County
    Goodfield, 71

Indiana, 112
  Cass County
    Eel Township, 35
  Clark County, 94
  Clay County, 91
    Brazil, 49
  Darke County
    Fort Jefferson, 123
  Dearborn County, 76, 93, 103
    Hubbell's Crossroads, 98
    Jackson Township, 72
    Kelso Township, 72
    Logan Township, 98
  Decatur County, 49, 50, 63, 64
    Greensburg, 49, 50, 123
    Milford, 50
  De Kalb County
    Jackson Township, 93, 108
  Delaware County
    Liberty Township, 89, 91
    Muncie, 124
  Elkhart County
    New Paris, 107
    Washington Township, 107
  Fayette County, 113
  Floyd County, 49–50
    Galena, 81
  Fountain County, 78
    Covington, 78
    Wabash Township, 78
  Franklin County, 50, 54, 63, 64, 81, 115
    Andersonville, 49–50
    Blooming Grove, 39
    Blue Creek, 84
    Brookville, 39, 41, 82, 84, 113, 115
    Fairfield, 52
    Metamora, 92–93
    Mount Carmel, 63
  Fulton County, 102
  Hamilton County, 61, 76, 92
    Adams Township, 81
    Noblesville, 31, 76
  Harrison County, 111

Hendricks County, 118
  Coatesville, 118
Henry County, 31, 56
  New Castle, 65
Jefferson County
  Shelby Township, 50
Johnson County
  Franklin, 38
Knox County
  Vincennes, 106
Kosciusko County
  Van Buren Township, 107
La Grange County, 89
Lake County
  Center Township, 123
La Porte County, 41
Madison County, 70
  Adams Township, 70
  Ovid, 70
Marion County
  Indianapolis, 91
  West Indianapolis, 91
Miami County, 52, 108
  Harrison Township, 52, 107
  Pipe Crick, 107
Montgomery County
  Alamo, 51
  Crawfordsville, 115
Morgan County, 65, 71
Parke County
  Jackson Township, 89
  Wabash Township, 75
Porter County
  Valparaiso, 63
Putnam County
  Fillmore, 89
  Greencastle, 89
  Greencastle Township, 89
Ripley County, 70, 76
Rush County, 76
  Carthage, 98, 110
Saint Joseph County
  South Bend, 58
Shelby County
  Shelbyville, 76
Steuben County, 62
  Brockville, 88
  Fremont. *See* Brockville
Switzerland County, 35, 49, 50, 61, 92
  Caledonia, 106, 107
Tippecanoe County
  Lafayette, 35, 71, 73, 89
Union County, 52, 64
  Brownsville, 111
  Dunlapsville, 64

Harmony Township, 45
Vigo County
  Harrison Township, 74
  Terre Haute, 74
Washington County, 49, 81
  Canton, 49, 123
  Salem, 89, 107
  Washington Township, 89
Wayne County, 31, 82, 92, 110, 120
  Cambridge City, 31
  Dalton Township, 58
  Germantown, 89, 91
  Green Township, 31
  Hagerstown, 71, 111
  Milton, 31, 84, 108, 120
  Richmond, 54, 65, 76, 96
  Washington Township, 98
  Williamsburg, 31
White County, 35

Iowa
  Jefferson County
    Fairfield, 109, 110
  Johnson County, 37
  Mahaska County, 31
    Oskaloosa, 64
  Scott County
    Davenport, 84

Kansas
  Crawford County, 50
  Douglas County, 31
    Clinton, 31
  Osage County, 31

Kentucky, 63, 88, 113
  Barren County
    Glasgow, 62
  Bourbon County, 51
  Fayette County, 51
    Lexington, 53
  Jefferson County
    Louisville, 74
  Pendleton County
    Falmouth, 118
  Scott County, 51, 74
  Shelby County
    Shelbyville, 118

Maine, 65

Maryland, 69, 110
  Baltimore, 61, 75, 76, 84, 113
  Carroll County
    Lineboro, 115
    Westminster, 63

Frederick County
  Beaver Dams, 62
  Graceham, 63
  Johnsville, 66
  Middletown, 46
  Walkersville, 122
Washington County, 95
  Boonsboro, 117
  Hagerstown, 63
  Leitersburg, 65

Massachusetts, 63
  Middlesex County
    Lowell, 50
  Suffolk County
    Roxbury, 53

Michigan, 31
  Branch County
    Kinderhook, 88
  Hillsdale County
    Pittsford, 120
  Oakland County, 112

Missouri, 58, 64, 91
  Livingston County
    Chillicothe, 38
  Saint Charles County
    Hamburg, 102

New Jersey, 77
  Bergen County, 45, 123
    Englewood, 46
    Norwood, 66, 67
    West Norwood, 66–67
  Burlington County
    Lumberton, 117
    Mount Holly, 54, 96, 117
  Camden County
    Camden, 41
  Cumberland County
    Bridgeton, 113
    Centerville, 113
    Dorchester, 91
  Hudson County, 123
  Hunterdon County
    Bethlehem Township, 50
  Passaic County
    Paterson, 102
  Somerset County
    Millstone, 32, 112, 113
  Sussex County, 95
    Montague, 110
    Stillwater, 110
  Union County
    Rahway. *See* Shotwell's

Landing
    Shotwell's Landing, 106
Warren County
    Asbury, 113

New York, 37, 49, 120, 123
  Albany County
    Albany, 95
  Cattaraugus County
    Gowanda. See Lodi
    Lodi, 45, 52. See also Lodi
      (Medina Co.), Ohio
  Cayuga County
    Auburn, 34, 38
  Chautauqua County
    Dunkirk, 78
    Fredonia, 78
    Pomfret, 78
  Chemung County
    Elmira, 46
    Southport, 46
  Cortland County, 72
  Delaware County
    Delhi, 71
  Dutchess County
    Fishkill, 113
  Erie County
    Boston, 111
    Buffalo, 81
  Genesee County
    Bethany, 32, 61, 63, 72, 84, 100, 117
    Mount Morris, 106
  Jefferson County, 42, 100, 112
    Butterville, 111
  Livingston County
    Dansville, 34
    Groveland, 32, 68
  Madison County, 118
    Cazenovia, 61
  New York City, 54
  Niagara County
    Cambria, 110
    Lockport, 63
    Pekin, 35, 66
  Oneida County, 42
    Clinton, 61
    New Hartford, 42, 51
    Oriskany, 42
    Utica, 40
    Waterville, 61
  Onondaga County, 95
    Pompey, 95
    Syracuse, 42
  Orange County, 36, 51
    Balmville, 63
    Little Britain, 31
    Middletown, 111
    Newburgh, 31, 63, 98, 118
  Orleans County, 73
    Kendall Mills, 106
  Oswego County, 111
    Lansing, 53
    Pulaski, 73, 84
  Otsego County
    Middlefield, 65
  Richmond County
    Rossville, 100
  Rockland County
    Tappan, 108
  Saratoga County
    Saratoga, 53
    Saratoga Springs. See Saratoga
  Seneca County
    Geneva, 109
    Ovid, 53. See also Ovid (Franklin Co.), Ohio
  Tompkins County
    Groton, 46
    Ithaca, 52
    West Dryden, 95
  Wayne County
    Palmyra, 66, 113
    Wolcott, 46, 72, 108
  Wyoming County
    Perry, 106
  Yates County
    Benton, 96

Ohio
  Adams County, 115
  Allen County
    La Fayette, 67–68
    Lima, 86
  Ashland County, 122
    Ashland, 40, 41, 82
    Hayesville, 69
    Loudonville, 66, 115, 122
    Nankin. See Orange
    Orange, 82
    Rowsburg, 115
    Sullivan, 78
    West Salem, 107
  Ashtabula County
    East Ashtabula, 120
    East Village, 120
  Belmont County, 84
    Armstrong's Mills, 110
    Farmington, 46
    Morristown, 38, 75
    Saint Clairsville, 41, 71
  Butler County, 70
    Hamilton, 38
    Middletown, 78
    Monroe, 73
    Somerville, 82
  Carroll County
    Carrollton, 32
    Center Township, 32
  Champaign County
    Johnson Township, 118
    Mechanicsburg, 108
  Clark County, 92
    Bethel Township, 92
    German Township, 98
    Madison Township, 92
    Midway, 118
    New Carlisle, 89
    Pike Township, 92
    Springfield, 36, 38, 51, 56, 109
    Tremont City, 98
  Clermont County
    Batavia, 69
  Clinton County
    Wilmington, 32, 67
  Columbiana County, 54, 100
    Chambersburg, 54
    Knox Township, 36, 117
    Lisbon, 45
    New Lisbon, 72
    North Georgetown, 36
    Perry Township, 82
    Salem, 70, 82
  Coshocton County, 52
    Lewisville, 77
    Pike Township, 81
  Crawford County
    Bucyrus, 96, 107
    Poplar, 70
    Vernon Township, 46
  Cuyahoga County
    Cleveland, 66
  Delaware County, 96
  Erie County, 34
  Fairfield County, 106
    Basil, 69, 70
    Bloom Township, 95
    Lancaster, 69, 70
    Lithopolis, 95
    Richland Township, 89
    West Rushville, 89
  Fayette County, 84
  Franklin County
    Canal Winchester, 34, 103
    Columbus, 34, 35, 36, 89
    Madison Township, 34

Montgomery Township, 89
Ovid, 52. *See also* Ovid (Seneca Co.), N.Y.
Fulton County, 41
Gallia County
    Gallipolis, 113
Geauga County
    Chardon, 96
Greene County
    Xenia, 49, 82
Guernsey County
    Cambridge, 94
    Madison Township, 94
    Winterset, 94
Hamilton County
    Cincinnati, 35, 38, 41, 45, 46, 50, 56, 58, 93, 107, 122
    Reading, 35
Hancock County
    English Township, 61
    Findlay, 61, 124
    Jackson Township, 88
Harrison County
    Cadiz, 51, 110
Highland County
    Greenfield, 110
    Hillsboro, 32
Hocking County, 110
    Logan, 37, 70
    Logan Township, 70
    Logan Village, 70
Holmes County, 42, 82
    Salt Creek Township, 110
Huron County
    Monroeville, 37
Jackson County, 75
Jefferson County, 74, 81, 84, 103
    Steubenville, 37, 64, 75, 78, 82, 84, 88
    Yellow Creek, 81
Knox County, 45, 73, 81, 110
    Clinton Township, 98
    Jackson Township, 122
    Mount Vernon, 34, 65
Licking County, 106
    Hanover, 120
    Newark, 37, 45, 56, 61, 89, 110, 111
    Utica, 82
Logan County, 78
    Bellefontaine, 82
Lorain County
    Huntington Township, 78
Madison County
    London, 95

Union Township, 95
Mahoning County
    Canfield, 31
    Cornersburgh, 42
    New Springfield, 39
    North Lima, 36
    Oldtown. *See* Weathersfield
    Springfield Township, 117
    Weathersfield, 124
    Youngstown, 42
Marion County, 61
Medina County, 36
    Brunswick, 73
    Chatham, 94
    Chatham Center, 94
    Chippeway, 94
    Lodi, 52. *See also* Lodi (Cattaraugus Co.), N.Y.
    Medina, 36
Miami County, 34, 49, 61
    Covington, 75, 109, 113
    Newberry Township, 75
    Piqua, 62, 64
    Troy, 49, 109
Monroe County
    Malaga, 93
Montgomery County, 31, 34, 76, 106
    Chambersburg, 70
    Dayton, 111
    Germantown, 78, 110
    German Township, 82
    New Lebanon, 106
Morrow County
    Chesterville, 46
    Woodview, 112
Ottawa County, 77
Perry County
    Reading Township, 61
    Somerset, 70
    Thornville, 46
Pickaway County
    Circleville, 70
Pike County
    Piketon, 61
    Saltcreek Township, 100
    Tarlton, 100
Portage County
    Franklin Township, 70
    Streetsboro, 92
Richland County, 45, 56, 58, 106
    Belleville, 84
    Blooming Grove, 120
    Franklin Township, 93
    Lexington, 36

Madison Township, 86
Mansfield, 86
Mifflin Township, 70, 89
Milton Township, 67
Olney, 69
Troy Township, 96
Washington Township, 105
West Windsor Township, 89
Ross County, 109
    Adelphi, 69–70
    Chillicothe, 41, 70
    Scioto Township, 41
Sandusky County
    Fremont, 84
    Washington Township, 84, 110
Scioto County
    Portsmouth, 96
Seneca County
    Attica, 106
    Bascom, 40
    Hopewell Township, 40, 91
    London Township, 37
    McCutchenville, 88
    Rome, 37
    Thompson Township, 102
Shelby County
    Sidney, 54, 65
    Springville, 109
Stark County, 73, 81, 84, 96, 108, 115
    Bethlehem, 107
    Canton, 51, 71, 81, 82, 86, 95, 107
    Canton Township, 95
    Greentown, 69
    Jackson Township, 81, 106
    Lake Township, 69
    Mapleton, 107
    Massillon, 61
    Navarre. *See* Bethlehem
    New Baltimore, 124
    New Berlin, 37, 81, 106
    North Canton. *See* New Berlin
    Osnaburg Township, 107
    Plain Township, 69, 82, 106
    Sucer Creek, 124
    Sugar Creek Township, 75
    West Brookfield, 71
Summit County, 110
    Coventry Township, 110
    Inland, 110
    New Portage, 42
    Norton Township, 122
Trumbull County, 112

Howland, 86
Vienna Township, 86
Tuscarawas County
  Bolivar, 38, 61
  Canal Dover, 41
  Dundee, 92
  New Philadelphia, 42, 118
  Shanesville, 42
  Strasburg, 63
  Zoar, 73, 93
Warren County, 82, 113
  Dunlevy, 36
Washington County
  Adams Township, 102
  Marietta, 34
Wayne County, 31, 40, 58, 81, 105, 124
  Bristol, 81
  Chester Township, 54, 98
  Cornersburg, 73
  Mansfield, 86
  Marshallville. See Cornersburg
  Perry Township, 67
  Plain Township, 110
  Salt Creek Township, 31
  Shreve, 41
  Sugar Creek Township, 122
  West Lebanon, 86
  Wooster, 67
Wyandot County
  McCutchenville, 61

Pennsylvania
  Adams County, 65
    Fairfield, 61
    Franklin Township, 37–38
    Germany Township, 46
    Gettysburg, 103, 105
    Hamiltonban Township, 61
    Hampton, 103
    Highland Township, 75
    Huntington Township, 65
    Little Marsh Creek, 75
  Beaver County
    Beaver, 110
    Brighton Township, 110
  Bedford County, 63, 65
    Bedford, 115
    Bedford Township, 115
    Harrison Township, 63
    Middle Woodberry Township, 74, 120
    Morrison's Cove, 74
    Woodberry, 74, 82
  Berks County, 54, 65, 69, 78, 98, 100
    Albany Township, 65
    Bethel. See Millersburg
    Bethel Township, 77, 107
    Centre Township, 75
    Friedensburg, 54, 68
    Greenwich Township, 65
    Hamburg, 81, 89
    Heidelberg Township, 66, 102
    Hereford Township, 45
    Kutztown, 88
    Lobachsville, 65, 68, 69
    Maxatawny Township, 65
    Millersburg, 39
    Oley Township, 68, 69
    Pike Township, 65
    Reading, 77, 104
    Robeson Township, 73
    Rockland, 68
    Schartelsville, 89
    Tulpehocken Township, 40
    Union Township, 81
    Upper Bern Township, 58
    Womelsdorf, 40, 74, 93
  Bethel County
    Millersburg [later in Berks Co.], 77
  Blair County
    Blair Township, 52, 88
    Martinsburg, 106
    Newry, 52, 88
  Bradford County, 73
    LeRoy Township, 73
  Bucks County, 42, 72, 73
    Haycock Township, 81
    Hilltown, 91
    Milford, 91
    New Britain Township, 65, 66, 82, 106
    Plumstead Township, 123
    Springfield Township, 37, 73
  Butler County
    Harmony, 71
    Old Economy. See Harmony
  Carbon County
    Weissport, 61
  Centre County
    Aaronsburg, 56, 115
    Haines Township, 56, 115
    Howard, 36
    Pine Grove, 89
    Salona [later in Clinton Co.], 84
  Chester County
    Brandywine, 95
    Bridgeport, 49
    West Caln Township, 95
  Clinton County, 98
    Bald Eagle Township, 58, 84
    Dunstable Township, 98
    Lamar Township, 58, 84, 103
    Larry's Creek, 98
    Mill Hall, 58, 117
    Salona, 58, 84, 103, 106
  Cumberland County
    Mechanicsburg, 105, 117, 118, 122
    Shippensburg, 70
    South Middleton Township, 61
  Dauphin County, 88
    Derry Township, 61
    East Hanover Township, 71
    Harrisburg, 36, 52
    Hummelstown, 61
    Middle Paxton Township, 112
    Millersburg, 96
    Susquehanna Township, 88
    Upper Paxton Township, 96
    West Hanover Township, 112
  Delaware County
    Edgemont, 62
  Fayette County
    Brownsville, 53, 94
    Tyrone Township, 62
    Uniontown, 62
  Franklin County, 34, 35
    Antrim Township, 39
    Chambersburg, 34, 70, 81, 93
    Fayetteville, 38, 49
    Fort Loudon, 49
    Greencastle, 31, 32, 39
    Green Township, 70
    Peters Township, 103
    Washington Township, 35, 38
    Waynesboro, 81
  Greene County
    Ruff's Creek, 62
  Juniata County, 54, 106
  Lancaster County, 78, 81, 112
    Brecknock Township, 109
    Cocalico Township, 81
    Conestoga Township, 122
    Denver, 81
    Earl Township, 91
    East Donegal Township, 63
    East Hempfield Township, 32, 78, 81, 82, 92

[ 147 ]

East Lampeter Township, 45
Elizabethtown, 71
Ephrata Township, 86
Kissel Hill, 52, 66
Lampeter Square, 122
Lampeter Township, 110
Lancaster, 39, 70, 74, 75, 103, 120
Leacock Township, 70, 98, 100, 120, 124
Lititz, 52, 61
Manheim, 39, 40, 104
Manor Township, 32, 120
Maytown, 63
Millersville, 92
Mount Joy, 40, 62, 64, 65, 70, 74, 81, 108
Mount Joy Township, 61, 62
Neffsville, 39
New Holland, 41, 72, 91, 100
New Providence, 70
Providence, 39
Rabbit Hill, 106
Reinholdsville, 81
Strasburg, 45, 70
Vera Cruz, 67
Warwick Township, 52, 66, 73, 86, 92, 106
West Cocalico Township, 67, 81
West Lampeter Township, 122
Willow Street, 122
Lebanon County, 58, 98, 115
Annville. *See* Millerstown
Fredericksburg, 77, 86
Heidelberg Township, 98, 107, 123
Jackson Township, 92
Lebanon, 86, 106, 122
Millerstown, 70, 86, 107
Myerstown, 92
Schaefferstown, 81, 98, 107, 123
Lehigh County, 58
Allentown, 45, 51, 62, 65, 68, 72, 81, 95, 96, 100, 104–105, 107, 115, 117, 120, 122, 123
Emmaus, 58, 61, 66, 88, 115, 122
Heidelberg Township, 88, 94
Jacksonville, 108
Lower Milford Township, 95, 96

Lowhill Township, 104
Macungie. *See* Millerstown
Millerstown, 38, 61, 62
Mountainsville, 124
Salisbury Township, 58, 66
South Whitehall Township, 95
Trexlertown, 68, 77, 117
Upper Macungie Township, 68, 77
Upper Milford Township, 115
Washington Township, 53, 94
Luzerne County
Black Creek, 65
Black Creek Township, 53, 65, 111
Nescopeck, 65
Sugarloaf, 53, 111
Lycoming County
Duboistown, 89
Level Corners, 82
Muncy, 82
Mercer County
Delaware Township, 37, 65
New Hamburg, 37
Mifflin County, 62, 89
Brown Township, 102
Derry Township, 118
Lewistown, 102
Milroy, 89
Strunk's Mills, 102
Monroe County
Jackson Township, 106
Montgomery County, 42, 88
Hanover Township, 107
Lower Frederick Township, 93
Lower Salford Township, 117
Norristown, 77
North Hanover Township, 75
Pottstown, 75, 117
Skippack Township, 45
Trappe, 63
Upper Hanover Township, 107, 109
Zieglersville, 93, 117
Montour County
Anthony Township, 65
Danville, 65
White Hall, 65
Northampton County, 81
Bethlehem, 78, 88
Easton, 45, 104

Forks Township, 45
Hellertown, 84
Jackson Township, 66
Lower Mount Bethel Township, 70
Lower Nazareth Township, 84
Lower Saucon Township, 58, 84
Machenoy, 66
Saucon Township, 84
Upper Mount Bethel Township, 70
Northumberland County, 66
Jackson Township, 73
Perry County
Landisburg, 118
Philadelphia County
Philadelphia, 34, 64, 104
Pike County
Milford, 110
Schuylkill County, 84
Orwigsburg, 66, 96
Schuylkill Haven, 84
Seneca County, 86
Snyder County, 32, 100, 102
Freeburg, 102. *See also* Freeburg (Union Co.)
Somerset County, 42, 63, 71, 100
Somerset Township, 42, 88, 123
Tioga County, 73
Union County, 45
Freeburg, 100, 102. *See also* Freeburg (Snyder Co.)
Lewisburg, 32, 100
Mifflinburg, 103
Union Township, 37
Washington Township [now in Snyder Co.], 100
Washington County, 62
Canonsburg, 35
Westmoreland County
East Huntingdon Township, 94
Salem Township, 58
York County, 110, 122
Carroll Township, 35
Codorus Township. *See* North Codorus Township
Conewago Township, 52
Dover, 71, 109
Dover Township, 108–109, 117
Hanover, 46, 66, 71, 77–78,

[ 148 ]

84
North Codorus Township, 105, 109
Paradise Township, 118
Shrewsbury, 56, 102
Shrewsbury Township, 56, 102
Springettsbury Township, 61
Strinestown, 52, 94
Washington Township, 35, 40
Weigelstown, 108–109
West Manchester Township, 39
Windsor Township, 61
York, 40, 68, 71, 72, 103, 104, 123
York Township, 110, 117

Rhode Island
   Washington County
      Kingston, 100

Tennessee, 92

Vermont
   Orange County
      Chelsea Upper Village, 115
   Windsor County
      Windsor, 106

Virginia
   Berkeley County
      Martinsburg, 36, 53, 108
   Harrison County
      Bridgeport, 41, 42, 46, 49, 67
   Jefferson County, 95
   Scott County
      Floyd, 115

West Virginia
   Berkeley County
      Martinsburg. *See* Martinsburg (Berkeley Co.), Va.
   Harrison County
      Bridgeport. *See* Bridgeport (Harrison Co.), Va.
   Jefferson County. *See* Jefferson Co., Va.

Wisconsin
   Milwaukee County
      Milwaukee, 81, 84

Canada, 63, 72, 109, 123
   Ontario
      Lincoln County, 34
      London, 42